The Rhetorical
Origins of Apartheid

The Rhetorical Origins of Apartheid

*How the Debates of the Natives
Representative Council, 1937–1950,
Shaped South African Racial Policy*

MIA ROTH

McFarland & Company, Inc., Publishers
Jefferson, North Carolina

LIBRARY OF CONGRESS CATALOGUING-IN-PUBLICATION DATA

Names: Roth, Mia, 1940– author.
Title: The rhetorical origins of apartheid : how the debates of the
    Natives Representative Council, 1937–1950, shaped South African
    racial policy / Mia Roth.
Description: Jefferson, North Carolina : McFarland & Company, Inc.,
    Publishers, 2016. | Includes bibliographical references and index.
Identifiers: LCCN 2016030199 | ISBN 9780786499823 (softcover :
    alkaline paper) ∞
Subjects: LCSH: South Africa. Natives Representative Council—
    History—20th century. | South Africa. Natives Representative
    Council—History—20th century—Sources. | Debates and
    debating—South Africa—History—20th century. | Political
    oratory—South Africa—History—20th century. | Rhetoric—
    Political aspects—South Africa—History—20th century. |
    Racism—Political aspects—South Africa—History—20th century. |
    Apartheid—South Africa—History—20th century. | South Africa—
    Race relations—Political aspects—History—20th century.
Classification: LCC DT1928 .R68 2016 | DDC 323.16809/044—dc23
LC record available at https://lccn.loc.gov/2016030199

BRITISH LIBRARY CATALOGUING DATA ARE AVAILABLE

ISBN (print) 978-0-7864-9982-3
ISBN (ebook) 978-1-4766-2204-0

Front cover image © 2016 chelovek/iStock

Printed in the United States of America

*McFarland & Company, Inc., Publishers
  Box 611, Jefferson, North Carolina 28640
  www.mcfarlandpub.com*

Table of Contents

Abbreviations and Terms

AAC: All African Convention

Agitator Number: A number given by the police to any African they considered might prove problematic to them at some future date.

ANC: African National Congress or simply "Congress"

Atlantic Charter: A document published by the Allies in 1942. It endorsed national self-determination, stating that people should have the freedom to choose the type of government under which they wished to live.

Council: Natives Representatives Council

CPSA: Communist Party of South Africa

CYL: Congress Youth League

ILO: International Labour Organization

Kaffir beer: A drink made from maize, traditionally brewed by Africans on festive occasions.

Location or township: The only place blacks in an area were allowed to live in pre–1989 South Africa.

MRC: Used to denote a member of the NRC (the equivalent of the Parliamentary "MP").

NRC: Natives Representatives Council

Oom Jan: Uneducated Afrikaner

Pass Exemption: Document given to Africans indicating that the owner was exempt from carrying a pass. Given to chiefs, members of the Natives Representative Council and a few other educated Africans.

Passes: Document that permitted an African from a rural area to travel to or live in an urban area.

Pick-up van: Police vehicles used to take Africans to jail who had no pass (see above).

Platteland: Rural areas

Reserves and Crown Land: Land set aside in rural areas on which Africans were permitted to reside.

Rooinek: Derogatory term for a British immigrant.

Preface

This anthology collects some of the most moving and important speeches made by African leaders from 1937 to 1950 and spoken during the fourteen years of an almost forgotten organization called the Natives Representative Council (NRC). The anthology is important not only because it gives us some memorable insights into the condition under which Africans lived before the advent of apartheid, but also because it tells us the origin of the ideas that its compiler, WWM Eiselen, used in the formation of this infamous system.

Because so little is known about the organization, I have added sections on its formation, function, and elections in order to clarify the context in which the speeches took place; this is Part One of this book. Part Two is divided into chapters on the various topics of importance that the NRC debated. Before each chapter of Part Two I have given a short introduction in order to clarify certain aspects of their speeches that may be puzzling to those who are not South Africans, and indeed also to the new South Africans born since the downfall of apartheid and the formation of a new South Africa.

What was the Natives Representative Council? It was a council formed as the result of the 1936 Natives Representation Act, the quid pro quo given by the white government to the Africans in exchange for taking away their status as Cape voters in the Union of South Africa's general elections. Natives Representative Council proceedings are verbatim reports of the speeches of the majority of the country's most important African leaders of the first 50 years of its existence. Its significance at the time of its formation lies in several features:

(a) It was the only institution up until 1994 in which the white government attempted to draw its black subjects into a regular constitutional relationship that ignored ethnic and tribal differences among the Africans.

1

(b) It was the only time the government instituted nationwide, free voting open to every African male over the age of eighteen.

(c) It was the first occasion on which African leaders, elected by their own people, were given constitutional recognition by a white government.

(d) It was the only body that the government promised might become the parliament of the Africans of South Africa.[1]

(e) It was the first time African political parties could have their policies brought to the government's attention by recognized constitutional means on a countrywide basis.

(f) The Transvaal Director of Native Education who heard their speeches was Werner Eiselen, the progenitor of apartheid. He attended NRC sessions and listened to the councilors for thirteen years. He was the only person of any consequence who was present both at its start in 1937 and at the Council's last session in 1950.

(g) The speeches were made at a time when South Africa's indigenous people changed from reluctant acquiescence to open rebellion against the white government.

The members of the Natives Representative Council wrote their own speeches. Most were not prepared texts, and their eloquence is the more remarkable when this is taken into account. The exceptions were the speeches made in the NRC in 1949 when the newly elected National Party government had already made the announcement that they were to abolish the Council; thus the councilors thought that this would be their last chance to put forward their views. Unexpectedly in December 1950, the apartheid government made another attempt to persuade the NRC to continue their work. The secretary of native affairs was now Werner Eiselen and Hendrik Verwoerd was the minister of native affairs. At this 1950 NRC meeting the councilors were adamant that that they would not be used as the African spokesmen for apartheid, and so these were their very last speeches in the Council and were probably prepared beforehand.

Some of the councilors were well-known figures in the African political scene of that time, and some were of lesser stature; but all their speeches offer powerful insights into the ideals and the motives of these men, all of whom played their part in the history of South Africa. Their speeches also show that segregation, the system that had been in place since 1910, did not initially appear to Africans to differ greatly from apartheid. Their speeches could not persuade the government to end discrimination; this took another fifty years. Eiselen, who listened to their speeches, tried to make apartheid acceptable by emphasizing what he termed its positive aspects, namely the rectification of many of the grievances expressed by the councilors in their speeches, without attempting to put right the core of the matter, namely discrimination on account of the color of their skin.

Nothing can give us a greater understanding of the black man's place in South Africa than these speeches. They come to us as advocates of liberty and defenders of the rights of their fellow citizens. Their words were eloquent, quietly spoken and in the main unheard by those on whose behalf they were delivered.

1

The Formation
of the Natives
Representative Council

In South Africa, since the days of European colonization, there was a majority black population and a minority of white people, who ruled the country and were determined to stay in charge. The Natives Representative Council was one way in which they intended to retain control, while at the same time giving Africans some say in government. The period when the NRC functioned was the only time under the Westminster system of government when the Africans as a whole had a place, however limited, in the parliamentary system of South Africa until the first free elections in 1994, nearly sixty years later.

The Natives Representative Council was the third chamber of Parliament by virtue of its function of examining pending legislation relating to Africans before such legislation could be put before the House of Assembly. This led to the widely held views among blacks that the NRC contained within it the germ of a black parliament. This possibility was supported by the Opposition under DF Malan, the South African prime minister from 1948 to 1954. Malan had mentioned this aspect of the NRC in 1936 and again in 1951. This is what the Africans clung to: the view that the NRC was the beginning of a black parliament, one that would be subsidiary at first but not forever.[1]

The value of the Natives Representative Council from the African viewpoint was that it contributed to a national consciousness among them. The holding of countrywide elections gave the Africans a keener awareness of their political status. For the first time since the formation of the Union of South Africa, black people had an official platform on which to express their views.[2] To the black leaders; the Council gave a platform to express their views to the government; it gave them added status among their own people; and perhaps most important of all, it gave them the opportunity to address their people at political meetings in their constituencies. Africans viewed it as the start of securing a place within the parliamentary system for Africans—either by strengthening the NRC until that organization was in a position powerful enough to threaten the domination of the white parliament or until they were able to replace the NRC and become a part of Parliament themselves. It was only after the abolition of the NRC that the Africans were forced to switch from parliamentary to other methods to gain equality. As NRC member George Champion pointed out, if constitutional means were denied to the Africans, other means would have to be found. The Council, once it came into existence, did not give them equality, and when they demanded this and refused to cooperate with the white government, the government abolished it 1951. What took its place was apartheid.[3]

When the Union of South Africa came into being in 1910, segregation was already firmly entrenched in South Africa. The Union's African inhabitants were largely without any franchise rights, the only exceptions being a relatively small number of Africans in the Cape Province who could meet the criteria for this franchise. From the time of union onwards, attempts were made first to circumvent the Cape Franchise, as this African franchise was called, and then (from 1926 to 1936) to remove it entirely.

The first forty-five years after the formation of the Union of South Africa in 1910 are noteworthy for the insignificant impact made on white political opinion by African organizations. This applies both to official organizations, such as the Transkeian General Council (Bunga) and the Ciskei General Council, and unofficial ones, such as the African National Congress (ANC). The only exception was the Industrial and Commercial Workers Union (ICU), which by 1937 had long passed its zenith. The All African Convention (AAC) was formed to counteract the abolition of the Cape Franchise, but by 1937 it too lost its initial significance. In fact, the formation of the NRC was expected to give any existing African political organizations a new lease on life. As *Imvo Zabandsunsu* put it: "The ushering in of a new era in the political life of the black races as laid down by the creation of the Natives Council or to be more concise, the Bantu parliament, has had the positive result of rejuvenating ... parallel organizations."[4] An exception to this dismissive attitude of the government towards African political organizations was the ANC deputation that went to Europe in 1919. It wished to present a memorandum to both the British government and the Versailles Peace Conference, to complain about the treatment of Africans by the South African government. One of the prominent leaders of that time, Sol Plaatje, pointed to the discriminatory legislation that had already been passed by the Union government and said that such measures were passed because Africans had no voice in the government.[5] Although the conference took no notice of the deputation, the British Colonial Office sent a strong message to the South African government to do something about the Africans' lack of representation.[6]

This influenced Smuts, the prime minister, in the passing of the Native Affairs Act of 1920, which laid down provisions for the formation of local councils in the rural areas and a general council for the larger rural tribal units in both the Transkei and the Ciskei. The act also provided for the convening of conferences to which Africans from all sections and areas of the country were appointed; these conferences were intended to ascertain African opinion on any matter the government would put before them. Conferences were held on a regular basis from 1922 to 1927, and many of the later NRC councilors were nominated by the government to attend them and give their opinion on proposed legislation.[7] Hertzog, South African prime minister from 1924 until 1939, thought of these conferences as forerunners of the NRC.[8]

No conferences were convened between 1927 and 1930, and one can infer that the rise of the ICU corresponded with the decline in using the conference system as a means of ascertaining African opinion. The government was worried that a militant opinion would be displayed at these conferences, even if its participants were all nominated. Act 23 of 1920 had erected two of the voting units of the NRC, namely the rural local councils, a mixture of nominated and elected members, often attended by the chiefs but presided over by the local native commissioner, and the general councils of the Transkei and the Ciskei.[9] Thus, rural Africans had some way of making known their wishes, while urban Africans still had no representation, even minimal. In 1923 the Natives Urban Areas Act was passed, one section of which made provision for the establishment of advisory boards. All its members had to be Africans, excepting the chairpersons, who as in the local councils were white officials. These boards were meant to act in an advisory capacity in regard to regulations passed by the urban local authority under which they fell.[10] The government was wary of the advisory boards in spite of the fact that they had no legislative or other authority of any kind and appeared quite innocuous politically.[11]

J.B.M. Hertzog, South African prime minister from 1924 to 1939, was committed to a policy of segregation and was determined to do away with the Cape Franchise, which he saw as a danger to white domination. He had read some of the resolutions of the ANC and, by 1923, said in the House of Assembly that it appeared to him that Africans would be satisfied with nothing less than direct representation on all legislative bodies; he said that something more would have to be done to avert "unrest."[12] In South Africa the word revolt or revolution was never articulated; the word used was always "unrest." On 23 July 1926, Hertzog presented the first of the four bills that would eventually, ten years later, lead to the Natives Representative Council, the abolition of the Cape Franchise and the formation of the Native Trust and Land Act. The latter act promised that land would be bought for African occupation and was the carrot dangled in front of the Africans in an attempt to get them to cooperate. Much handwringing went on in government circles before the all-white parliament would agree to the formation of any kind of a nationwide African council. After 1927 when the influence of the ICU was at its height, the popularity of the movement among the Africans was such that it made both Hertzog and Smuts, the leader of the parliamentary opposition, uneasy. The council concept suddenly became "premature" and the council was described as a place that would collect "Communist agitators."[13] Smuts said: "A wrong council may easily be a hotbed for agitation and bolshevism among the natives, who are at present law-abiding."[14] It should always be remembered that the South African government was prepared to provide machinery for consultation not because they were in any way willing to forego the authoritarian stance they had adopted since 1910, but because they saw that they could not successfully govern the African population without at least knowing black reaction to what they planned to do.[15]

All this, it was feared, was "intended to upset white civilization" and the Council bill was dropped in 1930.[16] Other schemes were mooted but none catered for the African intelligentsia, which had been the whole point of the original Council bill. By 1935 the dangers posed by the ICU had passed and the ANC, as the only other significant African organization, was in disarray. In the end it took ten years of discussion before the Natives Representation Act was finally passed in 1936.[17] This lengthy period of indecision resulted in a great deal of primary material being available not only from government archives but also from the private papers of those who sat on the NRC and of the white candidates who were elected to represent Africans in Parliament and the Senate after the 1936 Natives Representation Act was passed, such as Margaret Ballinger, Donald Molteno and J.D. Rheinallt Jones. Private collections were also left by the two ANC presidents, James Moroka and Albert Luthuli, NRC members, and other stalwarts of the ANC such as A.B Xuma and George Champion. Unlike the activities of African political organizations whose views and actions were generally only noted in the newspapers intended for African readers, the NRC's activities and sessions were also discussed in those newspapers intended for white English and Afrikaans readers. Thus from its inception the NRC received more coverage than any other African body had received up until then. This profusion of primary sources contrasts with the paucity of secondary sources, only three of which deal with the NRC to a significant extent.[18] Thus the attitude towards the NRC by historians was largely dismissive. Probably its failure to achieve any positive political results, its abolition in 1951 and the rise of militancy throughout South Africa and the African continent contributed to the many careless factual inaccuracies that abound in the secondary literature when any aspect of the NRC is discussed. This includes even such basic information as to the number of its official members,[19] the dates on which elections were held,[20] and even when it last meeting was held.[21] C.W. Tatz's large section on the Council[22] is marred by its reliance on another published and inaccurate source, that of Julius Lewin, who wrote an article on the electoral system of the Council that was not only inaccurate but was biased to such an extent as to give an entirely erroneous picture of the electoral system and thus of the 1937 election. Even his government statistics were inaccurate.[23] Unfortunately Lewin's study was used as a source by Tatz and others. They were cited to show that the elections were dominated by "backward elements in African society." They were, in fact biased in favor of the "progressive elements" rather than the farm laborers.[24] ANC president A.B. Xuma's NRC membership was said to give him access to the minister of native affairs; but Xuma was never a member of the NRC and had no access to the minister of native affairs.[25] Paul Rich held that the election of Self Mampuru to the Council in 1948 showed the support received by the African Democratic Party from the African electorate. Self Mampuru was defeated when he stood in the 1948 NRC election and was never a councilor. The most commonly cited error was that of describing the NRC adjournment as a reaction to the 1946 gold miners' strike.[26]

A common perception involved the supposedly conservative attitudes of the NRC councilors.[27] This was contrasted to the ANC, viewed as an organization, which under the increasingly repressive climate of the 1940s had reached the point of embracing a strategy of mass action. When it is understood that most of the councilors were not only ANC members but were all part of its national executive structure, such views do not make much sense. The very year the "Programme of Action" was accepted, Councilor Moroka was elected ANC president-general. The head of the Natal branch was then Councilor George Champion, who acted as deputy president-general in the absence of Xuma during the latter's presidency in the 1940s. From 1940 until 1949 Councilor Xiniwe was Cape ANC president, and on his death Councilor Z.K. Matthews became the head of the ANC in the Cape. What is more, during the period of the ANC's militancy in the 1950s and 1960s, it was led first by Councilor Moroka and then by Councilor Albert Luthuli, the Nobel Prize–winner, and yet another councilor who became a national figure only after his election to the NRC in 1946. This is not intended to minimize the role played by the Congress Youth League (CYL) during the late 1940s in the ANC. But the CYL, to which Nelson Mandela belonged, was a small group that could only have its ideas carried out under popular national leaders, and these leaders were all members of the NRC.

The African Mine-Workers Union was considered to be the catalyst that heralded the change in black attitudes after August 1946. The strike, it was agreed, was a failure, but it led to the adjournment of the NRC and to the events that followed on this adjournment, thus giving the Communist Party, which organized the strike, undeserved credit for radicalizing the Africans after 1946.[28] Some historians noted that the adjournment had nothing to do with the strike,[29] but others chose to ignore this opinion. In spite of the supposed popularity achieved by the leader of its union, J.B. Marks, he was not chosen as president-general of the ANC. It was instead the presenter of the NRC "freedom resolution" (as the adjournment resolution was called), James Moroka, who gained this honor. In addition, this election of Moroka, because of the basic misunderstanding of the importance of the NRC in the 1940s, puzzled many historians. Moroka had played a minor role in the All African Convention and had only joined the ANC when he was elected its head in 1949. Why was he the popular choice for this position? Not because he was willing to boycott the NRC, something that Moroka himself denies.[30] He was elected in 1949 and attended the last session of the NRC in December 1950.[31] Whether or not the NRC was radical or conservative can be finally judged from the councilors' speeches in the chapters that follow.

What the government hoped to achieve with the formation of the NRC was an institution that would provide what the government termed the African intelligentsia with an outlet for their political aspirations. They would achieve official recognition as leaders of South Africa's black population, and it was hoped that this would divert them from what the government perceived as more troublesome and dangerous activities. By the use of an efficient electoral system, these leaders would be pinpointed, another useful aspect of such a council. Xuma was in no doubt that the ultimate purpose of the 1936 legislation was to increase white control over the Africans—a desire on Hertzog's part.[32]

There had been a great deal of African opposition to the abolition of the Cape Franchise. Once the act was passed in 1936, African leaders faced the dilemma of whether to reject the NRC or whether to accept it in the hope that they could use it to good purpose.[33] They knew that they could not change the situation, and in any case their focus was on the retention of the Cape Franchise. The idea of a council such as the NRC had never been vehemently opposed by them, and there appeared to be certain advantages in its formation. Now, African leaders would have an official platform from which to state their aspirations, both political and social, and their status would be recognized, not only in their own communities but, for the first time, by the government as well.

In addition the African leaders of the 1930s recognized that the Council was a political institution in advance of anything then in existence in the rest of Africa.[34] In colonies such as Northern Rhodesia, no African had any kind of voting rights. In Southern Rhodesia, where there was a large settler element, power might be more evenly distributed between the white settlers and the British administration, but again Africans were excluded. In Nyasaland, Uganda and Tanganyika the legislative councils were all nominated. In Basutoland, the high commissioner legislated by proclamation and the Pitso was an irregularly convened council of chiefs. The Nigerian Legislative Council had four elected members who could but did not necessarily have to be Africans. In the Gold Coast the chiefs elected the six rural members. The three urban Africans were elected by a limited franchise only given to those Africans who occupied property valued at six pounds.[35] There were fifty-eight African voters in Southern Rhodesia in 1933. All the legislation in the French colonies emanated from France. The Belgian system was based on legislation by decree with no Africans in any self-governing institutions. The Portuguese colonies had an advisory council whose members might be of mixed descent but were not Africans.[36]

The formation of the NRC led African leaders to believe this was the beginning of African participation in the legislative process in South Africa.[37] They were influenced by statements made by members of the Native Affairs Commission who stated that although at that moment the NRC had no legislative authority, it had within it the nucleus of a black parliament.[38] Prominent African leaders such as Richard Godlo, who served as a councilor for fourteen years, held that although the functions of the Council were purely advisory, they were fashioned after the pattern of a parliament.[39] D.F. Malan (the South African prime minister after 1948) attributed the origins of this idea, that the NRC might one day assume the status of a parliament, to the then–prime minister, Jan Smuts, who promptly denied ever making such a statement. Hertzog, while prime minister in 1925, had actually promised that the Council as then envisioned would become an African parliament.[40] Newspapers published for African readers repeatedly referred to the Council as a "black parliament" throughout its fourteen years of existence. An indication of the importance that councilors attached to membership of the NRC was the addition of the letters "MRC" to their names in the same way that members of Parliament used "MP." Dr. Moroka, who was a councilor and African National Congress president, also emphasized the status attached to being a member of the NRC. He held the opinion that far more status was attached by Africans to the members of the NRC than to the heads of any other African organization of that time, including the ANC.[41] Thus the idea persisted and led to the NRC being commonly referred to as the "Black Parliament" or the "Third Chamber of Parliament."[42] The reports of the NRC were to be laid by the minister of native affairs upon the tables of both houses of Parliament, at their next session.[43]

In February 1936, the joint sitting of both houses of Parliament took place at which Hertzog, ten years after the introduction of these bills, finally managed to get them passed as the Representation of Natives Act and the Native Trust and Land Act. The latter was passed in the hope that it would create a "contented and prosperous black peasantry" who would no longer wish to leave the rural areas to compete with the poor white Afrikaners in industry.[44] The plight of the latter in the 1930s was considered a serious problem. The Great Depression of the early 1930s and the many years of draught had depopulated the rural areas, and Afrikaners as unskilled as their African counterparts were entering the towns in large numbers.[45] It was this section of the white population that the government was bent on protecting, and prevention of Africans entering the urban areas and competing for jobs with the equally unqualified Afrikaners was behind much of the urban legislation of this period.

The Representation of Natives Act provided for the formation of the Natives Representative Council. The Council was to consist of twenty-two members. Six of them were to be members of the Department of Native Affairs, namely the five chief native commissioners and the secretary of native affairs. The latter chaired the Council. These official members could speak but had no vote, with the exception of the secretary of native affairs who, as chair, had a deciding vote only. This deciding vote was never used in the Council's fourteen-year existence. The African councilors were to consist of twelve elected and four nominated members.[46] The electorate consisted of African males over the age of eighteen who had paid their poll tax; they could vote if they had the receipt. There were two rural and one urban seat for each of the four provinces. The Transkeian General Council elected three of its members at each election as councilors. Also, four chiefs were nominated to sit on the NRC, chosen by the Department of Native Affairs. The African electorate could also cast their votes for four white candidates who would sit in the Senate. In addition, the Cape Africans, who had been removed from the common roll, could elect three white representatives to the House of Assembly.

Thema realized the impossibility of such an idea's being workable in practice. He reiterated on a number of occasions that there could be "no two parliaments under the same government."[47] Malan, the first prime minister in the apartheid government after 1948, had from the first been against the NRC. In 1936 he said, "The natives when once they have the representative council will get no responsibility there because it has no effective say and they bear no responsibility for what they ask, accordingly he will always ask for more and more because it will cost him nothing to ask."[48]

By 1936, whatever the vicissitudes of the past ten years, a system had been put together that would result in the election of men who were to be consulted on every bill affecting Africans. They were to comment on each bill before it could be placed before Parliament. These comments admittedly only had the weight of opinions, but still they were the opinions of the eight million people whom they represented. It must be remembered that even this had been lacking in the 1910 constitution of South Africa. So Africans could, from 1937, by the formation of the NRC, at least "shout a little louder"[49] than previously.

2

Natives Representative Council Elections, 1937–1948

The NRC's electoral system was so complicated that it was misunderstood and easily painted as unrepresentative. If the Council was unrepresentative, the opinions of its members could be dismissed and there would be no point in publishing their speeches. This chapter will show that the elected councilors really were the people's leaders in the 1930s and 1940s, and that although the elections were unnecessarily cumbersome, their end results led to the most respected Africans of that time sitting on the NRC.

Three elections were held to choose the members of the NRC. They were held in 1937, 1942 and 1948. Before South Africa freed itself of white domination, they were the only elections ever held in which Africans could participate on a national level. The holding of such elections was itself an anomaly in a country that denied the electorate other basic freedoms such as freedom of movement, of speech and of assembly. In addition it was the only time up until 1994 that an attempt was made to ignore the divide-and-rule policy followed first by the British and after 1910, by the white South African government.

The system used to elect the African councilors was a complicated one and was widely misunderstood. C.W. Tatz in his book *Shadow and Substance* has, as previously mentioned, a large section on the Council, but it relies on another published but inaccurate source, that by Julius Lewin. Lewin wrote an article on the electoral system of the NRC that gave an erroneous picture of the both the system and the elections. Even his government statistics were inaccurate.[1] The election results were not dominated by farm laborers and other "backward and less progressive elements in African society,"[2] who, by implication, would elect the "wrong" people.

Twelve of the sixteen councilors were elected. Of these, nine were chosen by way of a system of electoral colleges. The first of these colleges was the Transkei General Council, which elected three of its members to represent the Transkei in the NRC. Of the three other electoral colleges, two were in the Cape and Natal, and one represented the Transvaal and the Orange Free State. The remaining three of the twelve elected councilors were chosen by the black advisory boards in the urban areas, who were themselves elected by the native inhabitants of the locations. There was thus one urban representative for each of the electoral colleges, the Transkei having no advisory boards and thus no urban representative. At the time of the initial discussions on the formation of what became the NRC, there were 5.5 million rural African voters and 1.1 million in the urban areas. The latter increased substantially in the intervening ten years between the first discussions by the government on the formation of the Council in 1926 and the passing of the bills in 1936. So even in the initial discussions about the Council, the urban Africans had one more member than their numbers warranted, strictly speaking. The main concern in the formation of the NRC was to give adequate representation to urban Africans, regarded as the element from which future problems for the white government would most likely arise. There was a widely held belief then that any revolt among the Africans would emanate from the cities, where the bulk of the educated Africans lived.[3] By 1936 all the electoral machinery, except the electoral committees, was already in existence. Local and general councils, as noted, had been established under the Native Affairs Act of 1920, advisory boards in the urban areas in 1923. The formation of the electoral committees was intended to be limited to those areas rural areas such as the white-owned farms where there were no other electoral units.[4]

In practice, it was not only the black laborers on white farms who were placed in these electoral areas, but also the majority of the urban Africans. This came about for several reasons. The first of these was the unwillingness of the Department of Native Affairs to approve the formation of the native advisory boards because of the suspicion and mistrust the department's officials felt towards the urban Africans. Once an African was given the status of an urban dweller, he could not be removed to a rural area. Thus the municipal authorities allowed only a small number of Africans to register in urban areas.[5]

This led to the absurd situation in which some magisterial districts only allowed one taxpayer to register in their urban areas. Durban, which by 1937 had 70,000 Africans, only allowed twenty-seven of them to register as urban dwellers. Johannesburg officially had only 719 Africans who were legally allowed to live there. Domicile for taxation purposes placed the Africans concerned on the appropriate voters' role.[6] D.L. Smit, the secretary of native affairs, maintained that it was a simple matter to transfer a man's tax registration from a rural to an urban area, but in actual practice this was fraught with difficulty because so few Africans were registered as urban taxpayers and were thus entitled to vote in urban areas; Africans had to produce their poll tax receipts before they were allowed to cast their votes.[7] In 1937 urban Africans registered in urban areas numbered only 14,865 out of 1,408,362 voters.[8]

The end result was that the electoral committees were swamped by the large numbers of unregistered urban Africans whom the government was now forced to place there. The candidates chosen by the electoral colleges thus turned out to have been voted in by the urban voters. The government was not happy, but given that the legislation had been passed, there was little they could do about it.[9] The electoral committees in the urban areas thus became mere extensions of the urban vote, a vote that had been intended to be limited to the advisory boards in the towns. The combined influence of these urban Africans, placed as they were in electoral committees and the advisory board electoral units, meant that their influence was greater than that of any other group. For example, B.B. Xiniwe, who lived in Kingwilliamstown and was the ANC president in the Cape Province, chaired the electoral committee of the Cape. He held the rural seat in the Cape until his death in 1949.[10]

Once voted into office, the African councilors held their seats for five years. In order to be eligible for election as councilors, they had either to be taxpayers or qualify as registered on the Cape voters roll. This effectively meant that all African males were eligible if they were over the age of eighteen, were South African by birth and were domiciled for two years previously in the electoral area in which they wished to stand for election. Place of birth could at times be ignored. Albert Luthuli was not born in South Africa, but he was not prevented from standing as a councilor.[11]

Sections 23 and 24 of the act gave the government extremely wide powers to control the membership of the NRC, including the ability to exclude candidates to the Council who had been issued with an order against them under the Riotous Assemblies Amendment Act of 1930 or the Natives Urban Areas Act of 1923. These powers were never used in practice. George Champion had been banned and deported from Natal for three years under the Riotous Assemblies Act, but there was no opposition from the government when he stood as a candidate in the 1937 election or when he was finally elected in 1942. Councilors Paul Mosaka and R.V. Selope Thema had been in jail. Henry Selby Msimang had an agitator number, as did Richard Baloyi. If such measures had been used, many of the councilors would not have been able to stand for election.[12]

The voting system used was first of all criticized on the grounds that the urban African vote would be minimized by the provisions of the act, a fear that proved groundless once the act came into practice. Both Xuma and D.D.T. Jabavu criticized the communal voting system, used due to the illiteracy of the population, claiming that it left too much to individuals who might be open to bribery. No evidence was ever furnished of a case of that kind. On the contrary, there is evidence that even in the case of the most arbitrary of the electoral units that voted through a chief, such chiefs had to heed the views of their followers when casting their votes.[13]

A more serious charge against the voting system was that of Z.K. Matthews, who held that voting by a show of hands, which occurred in both the rural local councils and the electoral committees, was unsatisfactory. Only the advisory board elections were held by ballot. But considering the illiteracy of the population, it is difficult to see what alternative method could have been employed. The use of pictures or symbols was an unknown and untried method of voting at that time.[14] What apparently happened in practice was that although the vote was by a show of hands, the result was recorded and placed in a sealed envelope and handed to the relevant authorities, so that the vote was as secret as possible given the circumstances.[15]

Another complication was that the elections were conducted in two separate stages. In the first stage candidates were nominated to stand for election by one or more of the electoral units. Some candidates put themselves up for nomination, while others were nominated by one or two electoral units, even if they did not want to stand for election. The latter happened to Xuma in both the 1942 and the 1948 elections.[16]

It is not certain why it was thought necessary to prolong and complicate these elections by having a nomination day. A probable reason from the viewpoint of the government was that they could gauge the national following enjoyed by Africans, especially those with "agitator" numbers, something that would otherwise have been difficult to ascertain. The advantage to the candidates in having a nomination day prior to the actual election was that they could gauge the extent of their support well before the day of voting. Candidates who were merely local notables were able to withdraw when lack of support from other electoral units became evident.[17]

This was of importance because the size of the electoral areas made it difficult and expensive for candidates to canvass the whole of an electoral area unless compelled by reason of the paucity of their support. J.D. Rheinallt Jones, for example, was not considered as having canvassed unusually extensively in having travelled 8,000 kilometers through the Transvaal and Orange Free State in March 1937, when standing as a candidate for the Senate. Besides travelling through the electoral areas themselves, the candidates appointed African political agents to canvass those rural areas that they themselves could not cover. At times the NRC candidates would align themselves with those for the Senate and act as a team. This enabled them to address a wider audience. However, candidates who worked as a team were not always elected as a team. Dube, who was the most influential African in Natal in 1937, stood with W.W. Ndhlovu, and both were elected. In 1942, however, Dube abandoned Ndhlovu and gave his support to Albert Luthuli. Dube retained his seat but Luthuli was defeated. The seat was won by George Champion. It was felt by the candidates that the support of a national figure such as Dube was a distinct advantage in the elections, but it appears that this alone did not ensure a candidate's election.[18]

Of the twelve elected councilors, nine were chosen by the votes of the electoral colleges. The first of these colleges was the Transkei General Council, which elected three of its members to represent the Transkei in the NRC. The three other electoral colleges were the Cape Electoral College (chaired by B.B. Xiniwe), the Natal Electoral College and one electoral college to represent the Transvaal and the Orange Free State (chaired by A.B. Xuma in 1942). The units that made up the other three electoral colleges consisted of the chiefs and their followers and the rural local councils. The remaining three of the twelve elected councilors were chosen by the advisory boards in the urban areas. There was thus one urban representative for each of the electoral colleges, the Transkei having no advisory boards and thus no urban representative.[19] In spite of the communal voting system and other controversial aspects of the electoral procedure, the Africans elected to the NRC by this system were regarded by the voters as their representatives. The only group who viewed those Africans elected to the NRC as unrepresentative of black South Africa was the white government after 1946.[20]

The attitude of the authorities towards the freedom of speech of those who stood for the NRC in these elections was ambivalent. There is no doubt that the speeches made by the candidates during the election campaigns were not the kind normally tolerated by the government.[21] A typical example was a speech made by R.V. Selope Thema in Benoni in 1937, in which he stated *inter alia* that the Africans would be perfectly justified in overthrowing their white persecutors; and when making reference to the police he said that they would be shooting children next. The 1937 election permitted political canvassing among Africans for the first time since 1910. This included the addressing of large gatherings by aspiring candidates; nothing like it had been permitted before. The whole matter was so hedged about by restrictive legislation that there was at first some doubt among candidates whether it could take place at all.[22]

The results of the first election were published in detail in the *Government Gazette* in 1937. Unfortunately this procedure was not detailed for the 1942 and 1948 elections. Thus no accurate figures are available for the latter two elections, making statistical comparisons of any kind very difficult. Although many of the results for the latter two elections were published in the newspapers, the figures given differed from each other, compounding the complexities in this connection.

The All African Convention, the ANC and the Communist Party of South Africa all put forward candidates for the 1937 elections. While the ANC and the AAC were both in some disarray in 1937, they made every effort to ensure that their candidates were elected, as did the Communist Party.[23] While the AAC and the ANC put forward prominent leaders such as James Moroka, R.V. Selope Thema, Richard Baloyi, George Champion, Josiah Gumede and Thomas Mapikela, the Communist Party nominated Edwin Mofutsanyana, at that time party secretary but by no means a national figure. The councilors who won the election were proven African leaders of long standing, all from an urban environment. Many of them had taken part in the agitation against the abolition of the Cape Franchise in 1936 but in spite of this, there was no talk of any boycott of the NRC elections.[24] The fact that four of the twelve elected councilors were newspaper editors is indicative of the influential position held by these men as regards political opinion.[25] Whatever political power was available to the African intellectuals of that time was to a great extent in the hands of the newly elected Natives Representatives Council.

The successful candidates in 1937 were as follows:

Elected Councilors

Transvaal–Orange Free State Constituency
R.V. Selope Thema, R.G. Baloyi and T.M. Mapikela

Cape Constituency
A.M. Jabavu, B.B. Xiniwe and R.H. Godlo

Transkei
E. Qamata, J. Moshesh and C. Sakwe

Natal Constituency
J.L. Dube and W.W. Ndhlovu

Owing to there being fewer than 2,000 registered urban voters in Natal, no Natal councilor for the urban seat could be elected until 1939.[26]

Nominated Councilors

Transkei
Chief Victor Poto Ndamase

Cape
Chief Samuel Mankuroane

Transvaal and Orange Free State
George Makapan

Natal
Chief Mshiyeni Dinizulu[27]

Even in 1937, it was clear that the party that emerged as the most favored was the ANC. Although the Communist Party put forward candidates in all three of the NRC elections, including that of 1948, they were always defeated.[28] By 1942 the relationship between the Council and the ANC was a close one. As Xuma wrote to Smit, the secretary of native affairs: "We are together. Our case is one. I am their national leader."[29] The election for the new Council was scheduled to take place on 4 November 1942. Xuma himself had declined to stand as an NRC candidate because he believed that the Council was hamstrung by the act that had created it, thus leaving the ANC as the more effective body.[30] The councilors in the 1942 election did not put out election manifestos but relied on their record in the NRC to ensure their re-election. Dube in 1942 had withdrawn his support of Ndhlovu and given it to a relatively unknown candidate, Albert Luthuli, who in spite of this was defeated.[31]

In 1942 the election results for the NRC were as follows:

Transvaal–Orange Free State
J. Moroka, R.V. Selope Thema and P. Mosaka

Natal
J. Dube, A.W.G. Champion and L.P. Msomi

Cape
Z.K. Matthews, B.B. Xiniwe and R.H. Godlo

Transkei
J. Moshesh, C. Sakwe and S. Mabude

Nominated Councilors

Transkei
Chief Victor Poto Ndamase

Natal
Chief Mshiyeni Dinizulu

Cape
Chief Samuel Mankuroane

Transvaal–Orange Free State
Chief Mohlaba[32]

The new councilors who were elected to the NRC rose to positions of importance within Congress. Champion and Matthews were to become provincial presidents of Natal (in 1946) and the Cape respectively (in 1949), while Moroka became president-general in 1949.[33]

By 1942 Prime Minister Smuts had already realized that African leaders could not be fobbed off (as he put it) with substantial economic and social improvements. What they wanted was not improvements but rights.[34] There was no hope of this, as the councilors had already realized by 1945. In August 1946 Xuma suggested that the members of the Council adjourn the next NRC session, that of August 1946.[35] There was now the problem of what to do in the next election. Should it be boycotted altogether? And if not, who should stand in the 1948 NRC election, once the Council had adjourned in protest against discriminatory legislation? After much deliberation on whether or not a boycott of the 1948 election was feasible, the ANC made the decision that all the councilors should be re-elected to the NRC in unopposed elections.[36] However, the ANC did not have enough support to ensure such a result. The only councilors who were in fact returned unopposed in 1948 were three of the twelve, namely Godlo, Champion and Luthuli.[37] There were a large number of nominations, especially for Xuma, which shows that while the voters supported the ANC, they were nevertheless prepared to ignore its resolution on the NRC.[38]

The election results as published in 1948 were as follows:

Elected Councilors

Transvaal and Orange Free State
R.V. Selope Thema, J. Moroka and P. Mosaka

Cape
Z.K. Matthews, B.B. Xiniwe and R.H. Godlo

Natal
A.W.G. Champion, A. Luthuli and H. Selby Msimang

Transkei
G. Dana, S. Mabude and T. Ntintili

Nominated Councilors

Natal
Chief Mshiyeni Dinizulu

Transkei
Chief Victor Poto Ndamase

Cape
Chief S. Mankuroane

Transvaal and Orange Free State
Chief F. Maserumule[39]

The AAC, which had changed considerably in its affiliations since 1937, did not put up any candidates in this election. The Communist Party put up three candidates, including for the first time Govan Mbeki as an NRC candidate for the Transkei.[40] As in previous elections, none of the communists were elected.

These results convinced the councilors that their stand had been endorsed by the electorate. Matthews said that the election results—that the councilors had not been changed—showed that the goals of the African people had not changed. They would thus appear before the new apartheid government of the National Party with the same demands for the abandonment of racial discrimination.[41]

3

How the Council Functioned

The sessions of the NRC were generally held in one of the government halls in Pretoria. The people present at the first session, besides the members of the Council and of the Native Affairs Commission (who had a statutory obligation to attend)[1] were the three native representatives from the House of Assembly and the four elected senators (elected by the same system as the councilors). Initially even the high commissioner for the United Kingdom came to listen as an interested spectator, but eventually the main spectators were Africans. There were generally a large number of Africans and a few Europeans who sat in the public galleries.[2] The opening session of the NRC was attended by Smuts, then deputy prime minister (a post he held until 1939), who gave a resume of the council system in his opening address, most of which was written by D.L. Smit, secretary of native affairs and Council chair.[3]

Deneys Reitz opened another of the Council sessions while Jan Hofmeyr, as deputy prime minister in the war years, replied to the August 1946 adjournment resolution in November 1946. In 1950 H.F. Verwoerd, then minister of native affairs, opened the last NRC session with a lengthy address on the mainly "positive" implications of apartheid. When a minister attended a session, he gave his address and immediately left, having no interaction with the councilors. Verwoerd was the only one who replied to the councilors' comments on his speech, an indication of the importance attached to this NRC session by the apartheid government.

The NRC's functions consisted of recommending to Parliament any legislation considered necessary in the interests of its constituents[4] and of examining and commenting on proposed legislation of relevance to Africans. Every bill relating to Africans had to be brought before the NRC before it could be placed before Parliament. However, from 1941 onwards the government started to consolidate and amend acts that it did not put before the NRC, stating that it was only necessary to go to the NRC in the case of bills and not in the case of amendments to existing legislation.[5] A few members of Parliament protested, stating that the minister of native affairs must by law allow the NRC to examine all proposed legislation whether it consisted of bills or of amendments to acts already passed by Parliament.[6] The 1936 act took it for granted that interests and indeed legislation could be neatly divided into those matters that affected blacks and those that affected whites. A leading Cape liberal, F.S. Malan, pointed out that there was not an act passed by Parliament that did not apply to Africans, but this obvious truth was ignored.[7] The report of the NRC was laid by the minister of native affairs upon the table of both houses of Parliament. This report did not consist of the verbatim debates themselves but were merely a summary in the form of the proceedings of the NRC.

However, it appears that the verbatim reports were read by at least two members of Parliament. In 1944, F.C. Erasmus (a member of the pro-apartheid opposition) made a speech on the native urban areas amendment bill. Arthur Barlow commented that Erasmus's speech was quite remarkable. He said that he puzzled as to why this was so until he read the NRC select committee report on the bill, which Erasmus had copied in his speech, almost word for word. Barlow then congratulated Erasmus on having the intelligence to read the views of the Africans on the bill.[8] Erasmus had obviously read this report with the initial intention of making political capital out of it rather than quoting from it. Perhaps other members of Parliament were also acquainted with the views of the NRC. The business of the Council took basically the same form at all the sessions. The agenda was divided into sections. The first consisted of business initiated by the Department of Native Affairs. It consisted of bills and draft ordinances that were of concern to Africans and thus had to be brought before the Council by law, before they could be passed by the Parliament.[9] After this the councilors dealt with the estimates of expenditure. Lastly the chair asked the councilors' opinions on any other matter they considered important.

The second section consisted, first, of information asked for by the councilors in regard to matters pertinent to African administration, and second, of motions formulated by any member of the Council including the native commissioners. In practice very few of the latter put forward any motions; nevertheless, their presence at NRC sessions led to useful informal discussions.[10] The yearly estimates of expenditure brought the provincial officials and those of the Department of Native Affairs in direct contact with the African councilors. This proved useful to the councilors who had never before had any accurate knowledge of government administration.[11] The officials who attended the NRC sessions were used to the Africans they administered obeying them without question. Fred Rodseth, for much of this time the undersecretary of native affairs, was one of these civil servants who had to report to the NRC. In his opinion, the mere fact that these officials had to report back to the NRC on a yearly basis encouraged them to make greater efforts in respect of the NRC resolutions than would otherwise have been the case. The officials were frequently taken aback by the debates and at a loss as to how to reply. Difficulties of that kind did arise in both the Transkeian General Council and that of the Ciskei, but as Rodseth put it, the native commissioners who chaired these councils would "just shut them up." This did not occur in the NRC.[12] Something of this kind was attempted by Smit when he chaired the 1938 NRC session, but the councilors were not so easily cowed.[13]

After the perusal of the estimates, the function of the Council was to discuss any pending legislation relating to African affairs. From the beginning the councilors used this part of the agenda to discuss not only pending legislation, but also past legislation. It was this function that gave the councilors the opportunity to raise matters other than those placed on the agenda by the government.[14] Both the press intended for African readers and the councilors themselves regarded the NRC as a black parliament[15] and called themselves MRCs (members of the representative council.[16] However, they acted in the Council more in the form of a parliamentary cabinet rather than as members of Parliament. Deneys Reitz, the minister of native affairs stated that he, too, viewed them as such.[17] NRC resolutions were usually unanimous, and the purpose of their debates was to emphasize relevant facts rather than different opinions.[18] Sometimes the members voting in favor of a motion were not all the councilors present, and it is obvious that the councilors would abstain from voting rather than register a negative vote.

In 1937 the Africans were prepared to accept the functions of the Council at set down by the 1936 legislation. By 1942 this had changed. The NRC was no any longer in the forefront of colonial legislation as relating to Africans, as had been the case in 1937. The outbreak of war, the Africans who joined up, and especially the publication of the Atlantic Charter by the allies in 1942, influenced the NRC. The second Council, elected in 1942, included a more forthright and fearless collection of councilors to add to the voices of Thema and Godlo, namely George Champion, Paul Mosaka, James Moroka and Z.K. Matthews. These formed a caucus of the NRC, with Z.K. Matthews as chair. A recess committee under his chairmanship then proposed certain changes to the NRC, changes that were endorsed by A.B. Xuma, president-general of the ANC.[19]

These proposals were as follows:

(a) Council membership be increased to no less than 100 members (the house of assembly had 1953 at this time)
(b) Public servants should not be members of the NRC, as they were at present, but should only attend to answer questions pertaining to their departments.
(c) The chair of the NRC should not be the secretary of native affairs but should be one of the African councilors.
(d) The venue should change from Pretoria to Cape Town, the same venue as that of the South African Parliament.
(e) Council sessions should be extended.
(f) The Council should be given statutory powers.[20]

As these proposals would have made the NRC a direct rival of the white parliament, there was no way these proposals could ever be granted. Nothing was done.[21] All that the government was willing to endorse, three years later, was the request for increased NRC membership.[22] The disillusionment of the Council can be seen from its speeches from 1942 onwards, and their attitude in 1946 is understandable. As the report of the recess committee indicated, they were eager to increase the power and prestige of the Council, which was in 1946—as indeed it was to be for the remainder of its existence—the only official propaganda platform available to Africans.[23] From 1942 until 1946 the legislation that the NRC was being asked to pass, and the amendments to legislation that the government did not place before the Council, increased the members' indignation. As their speeches reveal, they had hoped that the end of the war would lead to some easing of the restrictions placed upon the African population, but the contrary occurred. At last in August 1946 Z.K. Matthews, as the Council chair, prepared the following motion, presented by Moroka and passed unanimously, by both the elected councilors and the four chiefs:

> The Council having since its inception, brought to the notice of the government the reactionary character of Union native policy of segregation in all its ramifications deprecates the government's post-war continuation of a policy of Fascism, which is the antithesis and negation of the spirit of the Atlantic Charter and the United Nations Charter. The Council therefore in protest against this breach of faith towards the African people in particular and cause of world freedom in general resolves to adjourn this session and calls upon the government forthwith to abolish all discriminatory legislation affecting non-Europeans in this country.[24]

According to Smuts, Hertzog wanted the Council to function as an outlet for the expression of black opinion and make its contribution towards guiding public opinion and the opinion of Parliament into the right channels.[25] One cannot dispute that this was, ironically, exactly what the NRC had achieved. The 1946 Council adjournment that asked for the abolition of all discriminatory legislation was definitely "a contribution towards guiding public opinion and the opinion of Parliament in the right channels."

The next session of the NRC was held in November 1946. Before holding this session the government compiled an outline of what they believed to be the causes of the August adjournment, based on statements made by Z.K. Matthews to the newspaper *Bantu World*. These were lack of respect for the NRC, failure to consult the Council, lack of action on the Council's resolutions, and continued repressive legislation. Under this last section the government put such matters as the prohibition of all meetings in the northern Transvaal; prohibition of meetings on mining ground; the extension of the Pass Laws to the Cape; and restrictions on travelling.[26] From August to November a stringent control measure was passed in the form of a proclamation restricting the rights of Africans in urban areas under the control of certain local authorities.[27] Such a proclamation showed more clearly than any statement could have done how much notice the government intended to take of the Council's decision to adjourn its proceedings until the government had abolished all discriminatory legislation.

In November the councilors gathered in Pretoria to hear the government's reply. The deputy prime minister, Jan Hofmeyr, addressed them, an address that tabulated what the African people received from the government; it made no concessions and thus could not even be regarded as a reply to the adjournment resolution. Hofmeyr left the hall immediately after making his speech.[28] Hofmeyr was regarded as one the leading liberals of his day, and the absence of Smuts overseas led Africans to believe that Smuts had nothing to do with this reply—that the liberal Hofmeyr had written the speech himself. Although the NRC understood that the speech did not really reflect Hofmeyr's views, they were nevertheless disillusioned with the white liberals. It was thought that if Hofmeyr could sacrifice his principles to political expediency now, little would prevent him from doing so if and when he became prime minister.[29] In fact the reply to the NRC had been thoroughly discussed with Smuts. Indeed, it was Smuts who amended Hofmeyr's reply by making the statement "somewhat less apologetic in tone and somewhat stiffer, as it should be."[30] The councilors emphasized that they, as the only legitimate representatives of the Africans, freely elected by them, had no intention of resigning but would wait for the government to answer their demands.[31]The NRC then again adjourned, Chief Mshiyeni absenting himself before the second adjournment resolution was passed.[32] The NRC then sent a letter of congratulations to the UN on their work in connection with the dispute between India and South Africa.[33] Awkward questions had already been asked at the UN after the first adjournment of the NRC.[34]

Matthews had suggested in October 1946 that Smuts should have an informal talk with the NRC.[35] There was a great deal of discussion about whether or not the councilors should resign and refrain from standing in the 1948 NRC elections. Councilors and leaders of the ANC regarded an election boycott as impossible. It was also felt that the NRC was a weapon that could be used in the struggle for freedom and that it would be senseless to abandon it. ANC membership was limited, and it could not be said to represent the views of eight million Africans. In any case the ANC did not control the NRC constituencies, and the elections for the Council were too cumbersome to contemplate a successful boycott.[36] What the councilors wanted was to use the adjournment as a tactic to make the Council unworkable. It was thought that bills could not be bought before Parliament concerning Africans unless they had previously been put before the NRC, and thus that Parliament itself would find it impossible to pass certain legislation.[37]

The NRC was totally ignored during the royal visit of 1947. When the secretary of native affairs, W.J.G. Mears, went to the Liberian independence celebration, he was accompanied by ex-councilor and Chief Jeremiah Moshesh. *Inkundla Ya Bantu* was undoubtedly correct in maintaining that the government would have preferred to take along someone with the prestige of Prof. Matthews or Dr. Moroka, but were not sure whether these councilors would accept the idea.[38]

The letter sent by the NRC to the UN explaining the adjournment of 1946 had been a serious embarrassment to the government.[39] Cabinet minister Harry Lawrence attempted an explanation in a paper presented at the UN entitled "Request of the Natives Representative Council for Annulment of Discriminatory Legislation."[40] In addition, presumably also as an effort to offset the bad impression created by the NRC's letter to the UN, Smuts spoke at the UN exaggerating the powers of the Transkeian General Council.[41]

South Africa's trusteeship of South West Africa was increasingly coming under the scrutiny of the UN. When Paul Mosaka asked permission to visit South West Africa to see the conditions there, permission was refused.[42] One of the Indian delegates at the UN then pointed out that an African had been refused permission to enter South West Africa and that from this it must be concluded that the South African government did not want to have it known under what conditions Africans lived there.[43]

In May 1947 Prime Minister Smuts sent for Matthews and five other members of the NRC in order to put certain proposals before them. Matthews believed that Smuts needed the cooperation of the Council and that Smuts hoped to end the NRC adjournment before the next session of the UN, where it was certain that there would be a renewed onslaught on South Africa's racial policies. It seems highly probable that the Smuts proposals for the NRC, published in October 1947, were timed to coincide with the UN session.

Smuts was well aware that the publicized debates at the UN, filled as they were by talks of equality and non-discrimination, were having a great effect on Africans. Not only the NRC but Africans in general now felt it was incumbent upon them to inform the world of the South Africans' situation. What was more, they fully expected that world opinion would compel South Africa to change.[44] Smuts realized that Africans wanted rights but knew that their aim of equality would be politically impossible to implement in South Africa.[45]

All that the Smuts proposals contained was a policy of self-government in black areas under a reconstituted NRC. Thus the government was prepared to give blacks a greater share in their own administration. In this respect, by 1947 there was some resemblance between Smuts' ideas and those of Eiselen's apartheid policy.[46] Concerning the Smuts proposals, Paul Mosaka said the adjournment had been a matter of policy and that to ask the councilors now to help in the administration of a policy they did not support was to ask them to police their own people.[47] The Smuts government had discussed the option of abolishing the Council altogether but judged it unwise to do so at the first sign of conflict.[48] Thus the adjournment of the Council succeeded in making the government admit that a new "native policy" was necessary, but its dismissal of the NRC's demand to abolish discriminatory legislation made it impossible for Smuts' ideas to have any effect on the NRC.[49]

The attitude of the Opposition and the imminence of the next general election in 1948 made the government tread warily. For example, Hofmeyr's reply to the NRC in November 1946, in which he had enumerated what the South African government considered to be the benefits conferred on its African population, had not been included in the proceedings of the NRC placed before Parliament in 1947, probably in anticipation of the political capital that would be made of this by the National Party. Once the Smuts proposals became known, Smuts was accused of wanting to form a black parliament that would consolidate the eight million Africans under anti-white leadership; the NRC would become the medium through which the fight for equality would be carried out.[50]

In 1948 the United Party under Smuts was defeated by Malan and his National Party, under the banner of a new policy, that of apartheid. That year also saw the third and last election for the Natives Representative Council. No formal session of the NRC took place in 1947 or in 1948. Both the hopes of the NRC and the fears of the government—that no legislation affecting Africans could be passed unless previously commented on by the NRC—proved groundless. It appears that a legal loophole was found to circumvent this problem, as nothing more was heard of it. An NRC caucus met in Bloemfontein in July 1948. By this date the new National Party government had not met the Council, nor had anything been said about its abolition after the white elections in May 1948. Although the councilors did not want to retain the existing system, they were also not in favor of the abolition of the NRC.[51] It was still the only channel to both fight for equality and to make African views heard.[52]

In January 1949 Mears, the new chair of the Council appointed by the National Party government, at last called together the NRC. He stated that he had been instructed to deliver from the government the message that it was not prepared to accede to the Council's demands for the abolition of discriminatory legislation. Moreover, the government was of the opinion that the Council served no useful purpose and accordingly intended to take the necessary steps to abolish it.[53] It was clear at this meeting that the councilors were hoping that the NRC would not be abolished. They had asked for the repeal of discriminatory legislation, not the abolition of the NRC. Some held to their belief that no legislation affecting the interests of the Africans could be passed before having been placed before the NRC for consideration and report.[54] Xiniwe died in 1949, and in spite of all the talk of the abolition of the NRC, a by-election took place in 1949 and was won by S.P. Sesedi, president of the Advisory Boards Congress.[55] Articles and letters appeared in the press intended for African readers on whether or not they should resign, but the only significant pressure came from the Congress Youth League (CYL), of which Nelson Mandela and Walter Sisulu were by now prominent members. The councilors, on their part, held that they had a mandate from the people who had elected them, while the ANC and its offshoot, the CYL, did not; and they thus refused to resign from the Council.[56]

In 1949 a new strategy was endorsed by the ANC. In essence it was similar to the NRC's reasons for the adjournment of 1946. An added proviso however, was that freedom was to be achieved through militant action and that the NRC must be boycotted. Xuma publicly refused to subscribe to it, as did Matthews when approached by the CYL. The boycott of the NRC was also the only proviso not accepted by the candidates for office in 1949.[57]

Councilor James Moroka became the president-general of the ANC. He, too, did not accept the proviso to boycott the Council, a view that many found puzzling. If he did not accept the entire Programme of Action (as it was called), why was he made president-general of the ANC, especially taking into account that fact the he only joined the ANC at the same meeting where he was elected as president? The reason for his popularity was that he had agreed to read out the "freedom resolution," as the adjournment motion was called, in August 1946. There was a real fear among the other councilors that the presenter of the motion would be arrested, so he agreed to do it. He was a medical doctor with his own practice and not dependent on the government financially, as was the case with Chief Albert Luthuli. Neither was he dependent on a white institution, as Professor Z.K. Matthews of Fort Hare was. Moroka thus gained a reputation for being a militant national figure. Moroka said that he had no intention of resigning from the NRC in 1949 in order to become president of the ANC, an organization (in his view) of little influence and one that had less support than the NRC. This position he had made clear when approached by the CYL on the matter in October of 1949, but the CYL nevertheless cast their support behind him once they realized that one of the other candidates were prepared to boycott the NRC.[58]

Malan had said both before and after the 1948 election that the NRC would be abolished, but nothing had happened. The NRC had now ceased to function. E.G. Jansen, the minister of native affairs in 1949, said that there was no point in the Council meeting again while the adjournment motion still held good amongst them.[59] A surprising attempt at cooperation now took place at the instigation of the new secretary of native affairs, W.W.M. Eiselen, who had attended many sessions of the NRC and had been well received by the councilors.[60] As will be noted from the speeches of the councilors, they maintained that if they were forced to accept racial separation, at least it should be done on an equitable manner. Eiselen, his ideas obviously already focused on what would later become apartheid, emphasized that he was in favor African schools having an all-black staff, that all Europeans should leave the so-called black areas, and that African mechanics should be trained to work in African areas, among other ideas.[61]

Eiselen contacted Matthews and asked the NRC caucus to hold an informal meeting to consider ways of overcoming the impasse.[62] The councilors met and compiled a memorandum stating that they wanted to send a deputation to Jansen, then still minister of native affairs, to ask him to make a statement on the new policy of apartheid. Eiselen opposed this, as he did not consider Jansen to be sympathetic to the NRC, and the meeting did not take place. There was no publicity, and no report of the NRC meeting was made available.[63] Another informal meeting then took place in August 1950, this time in the presence of Eiselen. Although that government had given no formal indication that they were considering using the NRC as a channel for the implementation of apartheid, the renewed attempts to heal the breach by Eiselen indicate that he wanted the NRC to be a part of his policy of apartheid.[64] The resolution adopted at the informal meeting was that the minister of native affairs be invited to meet the NRC and that this resolution be brought to his attention. Jansen had meanwhile been replaced by H.F. Verwoerd, whose views were in tune with those of Eiselen. Eiselen subsequently wrote to Luthuli expressing his appreciation of the cooperative spirit expressed by the councilors at this meeting.[65]

The eleventh and last session of the NRC opened on 5 December 1950. The meeting was regarded as of some significance in that the Council would not be abolished if it cooperated with the government, but this in turn was dependent on the minister of native affairs making a statement on apartheid that would satisfy the councilors and enable them to withdraw from their previous standpoint. The English press held that the success or failure of the whole of the government's policy would depend on this meeting.[66] Jordan Ngubane viewed it as the turning point in black-white relations. On it would depend whether the future would lead to citizenship by reform or through revolution.[67] It was generally understood that the NRC were called together to hear an explanation of the policy of apartheid, the first ever addressed to the African themselves.[68] None of the Council members had resigned by the time the 1950 Council session was held.

Verwoerd gave his address and then left. He had clearly made a great effort to overcome the deadlock by saying that if this Council went ahead without an adjournment, the councilors were free to come and talk over any problems with him at the end of the session. However, Verwoerd made it clear that no minister of native affairs would participate in the NRC; that there was to be no discussion of politics; and that the order of business was to be at the discretion of Eiselen.[69] During the period when D.L. Smit was secretary of native affairs and chaired the NRC, the agenda was not strictly adhered to and councilors were given free rein to express their opinions at any time they considered relevant. This new ruling meant in effect that the councilors were expected to approve apartheid legislation without giving their opinion or objections to it as they previously would have been free to do. Eiselen insisted that they pass the apartheid legislation first, and only later would they be permitted to comment on it. The councilors refused to do so, and one by one they left the hall. Eiselen said that he would continue as long as there was a quorum, but in the end everyone had left the hall. So last session of the Natives Representative Council ended and Eiselen had to accept defeat.[70]

4

Members of the Natives Representative Council

The following chapter deals with the backgrounds of the councilors and the more important government officials, who as members of the NRC or as ministers of native affairs addressed the Council in its fourteen-year existence. The nominated councilors were nearly all chiefs, as were two of the elected councilors: Jeremiah Moshesh and Albert Luthuli. Chiefs were, by the time of the NRC's formation, all paid civil servants. Their stipends were dictated by the Department of Native Affairs, and the government also had the power to depose them if they deemed this to be advisable. In the case of the elected Councilors, all but a few came from poor, rural backgrounds. Many had migrated to the urban areas, where they initially found employment either in the mines, like George Champion, or as teachers or laborers, like Thema. Most had some missionary school education. A few, like Matthews, Moroka and Mosaka, had university degrees. Some like Jabavu and Xiniwe came from influential Cape families. Nearly all of them, by the time they stood as candidates for the Council, owned businesses, were newspaper editors, or had farming interests. As the African political organizations at that time were chronically short of money, it was essential for any African with political aspirations to ensure that he had some financial security before embarking on a political career; even voting rights in the ANC were only given to paid-up members. In spite of the material advantages that they had managed to secure for themselves, they felt at one with their constituents and were able to put the latter's viewpoints to the government so accurately because they were oppressed, as Thema put it, not as a class but as a race.[1]

The Elected Councilors

Richard Grenville Baloyi

In 1936, Henry Selby Msimang wrote to A.B. Xuma that the Transvaal branch of the ANC, then the most important of its branches, was hopelessly divided due to a disagreement between two of its most important members, Richard Baloyi and R.V. Selope Thema. Baloyi's importance in black politics at this time is shown in that it was only after the breach between him and Thema had been healed after the 1937 NRC election that the resuscitation of the ANC was possible.[2]

Richard Grenville Baloyi was a successful Johannesburg businessman. Baloyi was treasurer-general of the ANC in 1940, and it was he who proposed Xuma as president-general of Congress in 1940. He became the ANC treasurer, a post he held until 1948, after which he sank into obscurity as far as African politics were concerned.[3] He tried to get reelected in both 1942 and 1948 but was unsuccessful. Much has been made of his employment of J.B. Marks, a member of the CPSA (Communist Party of South Africa), as his secretary, but there is nothing to indicate that Marks had any influence on Baloyi.[4]

Baloyi's most notable contribution during his years as NRC councilor was his visit to the then–Basutoland (Lesotho). In February 1938, he visited Basutoland in secret to persuade Paramount Chief Griffiths and other leading Basuto to resist South Africa's attempts at incorporation by any means, including force of arms. The Basuto came away from their meeting with Baloyi totally convinced of the correctness of his views. After he returned to South Africa, a number of Basuto chiefs came to see him in Johannesburg, specifically to discuss the inadvisability of incorporating Basutoland as a part of South Africa. In April 1938, Baloyi again visited Basutoland. His visits alarmed both the British and the South African Department of Native Affairs. Baloyi was told that they did not consider it desirable for a member of the NRC to engage in political activities of this kind. Having said this, they could find no legal sanction to compel Baloyi to observe this warning; all they could do was keep a close watch on his movements and register him as "Agitator No. 628."[5] Baloyi's efforts in Basutoland are an example of the use made by the councilors of their NRC status to further their political agendas on behalf not only of their own constituents but rather of Africans in general. In 1943, when Baloyi was no longer a member of the NRC, he and seven councilors joined forces with six other African leaders and signed a petition to the British government protesting against certain proposals that the British High Commission Territories be transferred to South Africa.[6]

Alison Wessels George Champion

George Champion was eager to become a member of the Natives Representative Council. He was defeated when standing for the Council in 1937 and again in the by-election of 1939. He was finally elected in 1942.[7] He held this seat until the abolition of the Council in 1951. Champion was the chief trade unionist on the Council. He first gained some prominence in black affairs when in 1920 he was elected president of the Native Mine Clerks Association. In 1925, he was posted to Durban by Clements Kadalie as Natal secretary of the Industrial and Commercial Workers' Union (ICU). He became second in command to Kadalie but broke away and formed an independent and powerful branch of the union in Natal, the ICU Yase Natal.[8] Champion's activities in the ICU led to his becoming the first person to be banned under the Riotous Assemblies Amendment Act of 1930.[9] He was banned from Natal for three years. When his banning order was lifted in 1933 he returned to Durban. Champion had been a member of the ANC executive in the 1920s and again assumed this position in 1937. He became president of the Natal ANC in 1946 after the death of Dube and acting president-general of Congress in 1946–1947 during Xuma's absence abroad. After Xuma's return, Champion was regarded as vice-president of Congress.[10]

G.S. Dana

Dana was a prominent member of the Transkei General Council. He attended the last two sessions of the NRC, in 1949 and 1950. He was said to be a supporter of a strong Council, one that could be used by Africans to secure improved representation.[11]

John Langalibalele Dube

Dube studied at what later became Adam's College in Natal and then went to Oberlin College, Ohio, in the United States in 1899. When he returned to South Africa, he established a school for industrial education, the only one of its kind in Southern Africa at that time, the Ohlanga Institute. In 1904, he launched his newspaper *Ilanga Lase Natal* and remained its editor until 1934. He used the newspaper to criticize the government during the Bambatha rebellion of 1906, and was arrested. In 1912, he initiated the Natal Native Congress, of which he remained undisputed head until shortly before his death in 1946. Dube became the first president-general of the African National Congress in 1912. Under Dube, the Natal ANC was always semi-autonomous. In 1937, Dube won a resounding victory in the Natives Representative Council elections, beating his Natal rivals, Josiah Gumede and George Champion, by a considerable margin. Dube was reelected in 1942 and retained his seat in the Council until his death in 1946.[12]

Dube, Chief Mshiyeni Kwa Dinizulu and W.W. Ndhlovu were the first to report back on the 1937 session of the NRC. Before 1937, Africans were not permitted to hold political gatherings. The 1936 Native Representation Act gave them their first opportunity to hold any kind of political meeting. The police commissioner was present at the meeting, conducted in Zulu. He considered it to be of a "provocative nature," although he felt that the councilors had curbed themselves somewhat because of his presence. He explained that he wanted to report the meeting so that the police could decide whether all future meetings of NRC councilors should be watched. As all the subsequent councilor/constituent meetings held for the councilors to report on the NRC sessions were watched, it seems that this was considered necessary.[13]

Richard Hobbs Godlo

Richard Hobbs Godlo started his career as a reporter on the East London *Daily Dispatch.* He was the editor throughout the short but notable existence of the English-Xhosa monthly newspaper *Umlindi We Nyanga.*[14] Godlo was extremely active politically and was not only a member but also an important member of what seems to have been every political organization open to him in the 1930s. He was assistant secretary of the Cape Native Voters Convention; an associate member of the South African Institute of Race Relations; and recording secretary of the All African Convention and Chair of the Joint Council for Europeans and Africans in East London.[15] Although Godlo does not in 1937 even mention his membership of the ANC, he regularly attended ANC annual conferences,[16] attesting to the ANC's relative unimportance in 1937 at the time of the NRC's first elections. The most important political position held by Godlo in 1937 was his presidency of the Location Advisory Boards Congress.[17] He served as an NRC councilor from 1937 until 1951, when the NRC was abolished.

Alexander Macaulay Jabavu

Alexander Macaulay Jabavu was the son of John Tengo Jabavu and the younger brother of Prof. D.D.T. Jabavu. On the death of his father, he took over the editorship of his father's newspaper, *Imvo Zabansundu.* In 1926, he was elected senior vice-president of the ICU (Industrial and Commercial Workers Union) under Kadalie. In 1928, he founded and became the initial chair of the Location Advisory Boards Congress. From 1934, Jabavu was the leading African on the Ciskei General Council, as an examination of the debates of that body reveal, representing the Tamacha area.[18] The All African Convention, the Ciskei General Council, and the Cape Native Voters Convention all nominated him as their candidate in the NRC election in 1937. He lost his seat in 1942.[19]

Chief Albert Luthuli

Albert Luthuli was politically ambitious and tried for a number of years to gain a seat in the NRC. He was a minor chief in the Groutville area of Natal and on this basis asked the Department of Native Affairs to appoint him to one of the four nominated seats on the Council, a request that was refused. In order to stand as an elected candidate, in the 1942 election Luthuli had to apply for permission from the governor-general. As a chief he was technically a civil servant, and civil servants were not permitted to be part of any political body. In 1942 Luthuli lost the election to George Champion. At last in a by-election held after Dube's death, in 1946, he managed to get himself a seat on the NRC. He thus went to considerable trouble over a lengthy period in order to join the Council.[20] Although it has been suggested that Luthuli had so little political ambition that he only joined the ANC out of loyalty to Dube, this is not borne out by the above events. Joining the ANC at such a late date as 1945 indicates only the lack of importance he attributed to the ANC at that time, rather than any lack of political ambition.[21] Although Luthuli attended both the 1949 and the 1950 sessions of the Council, he rarely spoke and made little impact on the NRC. He never resigned from the NRC and remained a member until 1951.

Saul Mabude

Saul Mabude was elected in 1942 and held his seat until 1951. He worked as a secretary to Chief Botha Sigcawu in the Transkei.[22] Mabude's speeches in the NRC became more militant after the 1946 NRC adjournment, as did his speeches in the Transkei General Council, resulting in an increase in his popularity in the Transkei.[23] In 1947, he submitted a resolution in the Transkei General Council, spelling out his disagreement with Smuts's statement at the UN on the success of the latter as a vehicle for the representation for Africans in the Transkei. V.M. de Villiers, at that time the Transkei General Council chair, initially refused to accept Mabude's motion. When he was unsuccessful, de Villiers threatened to place Mabude under a banning order, unless Chief Secqua sacked him. Mabude lost his job as secretary to the chief but retained his popularity in the Transkei General Council, becoming a member of its executive committee in 1951.[24]

Thomas Mtobi Mapikela

Thomas Mtobi Mapikela was a carpenter by trade and worked as a builder and contractor. He had lived in Bloemfontein for forty years when he stood as a candidate for the NRC in 1937. Mapikela organized and convened the first meeting in opposition to the color bar legislation when it was first proposed as a part of the 1909 South Africa Act. In his 1937 election manifesto, Mapikela stated that he was a founding member of the first organized black political movement, known as the "Vigilant Committee," which developed into the African National Congress in 1912. He held various important positions in the Orange Free State branch of Congress. It was his position there, plus his linguistic abilities, which made him the natural choice for speaker at Congress conferences, usually held in Bloemfontein, a position that by 1937 he had held for twenty-two years. He also helped to draft the 1919 ANC constitution.[25] He was not re-elected in 1942; his seat was won by James Moroka.

Prof. Z.K. Matthews

Professor Matthews has been described as South Africa's most distinguished African intellectual, a guiding force in African politics in the late 1940s and the early 1950s. He was a serious contender for the ANC presidency both in 1949 and again in 1952.[26] It was his academic prominence that won him the leadership of the NRC caucus when he was elected to the NRC in 1942. At that time he was on the ANC executive.[27] Matthews justified his leadership of the NRC not only by his qualities of leadership but also by his efforts to present the motions put forward by the other councilors as clearly and accurately as possible. There is evidence from notes made by him on the subject that all the motions that he presented were backed by meticulous research.[28] In 1949, after the death of Councilor Xiniwe, he became president of the Cape branch of the ANC. During Luthuli's presidency, he acted as deputy president-general of Congress, a post he held until 1955. Professor Matthews, first African graduate at Fort Hare, head of the Cape ANC, has had much written about him, but his NRC speeches give us an additional insight into his views.

Dr. James Moroka

James Moroka held his seat from 1942 until his resignation from the NRC after its last session in 1950, when he was already president-general of the ANC. Moroka, a medical doctor practicing in Thaba 'Nchu, had first entered politics in 1936. When the All African Convention became organized on a permanent basis, he became its treasurer.[29] In spite of this he was relatively unknown and unimportant in black politics until his election to the Council. The decision to adjourn the Council was decided upon before the session opened; all that was now necessary was to decide who would present the adjournment motion. It was Xuma, as head of the ANC, who had first suggested that the adjournment of the Council might be an effective method of protest. Xuma did so with trepidation, as he feared that the councilors might well be arrested as a result. There was a real fear among the councilors at the caucus meeting that preceded that session that the person presenting it would be, if not immediately arrested, persecuted by the government.[30] The arrest of Mosaka during the Alexandra bus boycott and that of R.V. Selope Thema during the Pass Laws protest in Cape Town had shown that the councilors of the NRC were not immune from arrest.[31] Dr. Moroka said that he was late in arriving and the motion was thrust into his hands, although he had previously agreed that he had no objection to presenting it. It was his presentation of the adjournment resolution (called the freedom resolution)[32] at the 1946 NRC session that thrust him into prominence, giving the impression that he alone had the courage to present it to the government. It was this perception that led to his popularity and his election as ANC president-general in 1949.[33]

Paul Mosaka

Paul Mosaka was initially a teacher and exceptionally well educated for that time, having a university degree. He was elected in 1942 for an urban constituency, which included the industrialized Witwatersrand. The Witwatersrand already then contained the largest urban African population in the country. Shortly after his election to the NRC, he wrote to Xuma, then the ANC's president-general, offering to serve the interests of that organization on the Council.[34] Xuma's inactivity in replying to this offer led to Mosaka's forming the African Democratic Party with the then-senator of his constituency, Hyman Basner, in 1943.[35] The result of his actions on behalf of his constituents led to Mosaka's becoming an important figure in African politics in the 1940s. For example when there was a strike at the Brakpan location, Alport, chief native commissioner for the

Transvaal, asked Mosaka and Xuma to aid in mediation. They both addressed the crowd of over 3,000 who were protesting over the dismissal of a teacher. The teacher had been chosen to represent by the location inhabitants to represent them regarding their protests on the appointment of a new superintendant.[36]

The authorities used the support the councilors had among the Africans when it suited them to do so, but did not fail to arrest them if it did not. Mosaka, for instance, was arrested and jailed when he participated in the Alexandra Bus boycott in 1943.[37] Mosaka was one of the foremost opponents of the idea prevalent among the Congress Youth League to boycott the NRC after its first adjournment in 1946. He was not in favor of councilors' resigning from the NRC, either. It was Mosaka who took the lead in instituting the case against Eiselen and the government after the last session of the Council in 1950.[38]

Henry Selby Msimang

Henry Selby Msimang was elected in 1948 and held his seat until the dissolution of the NRC in 1951. Msimang had earlier contested both the 1942 elections and the Natal by-election held after the death of Dube in 1946 but was unsuccessful on both occasions. As early as 1919, Msimang was involved with Kadalie's ICU in Cape Town. He served on the ANC's national executive during the presidential terms of both Josiah Gumede and Pixley Seme and was Natal ANC secretary during the presidency of Champion.[39] In spite of only attending two session of the NRC, Msimang nevertheless made his mark on Council debates. Msomi lost his seat in 1948, and Msimang then took over as caucus secretary in 1949 and 1950. His attitude to the NRC was that it served as a useful "watch dog of the people" and ought not to be abandoned.[40]

Lancelot Peter Msomi

Msomi was elected in 1942 as the urban areas representative for Natal. Little is known of Msomi's background except that he had been a teacher for some considerable time before his election to the NRC. Matthews found him an invaluable caucus secretary and was eager to see him re-elected in 1948. Msomi was not an important political figure in Natal and had not managed to secure the support of Champion, his fellow councilor and Natal ANC president. Champion held that he could not support Msomi because Msomi was not a member of the ANC. This lack of support caused Msomi to lose the 1948 election.[41]

William Washington Ndhlovu

Ndhlovu came from Vryheid in Natal and was one of the two Natal members of the ANC who produced its 1919 constitution.[42] He was a leading figure in African affairs in the 1930s. In 1935 he attended the Natal Native Conference, called by the government to discuss the Hertzog Bills, and was appointed deputy chairman of the conference under Dube.[43] His popularity can be gauged by the fact that he defeated both George Champion and Josiah Gumede at the polls in 1937.[44] In 1938 and again in 1941 his opinions on racial matters at Council sessions set him apart from the other councilors, which may have been a factor in the loss of his seat in 1942.[45]

T. Ntintili

T. Ntintili was elected in 1948. He was not present at the 1949 Council session, thus only attending one meeting of the NRC, the last, in 1950. His views can be gauged by his speeches in the Transkei General Council. He was anti–Communist, showing a definite hostility to Govan Mbeki, his fellow councilor in the Transkei. The choice of Ntintili as a Transkei representative suggests that his views were shared by a large enough majority of the Bunga to ensure his election to the NRC. Five months before the adjournment of the NRC in 1946, he had moved a motion in the Bunga asking that the African people be given equal political rights, rights to which Ntintili thought they were entitled to as citizens of South Africa.[46] This was a radical resolution for that time and does not support the contention in *Inkundla Ya Bantu* that described Ntintili as a moderate of the mildest kind.[47]

Elijah Qamata

Elijah Qamata was elected by the Transkei General Council to the NRC but only retained his seat for one term. He had originally been a teacher but by the time he was elected to the NRC in 1937 was a tobacco farmer. A prominent member of the Transkei General Council, he gained more votes in the 1937 NRC elections than any other Transkei candidate,[48] but he was defeated in 1942. Although the reasons for his initial popularity are unknown, there were some exceptional aspects to his personality. The Department of Native Affairs' rehabilitation scheme in the rural areas met with a considerable amount of opposition in the 1940s. Qamata, however, did not merely complain about the situation; he actually took the trouble of conducting a census in his district that showed that out of 800 heads of families, 250 owned no land at all. He then pointed out that the rehabilitation scheme would be better received by the area as a whole if the government attended to the needs of this landless minority.[49] His view of the NRC was that it was an organization through which Africans might communicate their problems to the government, rather than an organization through which such matters might actually be redressed.[50]

Charles Sakwe

In 1918 Charles Sakwe was elected to what later became the Transkei General Council, on which he had served uninterruptedly for nineteen years by 1937, the time of the first NRC elections.[51] By 1937 he was also chair of the Transkei Vigilant Association and of the Transkei Native Voters, as well as being very influential on the Cape Native Voters Association, "an organization whose gallant defense of Bantu voter's rights during the last fifteen years has received scant appreciation from those whose interests it championed."[52] At the time of his election to the NRC, Sakwe was politically the most prominent African in the Transkei, a position he was to hold for some years.[53] Charles Sakwe was a member of the NRC from 1937 until 1948. Sakwe put much emphasis on unity among the Africans. This was one of the reasons for his strong support of the NRC. Known as the father of the Bunga (as the Transkei General Council was called), he initially regarded the NRC as the national manifestation of an accepted local body.[54]

William Buxton Xiniwe

William Buxton Xiniwe worked as a law agent in Kingwilliamstown.[55] His father was Paul Xiniwe, a hotel owner and a well-known figure in African circles in Kingwilliamstown, which was the seat of the Ciskei General Council.[56] Xiniwe was president of the Cape branch of the ANC from 1940 until his death in 1949 and this, together with his family's prominent position in the Cape, led to his nomination and later election to the NRC. He served on the Council from 1937 until his death in 1949. As far as can be ascertained, the only other post of importance held by Xiniwe was that of chair of the Cape Electoral Committee.[57]

Arthur Joseph Sililo

Arthur Joseph Sililo came from Durban and by his own account was an author by profession. It has not been ascertained what he wrote or whether anything he wrote was published. Since 1932 he had been a member of the Durban Advisory Board and had attended the national conference in Ladysmith. Besides his activities on the Location Advisory Board, there is also some evidence that he was fairly prominent in the All African Convention.[58] Too few Africans (under 2,000) had been permitted to register as urban dwellers in Natal, due to the unwillingness of the authorities to recognize the urban African population. Thus no one could stand for election in 1937. This led to an amendment of the Natives Representation Act in 1938. However, certain electoral irregularities took place during the 1939 electoral campaign, which led to the results twice being set aside. Thus it was only in October 1940 that Sililo won his seat on the NRC.[59] During his election campaign he stressed his interest in social welfare for Africans and emphasized that he alone of the candidates for the urban Natal seat neither shunned the white man nor regarded him as an enemy.[60] He won his seat over both George Champion and A.S. Mtimkulu but only held it for one session, that of 1941. His brief Council membership was terminated when he lost the 1942 election to L.P. Msomi.

Sam P. Sesedi

Sam P. Sesedi was elected to the Council in a by-election in the Cape in 1949, following the death of Xiniwe. He thus attended two somewhat truncated sessions of the NRC. Initially Sesedi had worked as a teacher, but at the time of his election he worked as a butcher. During his two years on the NRC he was a member of the ANC executive and was president of the Location Advisory Board Congress.[61] He too, like Luthuli, tried to get appointed to the Council but the Department of Native Affairs objected on the grounds that they suspected him of "communistic tendencies."[62] He showed no sign of this in his speeches when he became an NRC councilor.

Richard Victor Selope Thema

Richard Victor Selope was born in 1886 in the Peietersurg District of the Transvaal. He joined the African National Congress in Pietersburg shortly after its formation. He quickly gained a prominent position there and became the first general secretary of Congress when Dube was president.[63] In 1919, Thema was both spokesman and secretary of the deputation that went to London to complain of the unjust laws against Africans that had already by then been passed by the South African Parliament. The complaints made while he acted as deputation secretary are noteworthy in their similarity to those made by Thema twenty years later in the NRC. As a vehicle for his political opinions, Thema turned to journalism. He became the first editor of *Abantu Batho*.[64] In 1932 (with the help of B.G. Paver and Isaac Le Grange) he started *Bantu World*. He was the editor of a newspaper that by 1937 had the largest circulation among Africans in Southern Africa.[65]

From 1923, the government held a number of conferences in an attempt to gain African approval for its plans to remove the Africans from the Cape Franchise. Thema was a delegate at all these conferences, and as he himself wrote, "fought hard for the retention of the Cape Franchise." Thema pointed out that the concept of forming what was later called the Natives Representative Council would inevitably lead to such a council's being regarded as an African parliament and said, "We cannot have two Parliaments in one country."[66] In 1937, he won his seat on the NRC from forty-two rival candidates.[67] He was re-elected in 1942 and 1948.

The Nominated Councilors

George Makapan

George Makapan was appointed to the NRC by the government in 1937 and died in 1941. Unlike the other nominated NRC members, Makapan was not a chief but had been appointed to act as regent during the minority of his nephew. His ability as regent impressed the Department of Native Affairs and influenced it in his appointment to the NRC. Makapan held the regentship until 1927 and from that time until the formation of the NRC was active in African politics. During the 1930s, he acted as the financial secretary of the "upper house" of the ANC and in 1936, he became part of the AAC (All African Convention) executive. Makapan's views on forced labor, police methods and the pass system were such that there is every reason to suppose that had he not died in 1941, he would have held similar views to Mshiyeni and Poto in later years.[68] After his death in 1941, Chief S. Mohlatsa, a very old man, was appointed to take the place of Makapan. Mohlatsa said nothing at the NRC sessions and died in 1945. Chief Daniel More, also of an advanced age, was appointed in his place.

Chief Samuel Mankuroane

Samuel Mankuroane was a prominent chief from the Western Cape who retained his seat in the NRC from its inception until the government abolished the Council in 1951. The Department of Native Affairs favored him for this position initially, because all the elected councilors came from the Eastern Cape and they held that the Western Cape was thus under-represented.[69] Mankuroane participated in very few debates but when he did speak, he consistently adopted an anti-government stance.[70] By 1942, the government wanted to replace him. The last straw as far as they were concerned was a document signed by Mankuroane that stated, "The government is using the South African Native Trust as a tool for African exploitation." Smit, then Council chair, told Mankuroane that if that was really his view then he could not reappoint him to the NRC.[71] However, his removal would have laid the department open to the charge that it was only willing to appoint "yes men" to the Council, an impression that it wanted to avoid.[72] Thus, Mankuroane retained his seat in 1942 and was reappointed in 1948.

Chief Frank Maserumule

The government appointed Maserumule in 1946. Makapan's nephew was originally considered for this appointment but was rejected because he held anti-white views. It seems that Maserumule was appointed because it was hoped he would voice some pro-government views to counteract those of Mshiyeni and Poto.[73] They were disappointed in that he played the same minimal role in the NRC as had his predecessors. At the August 1946 adjournment session, Maserumule rose to speak but was prevented by the Council chair, Fred Rodseth. The intervention of Godlo, who attempted to persuade Rodseth to let Maserumule continue his address, suggests that the speech would have supported the adjournment motion. However, Maserumule later denied this and persuaded the department to overlook this incident. He was reappointed for a further term of office in 1948.[74]

Chief Mohlaba Shilubane

Chief Mohlaba Shilubane was appointed in 1941 after the death of Makapan. He was not the department's first choice. Initially Chief Mtha-helele was to have been nominated; however, he was then considered unsuitable because it became known that he was a supporter and friend of Thema, and the authorities considered that Thema had enough supporters in the NRC. As far as can be ascertained Mohlaba had never been politically active. He was seventy-eight when appointed to the Council in 1941 and died in 1944. He too played almost no part in Council debates.[75]

Chief Mshiyeni Ka Dinizulu

Chief Mshiyeni Ka Dinizulu became the Zulu regent during the minority of his nephew, Cyprian. He was a nominated member of the NRC from 1937 until 1951. In the first years of his Council membership, Mshiyeni held that in order to obtain concessions from the government, the best policy was that of cooperation.[76] This won him approval of the Department of Native Affairs and in 1939 he was appointed acting paramount chief of the Zulus, thus becoming the only recognized paramount chief in the country at that time.[77] By 1940, his stipend had been increased to 500 pounds per annum, making him one of the three highest paid chiefs in the country (Victor Poto was another).[78]

However, by the early 1940s, Mshiyeni began to take a more active interest in politics. In 1941, Xuma asked him to become the leader of the ANC's "upper house."[79] His attitude gradually changed and by 1946, he had entirely abandoned his former views.[80] As could have been anticipated, he was no longer regarded with favor by the department, which by 1948 was considering removing him from the NRC and replacing him with his ward, Cyprian. The only reason Cyprian was not appointed was that it was considered more economical to reappoint Mshiyeni rather than pay him the pension he would have received had he lost his seat on the NRC.[81]

Chief Victor Poto Ndamasa

Appointed in 1937, Poto remained a member of the NRC throughout its existence. In 1918, he was installed by the government as chief of the Pondos. He was one of the few chiefs granted jurisdiction over his area of Pondoland.[82] He was fully supportive of government agricultural endeavors and introduced the improvements suggested by the government. These were not his own innovations but were merely indicative of his support of government initiatives, in that since 1927 chiefs had been turned into little nothing more than civil servants. Initially, during the tenure of the first NRC, he was even more pro-government than Mshiyeni, but like Mshiyeni, his opinions gradually changed after 1942.[83] Poto was at first regarded as the ideal pro-government spokesmen on controversial issues, but his change of heart eventually became so pronounced that that by 1948 the Department of Native Affairs was considering replacing him as well.[84]

Chief Daniel More

Daniel More took the place of Chief Mohlaba on the Council, after the latter died. Smit said that More had served on the British side in the Boer War, and that he was loyal to the government and was a man who was not afraid to speak his mind.[85] More was of an advanced age and sat on the Council for less than two years, dying in April 1946. He had been a member of the Rustenburg Local Council but took little part in the debates and appeared overawed by the other councilors.[86]

Chief Jeremiah Moshesh

Jeremiah Moshesh, a great-grandson of the famous Moshesh of Lesotho, was an elected member of the NRC from 1937 until he lost his seat in the 1948 Transkei General Council elections for the NRC. He had succeeded to the chiefdom in 1915 and since 1918 had been a member of the Transkei General Council. By 1937 when he was elected to the NRC, he had been on its executive committee for three years.[87] In 1940, the Department of Native Affairs presented him with a medal for loyal service and in 1947, he was appointed by the department to accompany the secretary of native affairs to the Liberian centenary celebrations. Moshesh was a government supporter on a number of issues debated in the NRC and may be described as the most pro-government of all the councilors.[88]

Government Officials

W.W.M. Eiselen

W.W.M. (Max) Eiselen was born near Botshabelo in the former Transvaal in South Africa in 1899. He was the son of a missionary of the Berlin Missionary Society, as were the majority of the native commissioners before the advent of apartheid in the Department of Native Affairs. They were appointed because they understood at least one of the African languages due to their upbringing on a mission station. Eiselen spoke Northern Sotho. His field was anthropology and African languages, and in 1924 he received a doctorate at the University of Hamburg. After his return to South Africa he became lecturer and then professor at Stellenbosch University. He is infamous as being the compiler of the system known as apartheid. Given the impact that his ideas had on South Africa until 1994, the origins of Eiselen's ideas have been ascribed to his upbringing in Botshabelo, his studies in Germany, and the practical experience he gained both in his years at Stellenbosch University and through his work as chief inspector of native education in the Transvaal, at that time a province in South Africa. What has been entirely overlooked is the impact of his attendance at the multiple sittings of the NRC sessions that lasted for nine years, until the NRC adjourned in 1946.[89] This was also the year he resigned from the Broederbond[90] and from his job as director of native education. Eiselen then again returned to academic life, where he undoubtedly worked on his theory of apartheid. It could be that all this was a coincidence, but given the resemblance of the views of the members of the Natives Representative Council to the solutions proposed by Eiselen as a part of what he regarded as the "positive" aspects of separate development, the years in which he listened to and participated in NRC debates had a significant influence on him.

The major work that deals specifically with this aspect of apartheid, namely the question of how and when Eiselen formulated the views that had so much impact on South Africa, is a work by Cynthia Kros, *The Seeds of Separate Development: Origins of Bantu Education* (Pretoria, 2010). Eiselen was highly regarded not only by men of the NRC but also by liberal opinion in the 1940s, and yet what eventually emerged from his work was not a system that gave separate but equal quality of life to black and white but on the contrary led to war[91] and bloodshed. However, can Eiselen be blamed for the manner in which these ideas were applied in the following forty years? Kros has no doubt that he can. She compares Eiselen with Adolf Eichmann, the man who was at the center of the Nazi extermination program. Eiselen, however, renounced his German citizenship at the start of the Second World War because of his opposition to the Nazis.[92] He was also not in the center or even the periphery of any policy of murder. Kros spends three pages comparing him to Eichmann. The theory of separate development (the word *apartheid* is its literal translation into Afrikaans) degenerated into a brutal dictatorship, but never advocated extermination. This kind of hyperbole does nothing to advance our understanding of either Eiselen or apartheid and trivializes the Holocaust.[93]

Eiselen in his early twenties initially believed that there were differences in black and white physical and mental capabilities.[94] However, by 1929 he appeared embarrassed by his previous stance.[95] Between the two world wars, in the 1920s and 1930s, the majority of people held that African societies lagged behind those of the West. Eiselen regarded the 1936 legislation (the Natives Representation Act and the Native Trust and Land Trust Acts) as "morally suspicious."[96] and resigned from the Broederbond after ten years.[97] C.E. Byers Naude was a member of the Broederbond who resigned his membership after twenty-two years and became a much-revered part of the South African liberation struggle. So was President De Klerk, who began the reforms that led to the first South African general election in 1994, without ever apologizing for the original concept of separate development. A one-time membership in an organization does not indicate a lifelong devotion to the causes it espoused. No evidence is given that Eiselen ever belonged to either the New Order or any other of the quasi-fascist groups that arose in South Africa before and during the Second World War, and it also appears extremely unlikely that someone who gives up his German citizenship in protest against the Nazis would then join a fascist organization. There is also no evidence that he regarded Africans as mentally inferior to Europeans. In fact it seems that Eiselen cast doubt on the reliability of IQ tests at a time when their results were not generally disputed.[98] He was always at pains to point out that the so-called scientific evidence of Africans' mental abilities was inconclusive and called into question IQ tests. Differences, he maintained, were due to culture.[99]

A part of his duties and that of the other three directors of native education was to attend a Council session once a year, generally on the first day. There they presented their reports, waited for comments from the councilors, participated in the debate that usually followed and then they left. This happened for nine years in the case of the directors of the three other provinces. However, the Transvaal director, Eiselen, did not leave but went on to attend many more sittings of every session. Many of the debates at which he was present and in which he participated had nothing to do with education. Sometimes right at the start of a sitting, sometimes in the middle of a morning or afternoon sitting, it would be noted that "Dr. Eiselen has entered the room."[100] He was well received by the councilors; in fact one can state that of all the officials who attended the NRC sessions he was by far the most well-liked, giving every appearance of having a great understanding of their problems and aspirations in connection with education, and when he chose to participate in other matters as well.[101]

Eiselen became secretary of native affairs in 1949, and this made him South Africa's major administrator of South Africa's hated policy.[102] Although the NRC had been dysfunctional since 1946, Eiselen was convinced that he could persuade the councilors to reconsider. This idea must have been based on both his attendance at Council sessions and his interaction with councilors such as Z.K. Matthews after the NRC's adjournment in 1946. It was not only the liberals who were anxious to gain the cooperation of the African intelligentsia.[103] His efforts led to his financially enabling the councilors to meet in 1949, first at an informal meeting, without him, in Bloemfontein; then again at a meeting at which he was present. His private meeting with Z.K. Matthews and his efforts at getting Verwoerd not only to address the Council but also to reply to councilors' comments after he gave his speech were unprecedented in the Council's history. No other cabinet minister who addressed the NRC, including Smuts (deputy prime minister in 1937) and Hofmeyr (at that time acting prime minister), replied to the councilors' reactions to their speeches; only Verwoerd thought it important enough to do so. Thus both Verwoerd and Eiselen genuinely believed that certain aspects of apartheid would sway the councilors sufficiently to retract their former stance of non-cooperation. These were the aspects that had been debated in the Council since 1937, and had been incorporated into Eiselen's "great plan."

The National Party majority in Parliament in 1950 was so small that additional seats would have been useful. Possibly influenced by Verwoerd, they held it to be a possibility that Africans might vote for their candidates in the black elections held under the Representation of Natives Act. This act, besides leading to the formation of the NRC in 1936, also provided for the election of four white senators. The National Party then contested all the four seats in the Senate, although only the candidate in Natal had their official sanction.[104] Councilors Henry Selby Msimang, James Moroka and Paul Mosaka all took active steps to see that these candidates were rejected, and indeed, all lost their deposits.[105]

The main argument for territorial separation, as Verwoerd explained to the NRC, was political. D.F. Malan, the then–prime minister, said that either they would follow a course of equality that would end in suicide for the white race or they would implement a system of separate development in which each race would be protected with full opportunities for development without clashing with the interests of the other race.[106] In 1947 India became independent and began the bloody separation of Muslims and Hindus leading to the formation of Pakistan. In 1949 came the race riots in Cato Manor in Natal. These were acts of murder, rape, and looting by Africans against Indians who lived among them. Such occurrences, just at the time that Eiselen was presenting his plans for apartheid, were the examples that the advocates of apartheid had before them. Their fears then were not as far-fetched as they might seem to us today.

The Commission on Bantu Education,[107] the Eiselen Commission, was set up in 1949. The findings of this commission, arrived at through interviews and other research, reiterated many of the NRC resolutions on black education. This similarity would have led Eiselen to believe that the councilors and the African population in general shared his ideas on apartheid and that common ground might still be possible between the Council and the government as late as December 1950. The findings of the commission were published in 1951. The report stated that all aspects of black education should be controlled and coordinated by the state and that African parents should be involved in the educational affairs of their children. Eiselen believed that by firmly anchoring the schools in the life of the people, education would no longer encourage escape from African society but would fulfill its true function of uplifting the community as a whole.[108] All these findings resonated with NRC resolutions.

The only issue on which Eiselen differed significantly from the NRC was that of language. The NRC was not in favor of education in the vernacular, holding that if blacks could not speak English it would prove to be an economic disadvantage. Eiselen's idea of using the vernacular in the primary schools might have been educationally sound, but it was viewed with suspicion by the councilors as an attempt at segregation through language. The only benefit as far as the Council was concerned was that the insistence on mother-tongue instruction would ensure that more Africans would be employed as inspectors and also as teachers in African schools.[109] The issue concerning Afrikaans was more of an academic one, because most black schoolchildren never went beyond the first four years of schooling and were thus never taught in Afrikaans in any case. The matter was thus essentially one of principle. Councilors resented the attention accorded to Afrikaans as compared to the neglect of their own languages by the government.[110] In any case Afrikaans, not English, was seen as the language of the oppressor. Councilors were concerned that some children would now have to learn three languages. The matter of education without consultation was a sore point with the councilors, who continually complained that parents had too little say in the mission schools that their children attended.[111] NRC wanted education taken away from the missionaries, in line with Eiselen's views. However, they wanted it to be placed under the Department of Education, while Eiselen wanted it placed under the Department of Native Affairs. Smit, as secretary of native affairs, agreed with Eiselen. This was an important issue because under the Department of Native Affairs, education could be conducted in keeping with the country's segregationist policy.[112] All these concerns were dealt with in the Eiselen Commission.

Eiselen's ideas on the fostering of African custom were echoed in many councilors' resolutions. The NRC wanted the government to recognize polygamy. The denial of the legality of polygamous marriages led to difficulties in carrying out the customary laws of inheritance.[113] Not only the missionaries were against the recognition of polygamous marriages; the municipalities, too, used such marriages as an excuse to prohibit women coming into the towns. The Department of Native Affairs agreed with the Council and stated that any opposition encountered from the missionaries in this regard should be ignored.[114] Traditional herbalists, opposed by the medical fraternity of the day, were supported by the Council. Even Dr. Moroka declared that such medicines and traditions should undergo scientific testing before being condemned. In Natal, from 1927 to 1935, one thousand medicine men had their licenses scrapped. As Dube explained, in defense of his support of the herbalists, "We Zulus still cling to our old customs."[115] The African laws of inheritance divided the NRC, with the majority being in favor of its retention. Eiselen himself was in favor of such African practices as levirate marriages.[116] Other councilors considered such institutions no longer appropriate for modern women,[117] but Xiniwe, at that time the president of the Cape ANC, countered such statements with, **"I pride myself on my native law and custom."**[118]

Another bone of contention against the missionaries was their preference for employing white rather than black teachers, in spite of the additional cost involved. White teachers were paid three times the salary of African teachers with the same qualifications.[119] Eiselen was from the first in agreement with the councilors that all teaching posts in black schools should go to black teachers.[120] Mapikela explained, "We do not want the Europeans teachers in our schools, not that we hate them ... but justice has to be meted out to both sides. We did not want segregation; we did not claim segregation. You wanted it and now you are depriving us of our opportunities. A stop should be put to this."[121] Eiselen agreed; his strategy would put a stop to it. The NRC insistence that black interests could only be served by other blacks was questioned by the native commissioners who believed that their work was put in doubt by this attitude.[122] The chief native commissioners were all the sons of missionaries, and the paternalism that was still present in the Department of Native Affairs before 1948 led them to think of themselves as the "trustees" of the Africans and that what they did was for the good of their charges. However, their presumption that they were the arbiters of all knowledge about Africans irritated the councilors. Champion held that they were selected because of their knowledge of African customs, and this had nothing to do with, for example, the labor question.[123] They were of the opinion that senior administrative positions in the urban locations should be given to their own people: "We did not feel there was any necessity for a white gentleman to become the ruler of our settlement. Africans should be in charge of their own locations, they should not be run by ex-policemen"[124]; Moroka clarified the position by explaining that African advancement could not succeed because "no white man may serve under a native."

In 1945 the NRC was addressed in Afrikaans for the first and only time. This led Paul Mosaka to ask that he be addressed in one of the African languages used by the other eight million people who lived in South Africa.[125] It was the only time that approval of the use of African languages was mentioned in the Natives Representative Council.

Segregation placed Africans in their "own areas." But work in these areas was usually given over to white contractors. This aspect of segregation was one that led to many resolutions. Deputation after deputation from 1935 onwards was presented to the minister of native affairs asking that Africans be allowed to trade in the townships. Godlo called it one of the hardy annuals of the Council.[126] Eiselen's proposals would, if carried out successfully, have done away with such problems. Just as Africans would not be allowed to work in white areas, so whites would no longer be allowed to work in black areas. When councilors asked that an engineering faculty be opened at Fort Hare for the training of medical assistants, Smit said that there was no point in such resolutions, because graduates would not be employed in the private sector and no government departments, except that of native affairs, would employ them.[127]

A resolution to provide bursaries to assist men to train as sanitary inspectors was given the same reply: Where would such graduates find jobs?[128] Eiselen had the answer: In their "own areas." Africans under segregation had no opportunities to advance in any field and so were forced to remain in servile positions. Mapikela asserted that previously, work done in the urban locations had been given to African contractors, but on his visit to Orlando[129]Africans were no longer given such contracts.[130]

One of the earliest Council resolutions was that presented in 1937 by Makapan, who asked for the establishment of agricultural colleges. The establishment of both agricultural and industrial schools was in keeping with Eiselen's vision for the future of black education. This emphasis of Eiselen on industrial schools for African children was welcomed by Dube. His Ohlanga Institute, taken from the example of Booker T. Washington, taught tailoring, carpentry and shoemaking, but he complained that the color bar prevented those who had graduated from practicing their trade.[131]

The words "consistent" and "fair" were frequently heard in debates about job opportunities until 1946, when the NRC demanded the abolition of all discriminatory legislation. If just the white population was allowed to be employed and reside in the towns, then Africans should be given equal employment and opportunities in those areas where the government wanted them to live. They had no illusions about segregation. As Mosaka held, "They say, 'You can develop along your own lines.' Well, we know what that means. It means that the native can come and work for the white man, and after that he can be sent back to his *kraal*.[132] I contend that the African must be allowed to say what is good for him at a certain stage."[133]

The adherence to their customs was evident in many of the debates, cattle culling being one of them. The small percentage of land allotted to the Africans in the 1913 land act meant that overcrowding of stock was inevitable. The degradation of the soil that resulted led to repeated appeals by the Department of Native Affairs to cull cattle belonging to Africans in such areas. The Department of Native Affairs told the NRC to ask their constituents if they were willing to cull their cattle. African custom was strongly tied to the keeping of cattle, and all the councilors except for Jabavu, who was himself a farmer in the overcrowded Ciskei, reported back that their people had told them that on no account would they support cattle culling.[134] A councilor from the Transkei said during one of the debates on the customary law of inheritance (but it could equally be seen as relevant in the above case), "We are here representing our backward people."[135]

Councilors were not always consistent when it came to African customs. Sometimes, Thema could be vociferous in defending African customs, such as the lengthy debates on the brewing of traditional African beer. The municipalities had taken this lucrative means of making money for themselves by prohibiting illegal brewing in the townships and building beer halls. To add insult to injury, they did not use the monies thus accrued for the benefit of the African population but for roads and other such projects in white areas. It was an important source of income for urban African women, and the brutal police raids in the middle of the night and other harassment that took place as a result of this prohibition caused a great deal of distress. Beer was traditionally only made on festive occasions. "African people like their beer, beer was part of their father's food, and when the Europeans say, 'You shall not drink beer except the beer which is made by the municipality,' they simply show that they do not understand the position."[136]

When one compares the debates of the NRC with what were termed at the time "the positive aspects of apartheid," the conclusion is inescapable that his concept of "positive" apartheid consisted of much that the NRC had asked for during the nine years in which Eiselen attended their sessions. Eiselen could never admit that any of his ideas stemmed from NRC debates. The idea that anything said by an African could have such profound effects on government policy would have been unacceptable to the National Party and its supporters. Verwoerd and Eiselen's attempts at persuading the NRC to continue its work under the national party government show that Eiselen hoped that his concessions to NRC resolutions made before 1946 had been attended to, but they came too late. The Nazis had shown the world the horrifying results of a policy based on race, and no amount of "positive apartheid" could change this.

The Eiselen Commission was determined to get the African perspective, to address the problems of South African society. They wanted to lay the foundations of a viable plan that would be compatible with total separation, preparing the way through education for a separate development policy that would do away with the limited opportunities for Africans so far available to them. Large parts of the Eiselen report were penned by Eiselen.[137] Smit was one of the reasons that the NRC ran so smoothly from its inception until he retired. One of the first acts of the post–1948 government was to remove the new secretary of native affairs and replace him with Mears, who had previously been the chief native commissioner in the Transkei. Fred Rodseth deserved to be removed as secretary of native affairs. In November 1946, he was not only ineffectual but also inefficient, neglecting to provide translators for the four chiefs. He himself acknowledged his inexperience when the adjournment occurred and admitted that he did not know how to handle the situation.[138] However, Rodseth was never intentionally discourteous. The same thing cannot be said of Mears. He proved to be no better at the NRC session in 1949, so he too was replaced, this time by Eiselen.

In the NRC's history, the only motions proposed that appeared to ask for segregation were two entered by W.W. Ndhlovu in 1938 and in 1941. Ndhlovu moved for the removal of coloreds, firstly from Zululand, from which he wanted them "eliminated," and secondly from the black areas altogether. On Thema's protests on the dubious wisdom of such a motion, Ndhlovu agreed to amend it to apply only to those coloreds that refused to accept tribal discipline, but he refused to withdraw them altogether.[139] In 1941 he attempted to have the Council pass a resolution that would prohibit Indian men from associating with black women. Both attempts were heavily defeated in the Council.[140] Natal councilors who were said to have strongly anti–Indian views included George Champion, who was elected in 1942 and did not participate in these debates, but he never expressed such views during the time he was a member of the NRC.[141] The NRC made it clear that the Council as a whole viewed such resolutions with disfavor. Dube made a moving speech against these attempts by Ndhlovu.[142] He removed his support from Ndhlovu in the 1942 NRC elections and Ndhlovu lost the election.[143] Eiselen may have viewed such debates as more significant than they really were, especially after the anti–Indian riots in Cato Manor in 1949. There also allusions in the Eiselen Commission on the danger of continuing to withhold political rights from Africans, as well as fears by witnesses of social unrest due to the disintegration of African society.[144] In 1947 India was given its independence and the country was divided, with much bloodshed, into the new states of Muslim Pakistan and a smaller India. At the root of apartheid was the fear that South Africa might be torn apart if the political threat was not contained. This fear was not confined to Verwoerd or Eiselen or Malan but also had been expressed by Hertzog and Smuts in the 1920s.[145] One can thus view apartheid as yet another strategy at appeasing African leaders by giving them opportunities of advancement and leadership that they could not otherwise hope to attain in racist South Africa. The first strategy was the formation of the Natives Representative Council that drew its black subjects into a regular constitutional relationship that ignored tribal differences. Given the attempts at retaining the NRC by Verwoerd and Eiselen in 1950, perhaps they had in mind some kind of national council that would represent what were to become the Bantustans, but this can only be surmise.

Eiselen has been held responsible for all the resultant evils that emerged from the government's attempts at implementing apartheid. None of this was his intention, but intention is not everything. The members of the NRC were the original founding members of the African National Congress in 1912. Thema, Dube, Mapikela, and Ndhlovu were all founding members, with Dube as the first president-general of the ANC. If they could not be persuaded to accept segregation, what chance could there be that younger Africans would do so? Eiselen really did believe that segregation, if strictly and fairly applied with equality for both black and white, could succeed.

Of his "Great Plan," all that survives today are the remnants of the "positive" aspects of apartheid: the multiple universities constructed in the Bantustans and the African townships, the buildings that were constructed to house the administrators of the Bantustans, and the sports stadiums at such venues as Mmbatho; all these are what remain of his ideas. Eiselen died in 1977, a year after the Soweto uprising.[146] One aspect of the Council's views that he ignored was their objection to the teaching of Afrikaans. In the 1940s it seemed a minor matter, but the repercussions of the Soweto uprising against the teaching of Afrikaans resulted in the worst racial violence ever experienced in South Africa to date. The events in Soweto spelled the beginning of the end both for apartheid and for what turned out to be Eiselen's vision of a future South Africa that went horribly wrong.

Douglas Laing Smit

D.L. Smit was secretary of native affairs from 1934 to 1944 and thus chaired the majority of the NRC meetings. He understood the important part he could play when, in 1937, he wrote that the judgment of history on the South African nation would be dependent on the treatment of its Africans. Smit described his years in the NRC as one of the most interesting periods of his life.[147] Smit wanted the NRC to concentrate on matters of practical application, but he gave them great leeway in the Council debates. He was interested in the economic betterment of African life and chaired the Smit Report of 1942, which reflects his views. This committee was instructed "to explore possible ways ... of improving the economic, social and health conditions of the natives in urban areas."[148] On matters of policy he was not able to assist them, as the Department of Native Affairs could not remedy the policy itself. It was said of him that he was a liberal handicapped by his position.[149]

W.J.G. Mears and Fred Rodseth

On Smits' retirement in 1944, the chief native commissioner of the Transkei became secretary of native affairs and thus chair of the NRC. Rodseth became under-secretary of native affairs. In August 1945 Mears had caught the urgent undertone in the Council in 1945 when they asked that Smuts, the prime minister, should address them.[150] Smuts did nothing to fulfill this request in spite of Mears' attempts to have him do so. Rodseth had almost no experience of NRC proceedings when he took over the chair in August 1946, the time of the first Council adjournment. Both he and Mears had only chaired the Transkei General Council, and the technique used by them, according to Rodseth, was that the councilors were simply "shut up" if their speech was not to the government's liking.[151] There were also other incidents indicative of a general lack of respect for the NRC that angered the councilors.[152]

PART TWO: SPEECHES OF THE COUNCILORS

Introduction to the Speeches

The members of the Natives Representative Council wrote their own speeches. Most were not prepared texts, and their eloquence is the more remarkable when this is taken into account. The exceptions were the speeches they made in the NRC in 1949 when the newly elected National Party government had already made the announcement that they were to abolish the Council; thus the councilors thought that this would be their last chance to put forward their views. Unexpectedly in December 1950, the apartheid government made another attempt to persuade the NRC to continue their work. The secretary of native affairs was now W.W.M. Eiselen and Hendrik Verwoerd was the minister of native affairs. Together they had compiled their system of apartheid, separate development, a system that eventually led to South Africa's being completely at variance with a world that had witnessed the horrors that resulted from another system that viewed race as the defining aspect of a people, the Nazis. However, the compilers of the system of apartheid had no intention of exterminating an entire people, nor was there anything similar to the Wahnsee conference or any suggestion of such a thing as the "final solution."

By this, the last meeting of the NRC in 1950, the councilors were adamant that that they would not be used as the African spokesmen for a system such as apartheid, and so these where indeed their very last speeches in the Council and were also most probably prepared beforehand.

Some of the councilors were well-known figures in the African political scene of that time; some were of lesser stature; but all their speeches offer powerful insights into the ideals and the motives of these men, all of whom played their part in the history of South Africa. Their speeches could not change the minds of the white government to whom these speeches were addressed. That took another fifty years. Their words may not all have the poetry or beauty of great literature, but they have historical significance. Nothing can give us a greater understanding of the insensitivity of the whites in general to the black man's place in South Africa than these speeches. The segregation then in place was bleak and harsh but did not go as far as the crimes of the apartheid era. The councilors' speeches come to us at a critical time in South Africa's history. They were advocates of liberty and defenders of the rights of their fellow citizens. Their words were eloquent, quietly spoken and in the main unheard by those on whose behalf they were delivered. There was one man who listened, took part in their debates and was viewed by them as one of the few administrators, if not the only one, who understood the injustices they suffered. That man was the W.W.M. (Max) Eiselen, paradoxically regarded as the father of apartheid. It was he who listened and he who understood how important the rectification of their grievances was. He understood the injustice inherent in their complaints and made their rectification a part of what was termed "positive apartheid." Eiselen appeared to think, wrongly as it turned out, that this would satisfy the councilors, even if their demands for the abolition of all discriminatory legislation were ignored.

Each speech begins with the speaker, a short quotation from the speech, the date it was given, the page numbers on which the speech appears as published in the Verbatim Reports of the Natives Representative Council, and then an abbreviated version of the speech.

5

Education

The NRC believed that the key to freedom and equality lay in the education of their people. Z.K. Matthews' well-known comment was that in the South African context it had become accepted that the only work an educated African could do was to teach, preach and agitate.[1] It was this narrow basis that the Council tried to enlarge. They felt that Africa's whole future was bound up with the educational system. To the African education was everything, and nothing, as Moroka explained, was considered of greater importance. The situation, unsatisfactory as it was, was by no means unique to South Africa. Other African countries had the same problems. For example, in 1945 in British Bechuanaland (Botswana), at that time still under British administration, only 30 percent of children were at school, and of these well over 50 percent were in their first two years. Most classes had over fifty pupils, while 75 percent of the teachers had no qualifications. There were no secondary or technical schools.[2] This is not to condone the South African situation but merely to place it into an understandable context. Fort Hare in South Africa, which drew on the high school graduates of the entire African continent, had by 1945 only produced 72 black graduates.[3] The NRC's dislike of the missionaries was longstanding. The black community in general had many grievances against them, besides Dr. Bokwe's comment that the missionaries were more "mercenary than missionary." Issues such as these were articulated by the Council and undoubtedly noted by Eiselen.

The NRC was appreciative of what was being done in education when improvements were introduced, but not of the principles of differentiation that underlay these efforts. They did not believe there was such a thing a "native education." They resented the almost total segregation that had been achieved in the educational sphere. They believed that all the Africans needed to be the equal of the whites was education. The sums laid aside for black education increased considerably during the time of the Council. After the 1941 session it was announced that the Council's resolutions had been approved and that henceforth primary school education in government schools would be provided free of charge.[4] This was of course another reason for the unpopularity of the missionaries, who continued to charge African pupils educated in their schools. In 1945 J.H. Homeyr, then deputy prime minister, introduced a bill into Parliament that made the department of education responsible for financing black education, instead of the shameful previous situation where the African themselves had to finance the education of their children from the poll tax they paid.[5] So from 1945, black education was made the responsibility of the state. Africans would no longer have to bear the financial burden of their schooling.[6] Thus by 1947 Africans were receiving free primary school education, free books and free meals. In the high schools provision was now made for three times the number of pupils as had been the case in 1936. This was one instance when the government did take note of the resolutions of the NRC.

R.V. Selope Thema

"There is a great deal of injustice."
21 November 1938, 120ff

Mr. Chairman, if we speak so feelingly about this matter it is because we feel that insofar as education is concerned, there is a great deal of injustice. I won't repeat what the other councilors have said, but we see that we are not part and parcel of the population of South Africa as such. We are entitled, like other sections, to be treated in the same way.... I would like the Indian and colored people financed from their own sources and not from the source to which we also contribute. We do not only pay this poll tax to the state, we pay more than that, we pay in labor, the labor which has made development in this country possible.... I am not a racialist and I do not want to go into the question of whether the colored people should be taxed, but since it is the policy of the government that we should run our business along these lines, we certainly do feel that our education should be financed in the same way as that of the other sections of the community. We found also a differential treatment insofar as the teachers of our race are concerned. They are poorly paid; colored teachers are well paid and they even get a pension ... while the colored and Indian aged get pensions from the government, our aged people do not get anything.... Recently we had a conference in Johannesburg where it was stated that the native children are becoming uncontrollable running wild, they were doing all sorts of wonderful things—stealing and so on—and I would not be surprised if we were told that the reason is that we have come to the towns, if we had lived in the Reserves our children would not have come to the towns and got out of control. We came to the towns because the white people brought us there. Now it is the duty of the state to give us a chance, to give us the same educational facilities as it gives to other communities.

Chief Mshiyeni Kwa Dinuzulu
"Places are filled by Europeans."
21 November 1938, 98–99

There is this consideration which I think should not be lost sight of: We should bear in mind that education is something that advances—where are we going? ... I have come across Natives who have had excellent education but they are not able to get suitable work and therefore cannot earn money. In places where they might have had employment suitable to their education, those places are filled by Europeans. In our own native areas and at our magistracies, most of these posts are necessarily filled by Europeans; so too in dipping of stock, and that, of course, is rather simple work. What will be done with the education which has been spoken so much of when it has been given, seeing that avenues of employment are not open to us? It seems to me that the government, in making provision for the education of natives, should aim for fitting them for work which they will be able to do when they have finished their education so that they will not be at a loss.... In dipping services I may mention that we see natives taking the blood smear, mixing the medicine and counting the cattle, but there is a European placed over these people, who is in charge.... I shall be glad, sir, if employment can be found for our black people who have advanced sufficiently [to work] in our native commissioners' offices. I think the government should trust us in the same way we are trusted for doing domestic work in the kitchens.

Chief Samuel Mankuroane
"I am against ... the idea of ... separate schools for ... chief's sons."
21 November 1938, 101–02

It is our desire that we and our children should be educated so that we may be able to govern our tribes. Progress amongst people is the only thing that will save the people. Chief Mshiyeni has travelled beyond the proposals that were put before the Council. He dealt with the problem of children who have been educated and who are unable to get employment, but our trouble is to find education for our children.... It is true that if we intend our children to be chiefs to guide and lead our people, we must first train them to do so. What I do not support and what I am against is the idea of erecting separate schools for the training of chiefs' sons. The proper thing to do is this: that we the chiefs and our children should mix with commoners from our very childhood and as soon as the children have attained their majority we can give them some responsibility. I also support the idea that the chiefs' sons and the sons of headmen would be compelled to attend schools. I don't want to trouble you any more; the others have discussed the matter very fully.

Elijah Qamata
"The government is quite satisfied with building large prisons."
21 November 1938, 116–17

We do not say that the government has done nothing for the native people; what we say is this, that, in so far as education matters are concerned in respect of the natives, it is most unsatisfactory.... On my arrival here I met a large number of *amalaita* boys when I crossed the bridge. Those children would never have become gangsters if the government kept them in schools. The government is quite satisfied with building large prisons for a state of affairs which, in so far as the natives are concerned, is created by the government itself.

Thomas Mtobi Mapikela
"The Europeans ... cannot take everything for themselves."
25 November 1940, 63–65

The time has come when Europeans should realize that they cannot take everything for themselves ... that they should be consistent.... Africans have very few outlets. The Europeans can go where they like as teachers, etc. The Africans have very few opportunities. Even in offices, Africans are replaced by Europeans. In mechanical work, only Europeans are employed. Everywhere the Africans are excluded, however qualified they may be. I myself have been taken away. I am the man who made all the furniture for Grey College and the university, and the Europeans, some Europeans, asked why a native should be allowed to take the bread out of the mouths of their children. Not that I do not understand my trade. I know my work because my masters were very satisfied with me. A member of Parliament said that he would not allow a native to do the work, which should be done by Europeans. We are dismissed. You are running the whole show ... but please treat us better. If there is an opening for a native, do not take it away from him.

We do not want the Europeans teachers in our schools. Not that we hate them ... but justice has to be meted out to both sides. You cannot have it both ways. Our people should also be given a chance. We did not want segregation; we did not claim segregation. You wanted it and now you are depriving us of our opportunities. We do not want Europeans to teach our children if Africans are available. A stop should be put to this. We must speak frankly about these things. Give us a chance to do our work. Let this bad treatment come to an end; justice must be done. We are dictated to. This is not democracy. We are forced to certain things whether we like them or not; we cannot swallow everything. I urge that advertisements should be placed in all newspapers to the effect that African teachers would be appointed in African schools. All the European teachers are not graduates, only a few; the majority are ordinary teachers.

R.V. Selope Thema
"Civilization and barbarism cannot exist side by side without clashing."
25 November 1940, 121

Since the Council was formed we have been stressing the point that other sections are receiving more educational facilities that we, but we are also part and parcel of the population of South Africa and we are also contributing towards the development of the country. I think we have assisted more than other non-European section in the building up of South African industry, and therefore in this matter we have not been justly dealt with. One must not forget that civilization and barbarism cannot exist side by side without clashing. If we want to build up a civilized nation we must see to it that all sections of the population are civilized and educated. Only then will they become good citizens and will there be a real civilization in our country.

Thomas Mtobi Mapikela
"I move this motion with a sore heart."
25 November 1940, 52ff

Moves that the government's attention be drawn to the sad plight of the African teachers whose salaries are so low as the place them, as a class, among the unskilled laborers whose wages are now in some instances higher than the salaries of teachers; that the government be asked to give them some relief even during the war period. I move this motion with a sore heart. These people, these teachers are getting very little to live on... . Qualified teachers in many cases get only five pounds ten shillings, and even in secondary schools, they often get only about three or six pounds. We are never promised that these wages will be raised ... teachers remain in the same low position year in and year out ... many of the older men who have served the country faithfully are dying and are not getting a penny from the government.... Promises have been made, but now we are told that there is no money for them, and that there is no hope.... The white teachers are getting more than double what the Africans are getting although their scale of education may have been the same, and that is why we say that the European teachers should give our African teachers a chance.... We are given to understand that we have not got sufficient men to take up these positions, but when we look we see young Europeans from the colleges immediately being put into the schools to teach ... our people should be given the same opportunities. The work a man does and his abilities must be looked upon as the only qualifications. I say that this question of color must die away now. We should look at the question from this point of view: whether a man can do his work or not.

Paul Mosaka

"Sometimes ... we look like people who have nothing but grievances."
9 December 1942, 128

The native people are willing to be educated. We are not dealing with a people who have to be compelled to go to school, like the Europeans. Sometimes when we speak in the Council, we look like people who have nothing but grievances, grievances all the time to put before the government, Our expression of grievances is an expression of our desire to be uplifted so that we can make our contributions to the welfare of this country and not to be looked upon with scorn by other sections of the population. And therefore when we urge, particularly in this matter, that our education should be supported and financed on the same lines as the education of other sections of the community, we are not just making a complaint; it is not just a grievance: it is a desire on our part to be allowed to play our full share in the development of our country.

John Dube

"The white man ... shows his face
and the black boys are doing nearly all the ... work."
5 May 1943, 116

I stand up to welcome this [Dr. Eiselen's enthusiasm for building trade schools]. We have at Ohlanga tailoring, carpentry and shoemaking and the boys who are graduated from our industrial department, although they are hampered in their work by this color bar.... The white man simply stands outside, the white man simply shows his face and the black boys are doing nearly all the mechanical work behind.... They have been employed and they have done the work, but the face has to be there. That is the thin end of the wedge for us. and that has always been our difficulty in the past. But better days are coming, when all these color bars will be done away with. And when I see the government of the Transvaal (meaning Dr. Eiselen as director of native education) entering upon this venture, I am more than thankful, and although I have been discouraged in my own homeland, have had many sleepless nights trying to find money to carry on that industrial school at Ohlanga, I have never thought of giving up. I shall carry on because I think it is the rock on which the development of our country and the development of our people stand. Academic people are few in any race. It is the working people, the people that work with their hands, who are going to count above all. I have now started because I saw the need. I have started a school for teaching the boys and girls how to keep books, and how to do typewriting, shorthand and everything.... I believe that partly through the lack of proper bookkeeping, our people go down. Yes, they start well and they go under, they lose, because they are not able to keep proper accounts. Now this matter is being taken up by the education department and I therefore think that the future is hopeful.... This industrial school of mine has been going on for forty years. I got the inspiration when I was at college in the United States. I went over to Alabama and I became a great friend of Booker Washington's. I saw there, where color prejudice is not as strong as in South Africa ... negroes who went in for business. And it is something that we should welcome in this country because it will provide openings for our African people. We can talk a lot about our being able to do certain things ... but unless we can create things, we shall get nowhere. No matter how little it is—even if it is only a table that we can make—let us learn these things. And if the Department of Native Affairs are interesting themselves in this matter, I shall be very thankful, and in the afternoon of my life I am rejoicing that a scheme of this kind is coming into being before my bones are laid to rest.

George Champion
"The enmity [starts] in the classroom."
9 November 1945, 112–14

There was a time in this country when all children, white and black, went to the same school and were taught by the same teacher. These children were all together. They played together, and there was no spirit of ill feeling among them. For reasons better known to the government and other individuals, the children were segregated.... The white people went to their own schools and the natives went to their own schools, the Indians to their own schools and the colored people too. The native child was given an education which was supposed to be good for him, to enable him to develop along his own lines.... The native children were given the feeling that the other children were different from him. The enmity started right in the classroom. You will find that up to the age of 16 the native child is given a different education. In Natal and in the Free State too, I think he is taught in his mother tongue.... How these things were encouraged I don't know. Look at the position today. You have created people that hate everything that is white. You have stopped these people from getting the same quality of education.... You cannot bring these people back to the spirit of reconciliation and you can only do that by allowing the races to mix. At the back of all these laws, at the back of all these difficulties which we have, lies the segregation in the classroom. It is in the classrooms, in the primary schools that the trouble starts. I feel very strongly on this, Mr. Chairman, and I feel that the time has come when the schools should allow the mixture of children. Let the Zulu child, the Basuto child, the white child and the Indian child all mix together.... What I want to emphasize is the need for uniformity of education, the need to do away with this wretched segregation. I was a boy at Adams College more than thirty years ago. There were white boys at that college. We stayed together and we were friends. We know that Lovedale has produced some of the best men in the country. But what do we find today? Today we find white fathers and mothers teaching their children that the natives are a danger and a menace. That is the sort of education given the children today.

Paul Mosaka

"Keeping the *kaffir* in his place."
9 November 1945, 106ff

It was said by Councilor Moroka that it is a perfectly obvious thing that if this country is to progress, the African people must be educated; they must be brought up to the same level as the white people of this country. That is such an obvious thing that when it comes to the Europeans they take it for granted that a great deal of money must be spent on educating their children ... but when it comes to the native the same government does not think it quite so necessary or quite so obvious that these things should be done.... Well, I think we must try to find out why this should be so. I think it is because the policy of this government is based on two things. It is based on segregation—keeping the *kaffir* in his place. It is also based on cheap native labor.... Now by that the white people have created many dangers for themselves. They have made the native people a real danger to the white people. They have said to the native, "You must remain in your place, we don't want you." But because they cannot develop the resources of this country without the natives, they have found themselves forced to the position where they have to say to the natives, "Come along and help us to till our farms, and get the gold out of the mines." And by denying the African this fuller, richer life, as they call their Western civilization, they find that they have created conditions which are endangering the very life of Western civilization here. It is for that reason that the white people look upon the natives as a menace and a problem.... They find that in the ill health of the natives caused by the neglect in the Reserves, where they die of starvation and malnutrition.... The Reserves have become the breeding place of tuberculosis and of all manner of diseases ... a grave danger to the health of the white people of this country.... We cannot read with equanimity the statements in the press about the crimes committed by our people on the European public. Those crimes in fact are being committed on us in the native townships as well. But it is because the press does not generally report the murders, the robberies and the cases of rape in the Locations—it is because of that that we don't hear of these things. They are matters of no great importance but they become matters of importance when these same crimes are perpetuated on the European community....

Z.K. Matthews

"Why cannot we be compelled to do something ... for our benefit?"
9 November 1945, 102

If we are to live in harmony with the white man, it is important that we should be given the same opportunities as the white man. If we are to be respectable people then we must be educated, and that is the only way in which this land and the people in this land can ever hope to live in peace. We are compelled in regard to so many other things in this country, why cannot we be compelled to do something which is for our benefit? We are being compelled to carry passes; we are compelled to live in Locations; we are compelled to do all sorts of things—but we are never compelled to do something which will be of benefit for the African people and for the protection of the European people of this country. People who have studied the question will tell you that of our present population, the majority of our native population are completely illiterate people, people who have received no education whatever. Although this fact is not realized by many, those who have been educated are making a fair contribution to the welfare of this country; and I say this without fear of contradiction:

that they are the most orderly and the most law abiding people of this country. I submit that the European would be doing himself a good turn if he insisted on the education of all the African people of this country. We read the headlines in the newspapers and we see how nervous the Europeans are becoming about the criminal actions, the crimes perpetrated by some African people. We do not subscribe to these things, but we say how can you expect a man who lives under conditions such as conditions lived under by the Africans of this land not to produce that class of people, and we are asking the government to take drastic measures for combating criminality among the people—we are asking the government to give our people better education, give it to all of them, and we feel that it would be a step in the right direction to dealing with the criminal classes. As an educationist myself, I speak with feeling on this subject ... of compulsory education. We would make every individual more valuable to himself, and more valuable to the community to which he belongs, more valuable to the nation to which he belongs.

James Moroka
"African people should be made literate."
9 November 1945, 97ff

We medical men of South Africa, both black and white, are agreed that one of the great causes of tuberculosis in South Africa ... can be found almost entirely in the fact that the Africans are so ignorant that they cannot follow us when we try to help them. We have found out that in the majority of cases when these people come before us and we try to give them advice in matters that concern their health, as a result of their ignorance they are not able to follow our instructions, and we are agreed that the only way to combat this kind of thing is that all the African people should be made literate. A doctor cannot do everything himself without the cooperation of the patient concerned, unless the patient is in a position to.... It is almost impossible for those people to carry out our instructions, which is due to the fact that they are illiterate and cannot read and write even in their own language.... It must be borne in minds that the majority of these native children who don't go to school, do not go to school, not because they are not willing to go, but because their parents are so very poor that they are unable to give them the necessary clothing to go to school. It is not only a question of paying for the books, or paying the fees—they cannot clothe them sufficiently to enable them to go to school. Apart from that we know that one of the reasons why some of these children do not go to school is because the government has up to now failed to provide sufficient schools for African children.... The missionaries have tried for a hundred years to educate the African children but they have now come to the stage where they can pay no more, that they cannot afford to put up more money for the education of the children.... I maintain that if the government were to do as much as the missionaries have done, if the government were to put up as many schools as the missionaries have done, or as many boarding schools as the missionaries have done, and were to put up private schools, we would be able to put another 30 percent or 40 percent of the African children into schools. Mr. Chairman, it is the duty of any government to attend to the education of the children of the poorer section of the community in the land, and in South Africa the natives are the poorest.... The majority of these children today, even if they are told to go to school, have not got the clothes, but some of them have. Others again have not got the books they need, and that is why I have included this in my motion ... that free books should be provided. It is being done for European children and it is being done for colored children ... why then does not the government do it for the African people? We do not want to come here every day and cast stones as the government. We would like the government to know its duty, and it realize that the duty of the government is to see that the poorest of the poor are provided for better than other sections of the community, better than those sections that are able to do something for themselves. I maintain that the African people are like other people ... that is to say all of them will not go to school unless they are compelled to do so. That is why compulsory education must be introduced in this country.... It has not happened in the case of the white man or the colored man, and it is not likely to happen in the case of the African. So the one thing which the government must do is provide free and compulsory education for all the African children in South Africa. But free and compulsory education should first start in those areas where there are a large number of African children—in places like Johannesburg and the Witwatersrand ... and those big centers where you get large numbers of children not going to school, running about the streets, smoking, and playing cards, drinking, picking up cigarettes and cigars thrown away by Europeans. You get your juvenile delinquents there, you are getting criminals there, and in fact you are breeding them. You must get the children together and if you don't teach them, they will teach themselves. What else can you expect? And what annoys me often is that the Europeans in this country have the audacity to go about and say, "You see, the natives are the cause of all crime—their children are criminals, they grow up as criminals, they break into houses and do all sorts of wrong things," when in actual fact the fault lies with the white man. The white man has come to this country and has taken unto himself the right to run the natives.... Well, if he wants to run the native then he must do it in such a way that the native will become a respectable person.... If he does not do that it is his own fault. The native cannot do what he likes in this land. He is debarred. The faults which he has are attributable to the fact that the people who look after him do not look after him sufficiently well, they do not train him sufficiently.... My contention is that until the white people of this land realize that they cannot get rid of the African, until there comes a change of heart, and they look after the African as a human being ... until such time there will be no improvement in the general position.... Until that time comes we shall never see happiness in this land and, sir, let me say this, we shall never get the African to trust the white man.... Now, what happens in South Africa? We are not blind. We see what happens. We see large sums of money spent on European education. We see large sums of money spent on colored education, but against this we see very little spent on native education.... If you are fair-minded you cannot help realizing that there is something wrong somewhere, that justice is not done. If a man is not able to see that, then I say he is not prepared to see the truth. What I am pleading for ... is fair play ... we want equal opportunity—that is what we ask for. We want to be treated on exactly the same lines, we want to receive the same education, and we want to receive equal opportunity so that the white man in the long run will not be able to say that he is better than we are. Everything must be done purely on merit.

Z.K. Matthews

"In the olden days ... there was better
mutual understanding and ... mutual confidence."
7 November 1945, 23–25

We, Mr. Chairman, realize—having been produced by these missionary institutions, having lived in them and having known intimately the people who work in them—we realize the service which is being rendered in these institutions ... and I am sure the last thing we ... would wish to do is anything which might harm those institutions. All that we have said here ... has been said with the idea of trying to contribute something towards the better administration of the institutions.... The people who run them, as you know, are not so much concerned with money as with the upliftment of the African people, but what we say, and what we shall continue to say until the matter is put right, is that the African people themselves should be more closely associated with the government of these institutions. I want to assure you, Mr. Chairman, that in matters of discipline it would not be found that the African people are less strict than the people who are responsible for these institutions.... There is no longer proper mutual consultation between the people who work in these institutions, and the parents who do not seem to be taken into the confidence of those who run them; the teachers do not seem to be consulted ... and all we can say is that something must be done to breach that gulf. These institutions must be run as they used to be run in the olden days when there was better mutual understanding and better mutual confidence between those who were concerned in the work of education and the people.... I think that ... however hard it may be for them they must try and draw into the government of the institutions the African people who work there, and also those who are members of the churches that run the institutions outside. It is a combined effort, and we have recently suggested that it would be a good thing if the authorities of these institutions could have a conference with the leaders of the African people with a view to straightening out their difficulties. They might in that way get suggestions as to what are some of the root causes of these disturbances which have taken place in institutions.... We do not like these disturbances, and anything that can be done to remove them would be a contribution towards the development of native education. These institutions are an asset, Mr. Chairman, which we would not care to lose, and it must not be supposed that whenever we make our views heard on these matters we just do so with a view of criticizing the people who are doing their best under difficult circumstances. That is not so. We, the African people, would like to shoulder some of the burden together with those people, in the management of these institutions. Some of us have worked in these institutions and know how much trouble some principals take to try and carry the African people along with them—not to drag them along like unwilling horses, but to work along with them. It has been extremely successful in places where it has been tried.

James Moroka

"The work of educating the African people is beyond the missionaries."
7 November 1945, 28ff

I am more convinced than I have ever been before that the missionaries have done their level best to help educate the Africans. And I am also more convinced than I have ever been before that the work of educating the African people is beyond the missionaries. I think that it is now time that the government should do one of two things. Either the government must put up training institutions and put up boarding schools, or the government must come along and give more help to the missionaries to provide for native education. Mr. Hobson [on behalf of native education in the Cape] has told us today that in a big province like the Cape, a province which started native education as long ago as a hundred years back, a matter of 164 Africans will be writing the matriculation examination at the end of the year. Now, I look upon this as a very serious thing indeed. If, after the efforts of the missionaries over a period of over a hundred years, the schools in the Cape Colony can only send for the matriculation examination a matter of 164 students, then it surely shows that although the missionaries have done their level best they have not been able to satisfy native education. There is a great cry from the Africans for educations. Thousands and thousands of African children are kept out of mission schools because they have no accommodation for them. And if you want to produce the teachers who ... are needed, then it is my contention that the government must come along and do its duty and not throw that duty on the shoulders of the missionaries. It is not the work of the missionaries to educate the African people. The missionaries came here to Christianize the African people. It was merely because they were great-hearted people that they did not only teach the African children the Bible but that they also started teaching them various ways of making a living.... Either the government must step in and do it themselves, or they must enable the missionaries to do it. Where do we want the African people to get? We want the African people to get where other people are getting; we want the African people to be as educated as the European people of this country.... All we are asking for is that proper provision should be made for the African people.

Paul Mosaka
"Beware of the women!"
7 November 1945, 31

I just want to make ... very brief observations, first of all in regard to the riots at these institutions, and the suggestion of two institutions changing over from boys' to girls' schools. I should like to ask Mr. Hobson [chief education officer of native education in the Cape] to give these institutions very serious warning if they want to change over to girls' institutions—let them beware of the women.

Lancelot Peter Msomi
"All of us in this land are members of one human family."
9 August 1945, 67–69

Personally, I think that the whole trouble in this country arises from the fact that there is in existence in this country a type of education called African education. Yet we breathe the same air as the ruling class, we have the same sun shining above our heads; in case of disease we suffer in exactly the same way as they do. We are the same in every respect except that we are black and they are white. Except that they are advanced because of opportunities and we are backward for lack of opportunities. I disagree with those who contend that the white man came to this country because of his greater wisdom. I contend that our lot is governed by providence, by destiny. All of us in this land are members of one human family; we all have a duty to perform. The white man brought education to this country, he brought learning to us. Now we knew nothing about education, but from their teaching we came to understand that education is a means of preparing oneself for life, by going to school we became better prepared for life. If that is the case why should a child, simply because he is a black child, not be prepared in exactly the same way as the white child is prepared for life. We look upon the white people as Christians—our government is a Christian government. When we open this Council we pray because we all believe that we are responsible for our actions to a supreme being, so that whatever we do we act as Christians. We can hardly believe that in their actions towards the Africans the white people are actuated by any motives except those of fear, because they are great believers in that old saying about the survival of the fittest. We believe that what they are aiming at is to make themselves more fit that we are because it is the weakest that will go to the wall. It is not in the interests of the state itself that that the education of the greater number of the population should be an inferior education.... We see that the world is rapidly becoming a very small ball wherein people in South Africa can no longer hope to follow a policy of isolation for all time, and pursue a certain policy which is going to keep the greater section of the people of this country in a low state for all time. This country has to take its place in the sun along with other countries.... We Africans should not be given an education which makes us subservient, but an education which will make us independent in all aspects of life.

George Champion

"The native child [is] always ... the hewer of wood and the drawer of water."
15 August 1945, 89

In Natal ... the Bantu child who attended the same school as an Indian child and a white child ... was told to go to the native school, and so we found that instead of education, such as we know it, there was established what we know as native education. We were told that in the native schools the teachers must speak to school children in their mother tongue, and not only that, but the text books were translated into Zulu so that children in the native schools should be taught in their mother tongue. Now, what has that led to? It has led to children leaving a school without being able to express themselves in English. We find that ... the children in the native schools were told to go out and work ... and make the trees into *kerries.* We found that our children had gone to the rivers and collect clay to make images of oxen and goats. That was the kind of education which was regarded as suitable for African children—that was so-called native education. The girls were taught not to use the needle—no, they were taught [to] go out and collect grass for the purpose of making mats, such as those are used in the primitive life of the Zulu—that was native education.... The object, of course, was ... to make him the servant of someone else, not to put him into a position where he might compete with the others. The native child was always to be the hewer of wood and the drawer of water.

Paul Mosaka

"All we require is the opportunity to develop."
10 August 1945, 85

This motion raises the question of the ultimate goal of native education, and in that sense, what is the ultimate goal of that civilization of white and black in this country. What is the final structure of native education that we envisage? It says here that native education is different in scope and character from the education of other races. Now this view is a view on which we feel very strongly in South Africa. There is the view generally represented by the Nationalist Party ... who support this view that because there are differences in color, difference in economic development, differences in background, habits and customs and traditions and because these differences have always existed, they must be perpetuated.... It is said ... that the policy of segregation is brought about by the sociological and anthropological considerations in our social structure in South Africa ... [which] must be recognized in any policy of administration.... These differences have been used by the government to establish this policy of segregation ... which in the economic field has been made use of for the purposes of exploitation.... Now the opposite is of course the policy of assimilation, the policy that says that we are all of the same human stock, we are all capable of assimilating; all we require is the opportunity to develop, and we say the policy of the country should not take account of racial differences. There should just be one law for all.... The segregationist holds that the policy of assimilation in one which will lead to the complete destruction of the African, that a backward people cannot be overnight be brought under the Western stream of segregation.... It is maintained that you cannot teach an African child English and Afrikaans in the lower standards.... I want to say that when we speak about a policy of adaptation it must be understood that we really mean that the people concerned should be free to choose for themselves what is good for them. They say, "You can develop along your own lines," but at the same time they want to say, "We are the ones who shall lay down the lines along which you are to develop." Well, we know what that means. It means that the native can come and work for the white man, and after that he can be sent back to his *kraal.* I contend that the African must be allowed to say what is good for him at a certain stage.... We are looking forward to a time when the whole of the African culture with everything that is good in it will be assimilated into European culture, and it will be the contribution which the African people will make to the enrichment of European culture.

James Moroka

"It is the policy of this land that no white man shall serve under a native."
9 August 1945, 50

I come from the Free State as you know, and I know that in that province it would be well nigh impossible to any missionary institution to appoint a native principal. You know it is the policy of this land that no white man shall serve under a native. That is the accepted policy of this land. And it is for that reason that most of these missionaries are placed in a position which will mean that they will have to get rid of all the European teachers in the mission schools before they can appoint a native principal. That is the whole crux of the matter. Until the Europeans of this country are prepared to work side by side with the native people we shall never be able to achieve what we have in mind. The policy is there and it is just as well for us to be manly and face the position. The Europeans of this land simply say that if that policy is carried out, if that policy is carried out we shall be dominating them, and they are not going to allow any European to take orders from a non-European.... To my way of thinking that is the crux off the whole matter.... And let me tell you, Mr. Chairman, what the position is: the white men of this country are afraid of the native. Yes, he has an inferiority complex—it is the white man who has the inferiority complex. If he were not afraid he would give the natives equal opportunities, but it is because he is afraid that he wants to keep the native down.... It is for that reason that the European lays down the rule that in everything the native must take second place. No sane man can contradict what I am saying. That is the policy of the land and we simply have to submit to it. We cannot blame the missionaries; we must approach the government and prove to them that the policy is wrong, this policy of segregation, this policy of saying that because a man is a white man he is essentially a better man than the native. I don't agree with that contention.... He may, in certain circumstances, be a better man because he gets better opportunities. But that is all.

James Moroka

"It is absurd ... to say that because a man is an African
he can make do with less education and with less money."
9 August 1945, 65

My own personal opinion is this: that if the Europeans of this country are satisfied that they are so much better than we are—as they claim—then surely there is no need whatsoever to come to us and say, "You must not be given the same education as we get." If they know that they are better—as they claim to be—they will always be ahead of us. My own personal opinion is that the reason why the Europeans are now turning round and saying: "You must not follow us, you must have a different education from what we get, you do not need what we need, it has taken us 2,000 years to get where we are, and you must also take 2,000 years to arrive at that stage of civilization where we are..."—well, I think it is a most terrible thing to say. What I want to emphasize is that this is not a European civilization, it is a world civilization; and no one should be deprived from acquiring it. And I say that if we want the best in this land, if we want peace here, if we want white people and the black people to live side by side, then they must be given the same education so that they can understand each other. It is absurd for people to say that because a man is an African he can make do with less education and with less money, that his children need not get the same food as the children of the white man ... and have a decent house to live in.

Saul Mabude

"No race can achieve full and permanent success under alien leaders."
8 August 1945, 32ff

It would appear perhaps that I am out on a fight against missionary bodies. I wish to say at the outset that it is far from the average African mind to forget that deep debt of gratitude which he owes to the missionary societies in this country, both spiritually and educationally, but I want to say that certain unfortunate impressions threaten to estrange ... the missionary and the African. The present day missionary assumes a rather lukewarm attitude in regard ... to the appointment of head teachers in the denominational post-primary schools, more particularly in training schools. No race can achieve full and permanent success under alien leaders.... In the missionary institutions ... it is necessary that the interests of the African people should be paramount. The disease of color prejudice has crept in and is creeping into the missionary institutions. Political issues in regard to the native problem have found their way into the church and the missionary institutions.... The classroom and the pulpit have become the battleground for political differences. One of the fallacies that still obtain in the mind of many Europeans is that the mental potentiality of the African is limited, that he can only advance to a certain point and no further. There is unfortunately no drastic cure for the color prejudice disease. But I submit that in any event the Church is not the right place for such a disease. These are painful facts to emphasize, but one feels that one must emphasize them. Now what is responsible for this unsound state of affairs? I think it is the disease of color prejudice. This disease probably originated in the innate feeling of superiority which any one race has towards another race. As it is, color prejudice has permeated the whole white structure to such an extent that even the most uneducated and desperately low type of European sincerely believes that he is superior to any black man, no matter how good a citizen, how well educated that black man may be.

Z.K. Matthews

"We know that people make mistakes ... but we don't damn them forever."
8 August 1945, 17

We have recently had a number of disturbances in institutions, disturbances which have caused much grief, both to educational authorities and to parents, as also to the children in these institutions. These disturbances, by the way, have also have also been referred to in higher places, in the Assembly and in the Senate, and remarks have been made ... attacking teachers and others in regard to what is happening in native institutions.... What this particular motion is concerned with is the disciplinary action which is taken when these disturbances have taken place, and the mover points out ... that where a child has been dismissed from one school, that child is not to be admitted to other schools. I contend that that is a most serious thing for any child. An educational institution is a place of training where we expect the teachers and others to do what they can for that child to continue in that particular school; it does not seem reasonable that all further opportunity should be stopped.... We know that people make mistakes, serious mistakes, and they have to take their punishment for these mistakes, but we don't damn them forever. We do not even do that to criminals. When they have paid the penalty for their offence and if they reform, we receive them back into society—we allow them to become members of Parliament ... but children are debarred from further education.

6

Rural Issues

The speeches below deal with those Africans who lived in the rural areas either on Trust Land or on farms. The government was always wary of African ownership of what had been their own land. The only reliable census was that taken in 1951, by which time nearly three million Africans dwelt on Trust Land (that is, land owned by the state); three million dwelt on white-owned farms and only 342,000 were on land either owned by an African or under a chief.[1] The whole land issue was a constant bone of contention in the NRC, the councilors being against both the 1913 Land Act and the 1936 Trust and Land Act. The NRC was of the view that Africans had been relatively well off before the advent of the 1913 Land Act and that this act had been passed to provide labor for the mines. They repudiated the government's stated motive behind the passing of the Trust and Land Act, namely that this was passed to protect Africans against white acquisition of their land. There view was that on the contrary. Africans were so successful at buying land from the white landowners that it was passed in order to safeguard the acquisition of land by the whites.[2]

The NRC favored individual land tenure. They regarded Trust Land as government land and held that there was no security of tenure under such a system. The Council believed that their traditional communal land holding had facilitated the land's falling into the hands of the Europeans. All their efforts in the NRC were thus directed at helping the individual black farmer. At this stage about one-seventh of all the land in South Africa was still in African hands. African land purchases at the time were limited to black land companies, who by means of collective finance managed to acquire a number of large farms. They leased these to individuals who paid them a high rental. This enabled these companies to purchase more land from time to time.[3] These land companies were not mentioned in the debates on the land issues, and it is thus not certain what the councilors' attitude to them was. In spite of the fact that the government was supposed to provide finance for black farmers to buy land (according to the legislation of 1936, the only loans given were to black farmers in white areas. These loans made the black farmers indebted to the government. In 1938 an amendment made to the 1936 Land and Trust Act was passed that made it compulsory for the government to buy out black farmers on so-called white land. Africans who did want to farm were frustrated by the lack of help given to them and especially by the severe restriction against increasing their holdings. The government's interest lay in settling homeless people in an environment in which they might succeed in growing just enough food to prevent them from leaving for the urban areas. This stress on the provision of plots for the destitute rather than any genuine attempt to encourage the establishment of an independent black farming community was the main reason for the low productivity of these Trust Lands. The able farmers could not succeed under these conditions, while the majority of those who lived there had no wish to become farmers. The system was both wasteful of manpower and ruinous for the land. The Department of Native Affairs was well aware of this but was unable to do anything about it.[4]

Richard Victor Selope Thema

"Ownership of land is the only incentive."
24 November 1938, 347ff

To own land amongst our people ... the ownership of land is the only incentive of improved developing and competently administering the use of land profitably to us natives.... It is a right natives have had and should not be dispossessed of as they never rebelled against the government.... In any other government, even in the European countries, it is almost the sole reason why a human being may be dispossessed of the right of purchasing land—as they are rebellious against the government. I do not remember that any of the native races for the last fifty years have rebelled against the government. It seems unbelievable today that we must be put in a position that we cannot buy land in this country. Legislation is there but the policy is intervening. We really want to stress the importance of our ownership of land. No people can pride themselves in land that they have to pay an annual quitrent for and to think that other generations will have to do the same ad infinitum. It is a very regrettable state of affairs. And I do not think that a state of affairs of that kind should exist.... Our people are being educated through agricultural systems and methods which are up to date. What is the use of teaching our people all these fancy ideas of modern cultivation when you tell them that the land cannot belong to them and that no one in the future is to own any land.... It is no encouragement to our people to work the land profitably and in a reasonable manner. We really think that the government should put into practice what has been provided by law and carry out the promise that the minister gave in Parliament.

Richard Hobbs Godlo

"Laws ... restricted the acquisition of land by natives in urban areas."
29 November 1938, 576

Mr. Chairman, as you are no doubt aware, the Native Laws Amendment Act [of] 1937 restricted the acquisition of land by natives in urban areas. For the first time in the Cape Province, Africans were debarred from acquiring a property in town. Now the amendment went further than that; it stated that even such societies or institutions as building societies and savings banks can acquire land in town on one condition and that is that the savings or deposits of Africans in these societies do not exceed 20 percent even if it is a European organization. As long as the deposits or savings exceed 20 percent that association or bank has no right to own property in town. As a result there are certain organizations which think it is not worthwhile accepting deposits from Africans. One can really sympathize with business men; they do not have the time to look up their ledgers and balance sheets whenever an African comes to make a deposit to see that the total of the deposits made by natives do not exceed 20 percent. I am really at a loss to know ... what the intention of the legislature was in that respect. Some of our people are beginning to think that the intention of the legislature was the Africans should not save money, in fact that they have no right to possess any money at all.

George Makapan

"Securing the land which they live on."
30 November 1940, 196

Moves: That this Council again respectfully requests the government to evolve a scheme under which Africans can obtain loans from the government to purchase small urban holdings and plots and build their homes thereon. That the government's special attention be drawn to the fact that the severe restrictions imposed by Parliament on the right of Africans to buy land, whether in urban or rural areas, is causing the price to be driven excessively high for Africans, as a result of which they become desperate and fall into the hands of the money lenders, who mercilessly exploit their difficulties.... The native population of the urban areas should be given the opportunity of securing the land which they live on. We must be able to buy ground in urban and rural areas. We live there, we have our places in which live and we should be allowed to own that land.

George Makapan

"Teach our children how to use the ground."
29 November 1940, 162

I moved in 1937 that the government be requested to establish more agricultural colleges in all the provinces, to teach our children how to use the ground. Nothing has been done since I moved that, and I am now moving the same resolution again.... If our people knew how to use the ground. I am sure everybody would benefit. In every way the first thing we must have and the first thing we have to think of, when a state of war has been declared, is to have as much food as we can so as to be able to carry on the war successfully. You can supply all the war materials, all the munitions, all the guns and everything, but if the stomachs of the soldiers are empty they cannot do anything.

Lancelot Pater Msomi

"It is no use [applying] the measures of fifty years ago to the African of today."
14 August 1944, 127

It seems to me that they [the government] ... are not keeping pace with the progress that is so much in evidence among the non–European races, not only in this country but also throughout the whole of this continent. It is no use trying to apply the measures of fifty years ago to the African of today unless you maintain the African in the spirit which prevailed in the olden days. You do not recognize that fact that the African who has lived on the farm for many years, on the farm where his fathers and forefathers have lived, looks upon that farm as part of himself. It is for these reasons that we feel that something should be done to maintain that old spirit of understanding, which was so pronounced in days gone by.

Paul Mosaka

"Repeal all discriminatory laws
which curtail the rights of Africans to buy ... land."
9 August 1944, 34

[My resolution is] that this Council is fully aware of the misery and the conditions of economic slavery existing among the African people and requests that the government, in recognition of the distinguished and meritorious services of our boys serving with the Union Forces in North Africa and Italy ... repeal all discriminatory laws which curtail the rights of Africans to buy, own, rent or lease land as well as laws which restrict the rights of freedom of contract. We have found misery, homelessness, trouble among our people ... and all that must be attributed to nothing else but the Union government.... The acquisition of land is one of the elementary privileges which a democratic government should respect without regard to color or race.... It does appear that if you refuse the people these rights you reduce them to a state of slavery, total slavery—you tie them down to a position where they cannot move.

Chief Samuel Mankuroane

"There is little stock to reduce."
24 November 1938, 236–37

With regards to the remarks by the commissioner of the Ciskei, so far as our reserves in Kuruman are concerned, they are not favorable to the reduction of stock.... They say the land is quite capable of maintaining their stock. In our district the magistrate there also went over the district with us and explained this matter to the natives. He even went so far as interviewing the sheep inspector to give us the number of stock in that district—sheep, goats and cattle. He gave the figure as 24,000 and there are 24,000 taxpayers in the area. That means ... that each man only had one head of cattle. The same conditions apply in Griqualand West.... That is why they find it difficult to support the scheme because there is little to reduce.

George Makapan

"They will not reduce their stock."
23 November 1938, 237–38

Our Locations are fenced; they were fenced in 1910. After that a lot of our cattle died. If we had not lost so many cattle we would not have come to town; we only came to town to get money to buy more cattle.... The fact of fencing the Locations has had the effect of killing some of our cattle—they die. That is what we are afraid of. There are some people asking for more small pieces of land and these lands are going to be fenced, but we are always afraid that the fencing of Locations will have the effect of reducing stock. If the cattle die there will be starvation in the Locations. If the people could be given a small piece of land to plough they will be satisfied. They will not reduce their stock.

Alexander Macauley Jabavu

"At last we are going to be delivered from self-destruction."
23 November 1938

When this proclamation was brought up here I felt that it was at one of those stages when our great poet Shakespeare said:

> There is a tide in the affairs of men
> Which taken at the flood leads to fortune;
> Omitted, all the voyage of your life
> Is bound in shallows and miseries

The matter [of stock limitation] was submitted to the chiefs and ratepayers in the Reserves; to them it was a blessing in disguise. I am not trying to influence anybody; I am just telling you what the feelings were amongst the people in my area, and I am glad to find that at last we are going to be delivered from self-destruction. At first the matter was rejected by the chiefs and headmen, the method of approach was not for me to question....

I have written down the reasons that those who accepted it gave because it is very important.... At present all classes of stock, sheep, goats, donkeys, horses and pigs overrun the commonages to the detriment of cattle which eat longer grass. I wish the councilors could see the difficulty we are having in our area. I am a farmer and have had experience, so I know what I am talking about. Cattle, as you know, will eat grass only when it gets to a certain height. The others eat it right down from the bottom, and the cattle simply cannot live when they are put on the commonages. The result of this is a large number of cattle for the last ten years have had to be put on hired grazing at coastal farms at a fee.... Huge numbers have had to be paid at the coastal farms ... the chief native commissioner will bear me out in the number of native cattle at the coastal farms for which grazing is hired. For the last ten years—I would like that to be observed. On the coastal farms grazing became denuded also.... Representations were made to the government for more land without number, Mr. Chairman, but it seems that with uncontrolled ownership, even when additional land is made available the same will occur. It is quite apparent that even if the government did buy more land as it is doing now, the same will occur; in fact it is occurring, as I am going to show.... You will be surprised to hear that twenty farms have been bought by the Trust in the East London and Kingwilliamstown districts; farms which had quite a lot of grass have been denuded. Within two months of the government allowing the cattle to graze on these farms, they had to be driven away because the officials found that the cattle had eaten so much of the grass that unless grazing was rested the farms would be practically deserts…. I just want to show that the cry for more land is not going to help us very much if we are not going to control ownership of cattle. I say this from experience. I have not been influenced by anybody, I say to you—gain the benefit of the experience of a fellow councilor who is a farmer. I think the whole matter boils down to this—it is not a matter of limitation but of common sense…. I am going you the benefit of the experience we have had in the Ciskei, and we feel that if the government could expedite this matter of fencing our commonages we could be protected against ourselves…. The position is almost intolerable, and unless we in the Ciskei can adopt a method of limiting our stock it will simply mean that the people are going to die—following their own cattle…. I feel that if I cannot tell my people who have elected me to represent them in this body, what should be done, I am not fit to be here. I am talking about myself. If when people ask me about this proclamation … and if I do not tell them what I think about it, I am not worth my salt and I should not be on this Council…. What am I here on this Council for? To tell them what is right. I know that I have to express my peoples' opinion, but that is not the only thing to be done. These people elected me to see what danger was lurking ahead of them…. I found it was the danger of suicide. It is suicide to my mind for them to allow their cattle and money to be taken away by firms year after year for the past ten years…. It is time we called a halt to that sort of thing.

E. Qamata

"We are bound to … bring before this Council what the people have told us."
23 November 1938, 246ff

Mr. Chairman, I do not think there is any one as blind as not to admit the force of the facts as placed before this council by Mr. Jabavu. Notwithstanding what he said, we are bound to say or bring before this council what the people have told us. We have given this matter full consideration in the Bunga and the General Council and at meetings at home with the people. At all of those meetings their views have been to this effect: "We do not want a reduction of our stock at all." … They submitted that they could not move their cattle to markets…. They further reported that they were willing that there should be some voluntary reduction of stock like donkeys and goats but there should be no compulsion to do that. The General Council agreed that some small stock such as donkeys should be reduced or perhaps limited…. We are willing to cooperate with the government…. The only thing that we ask is that the number of stock should be fixed for each owner…. Those are the definitive views of the stock owners of the Transkei.

Charles Sakwe

"If we go against [the people we represent] they will not elect us again."
23 November 1938, 248ff

The people say if you are going to take away some of our stock, well you must substitute something for them. There is a proposal for reducing stock, but there has been no substitute proposal by the sponsors. They are quite prepared to meet the government in its proposals if the government wants to help them. The natives sell their wool, and that is how most of them get their cash. Most of our people do not earn wages.... They have expended money on buying stock-cattle and sheep—and also to battle stock diseases.... Now you come along with this proposal, you say, "Look here, reduce your stock, do away with some of your cattle," and you propose that in a manner which will not bring in any return to them.... If you had said, "Look here, we are going to open markets for you where you can sell your stock and get money for it," there would have been no necessity for a proclamation like this one.... In the Transkei, sir, we produce from 25,000 to 30,000 bales of wool a year—from the Transkei alone. Now this has increased for about a million for last year.... I am giving these figures and facts to show that if there is a proposal from one party to do away with this thing, it must be replaced by something with which we can live. We are being accused of ignorance but I have to place these facts before you.... Another thing, we are afraid of the people who we represent; if we go against them, they will not elect us again. If we do not give the exact views of the people who sent us here, are we doing our duty? We have to put their views before you and add our own individual opinion.... As far as we are concerned, we are doing our best to uplift the people of the Transkei. We have told them of the stock proclamation for culling and introducing good bulls; we are trying to educate the people of the benefits of the proclamation; and they are only just beginning to cull their cattle and are getting better brands for themselves. As soon as we have got to that stage they will do away with scrub cattle.... We have been given this opportunity to tell you that this matter will come along slowly and leisurely to the people, they do not want to be hurried.

John Dube

"The Zulu people [are] against it."
24 November 1944, 234–35

I think there was an assurance last year from the government that the limitation of stock would not be forced on any people, Bantu people, but that it would have to be accepted by them, having seen the benefit of it from other districts. With regard to Natal and Zululand I may say, because we have recently toured all the provinces, three of us native representatives, and wherever this matter of the limitations of stock was introduced the Zulu people were against it…. Mr. Ndhlovu has said they are conservative; to them their stock means everything, and therefore I think we are saying practically what Chief Mshiyeni would say if he were present. They need a great deal of education in our part of the country to convince the people that it is for their benefit to reduce stock.

George Champion
"I cannot leave without asking the permission of the landlord."
26 November 1946, 47

Now, I want to go back to 1932, and I want to refer to the Natives Service and Contract Act—Act 24 of 1932…. Now that act was introduced in Parliament, not by the minister of native affairs but by the minister of justice…. On the back of my poll tax receipt I am reminded or the Pass officials are reminded that they must inquire whether I reside on private land or whether I reside in a Location. And if I reside on private land I cannot leave that private land without asking the permission of the landlord no matter whether he is a native, European, or Indian. I don't know what the minister of justice had in mind, but I do say that it is political legislation of the worst kind…. In this act a native is created a tenant on a farm—he is a labor tenant, and the agreement is from month to month. It does not matter whether he has fifty head of cattle or a hundred head of cattle, whether he has cultivated lands or not, whether his crop is large or small—the farmer can just say to him, "I give you thirty days' notice and then you will have to quit." The native may say to the farmer, "My crops are standing on the land; how can I leave them?" Well, the farmer will say, "I shall look after your crops." We know what that means. He will simply let his cattle graze on the crops. It has been done. The position becomes even worse if the native has cattle. His master gives him a Trek Pass, but when he wants to leave with his cattle he will be told, "Oh, no, you cannot take your cattle; the farm is under quarantine." Well, then the native has to go to the farmer and … the farmer will charge him 2/6d per day. 2/6d is one pound in eight days. All this is provided for in the act.

Lancelot Peter Msomi
"The people … are denied the right to settle anywhere."
25 April 1946, 50–51

It seems the government is embarking on a policy somehow or other of getting rid of the native, so that eventually the native will have nowhere to go. And let me say this, the result of this policy is that some many criminals are roaming about the streets in the towns today. This sort of thing leads to demoralization. It leads to a breakdown of orderly life of the native people of those country. The trouble is due to one fact and one fact only, and that is that your African people, the first people of this country, the people who have no other home to go to, are the people who are denied the right to settle anywhere.

Chief Mshiyeni Kwa Dinuzulu

"Wild animals have their holes in which they can rest."
14 August 1944, 120ff

The people are suffering very great hardships, and we have on many occasions raised this question and pointed out the necessity of giving relief to farm laborers. The position is getting worse and worse owing to troubles over which the people have no control.... Where the chiefs have no land on which to place their people, these men have to go and look for work elsewhere. Now today we find that farm laborers who are working for farmers are being driven off the farms without any valid reason and their cattle are being left behind on the farms. And then the cattle are confiscated by the farmers on the grounds that they have to pay for the grazing and dipping. That is why we ask you to give this matter your careful attention. Practically all our cattle have died of disease. We have dipping tanks, but in spite of our cattle being dipped, they are still dying in large numbers. They have ticks; in spite of our having these dipping tanks we still have to take the ticks off our cattle.... Who can ever cure that disease? No one has ever been able to do so. My people are suffering great hardships as a result of the conditions prevailing on the farms. Wild animals have their holes in which they can rest and then at night they go out and get food. But as far as they are concerned, I doubt if there is any race living under greater hardships than the Africans are doing today. No, this is going too far, and things are getting worse.... We are simply slaves today, and we want to tell you that we are suffering hardships.

George Champion

"These laws have reduced our people to a state of ... slavery."
9 August 1944, 24–28

My resolution [repeal of the 1913 Land Act] says that these laws have reduced our people to a state of economic slavery—[not only] economic slavery but slavery in all its forms—because a farm laborer has no say whatsoever over his working conditions, or over his living conditions. He has to get up in the morning when the owner of the farm tells him to get up. He has to eat at a time which suits the convenience of the farmer. His children ... can be called upon to render any services required by the farmer. There is no wage legislation controlling the wages of that laborer... . In effect, a native farm labor tenant is in no better position than a horse or a cow belonging to the farmer—as a matter of fact he is worse off. I have come across instances where a horse suffering from open sores ... cannot be made to work. I have not come across any instance where a farmer can be charged if he compels his servants to perform any kind of work when they are ill. I say definitely that the position of a native on a farm is no better than that of a slave.... The farmer can do with his as he pleases and if they do not like it they can go. That position was created by Law No. 27 of 1913. Here we have a state of affairs where the people who originally owned the country are reduced to a condition which can only be described as slavery. These people are not allowed to buy land in a country that was originally owned by their forefathers. How long is this country, which is governed from the point of view of the farming community only, going to stand for these things? We were told by a professor this morning that he held no brief for agitators, but the man who is speaking now—that is me—is an agitator, and I want to say that no country can make progress without agitators.... I say that these laws are undemocratic and Hitleristic.... We know that the white farmers of this country are spoon-fed by the government. How long is this spoon-feeding to go on without causing an upheaval in the minds of the people, who have suffered so much at the hands of the white farmers? Many of our sons have shed their blood up north; many of them are prisoners of war. You speak of social security, but how can we be part and parcel of that ... if these things which I have mentioned are allowed to continue?

Richard Victor Selope Thema

"Is white South Africa going to support a system of enslavement?"
14 August 1944, 123–25

A number of resolutions will be put forward at the Farmer's Congress on the 17th.... Imagine! They are going to ask that little black boys should be apprenticed to farmers, which of course means that they will be enslaved.... Is white South Africa going to support a system of enslavement of this kind? If South Africa is going to do that [it] will be doing a great disservice to its own cause on this continent—it will create hatred and bitterness. One should not forget that South Africa is no longer far apart from the rest of the world ... white South Africa cannot afford to incur the hostility of the rest of this continent. We are not saying these things from any spirit of antagonism to the farmers; we are only asking that the farmers should do what is right.... But now they not only want the services of the natives, they also want to enslave the children. How would the farmers like it if we passed a resolution that white boys should be apprentices or enslaved too? There would be uproar in this country. Well, we feel the same way about it.

Richard Victor Selope Thema

"We have ... little reserves for tribes
and [nothing] for the whole of the African people."
6 May 1943, 136

The whole native policy is based on the fact that there is sufficient land for the African somewhere in South Africa. But in practice we find there is no such land.... What we have under the Trust and Land Act is nothing but little reserves for tribes and not for the whole of the African people. These reserves are today congested, and even those which will be bought at some future time will be bought when they are already congested, when there are already people living on the land. And we find that the land is not sufficient for the whole of the population. There are several millions of African people who will never have land in the reserves.... There are half a million people living on European farms who will be forced to live there whether they like it or not—there are thousands of people who have got old on these farms, and as soon as they get old they are forced to leave because their services are no longer required. And the only places they can go to then are the industrial centers where they may be able to earn a living. We have come to these urban areas, not because we want to do so, but because we are forced by legislation. And there in these urban areas we also find that we have no home, we have no home which we can call our permanent home. And in order to control and to be able to exploit our labor, the municipalities have proposed that we should have our own Locations built and erected, where we have to pay rent all the years of our lives. I always wonder why the Europeans are so short-sighted. Where their interests are involved they do not want to follow a policy such as they are following today in the urban areas. In the Transkei we are told that these territories are purely native territories, and yet we find European towns there, where Europeans own land. To be consistent, the Europeans in the Transkei should be living in Locations— that should be the position if we pursued this policy to its logical conclusion, but no; they live in the towns there and they own their homes there.

Why then cannot we own our homes in the urban areas of the Union? ... I don't think we are opposed to that [residential segregation], as long as it will give us a permanent home in the urban areas. If I have to go to a Reserve today I find that I have no place to live ... because the Reserves are congested. And if I go to the urban areas I am told that I can only live there so long as I serve the European interests. Otherwise I have no right to be there. We feel that the time has come when such a policy should be abandoned and when the Locations should become the permanent homes of the African community.

7

Urban Issues

The difficulties encountered by Africans seeking permanent residence in the cities was entrenched in legislation, legislation whose purpose was to allow few Africans permanent settlement in the cities. The urban areas were regarded as white areas to which blacks could only be admitted as servants of the white man. Africans who could not prove that they were employed were regarded as "surplus" and driven out. The NRC held that the demand for cheap labor for the mines lay behind the attempts to discourage Africans from leaving the rural areas for the towns. Cheap labor for the mines was recruited from the rural areas, and the government feared that this would diminish significantly if the Africans were allowed to enter the towns and work in industry.[1] Cheap labor was one aspect, but there were others. Another difficulty perceived by the government was that if they allowed Africans free entry to the urban areas, the farmers would protest. The continual complaints of the politically important white farming community meant that they would undoubtedly have withdrawn their support from any party that did not discourage rural migration to the towns.[2] In 1947 a regulation was passed that allowed the railways to refuse to sell tickets to Africans wanting to travel from the Ciskei and the Transkei if they had not secured employment before coming within the municipal boundaries. If they were caught by the authorities they would be jailed and, after being fined by a magistrate, would be thrown out of the municipal area. Sometimes whole areas were out of bounds.[3] Smuts said in Parliament that it would not be necessary to achieve territorial separation of black and white by force. This would happen in a natural way by applying the provisions of the Slums Act on the one hand and supplying housing in government-approved areas in the other. A census was taken in 1937, and from this the government was able to ascertain the number of "surplus" Africans living in the urban areas. This led not only to a large number of expulsions from these areas from 1939 onwards, but also to a determined effort by some municipalities to reduce the number of Africans who had previously been granted permission to live there. The NRC tried its best to make the government and especially the municipalities aware of how much misery was created by the legislation against Africans living in urban area.[4]

Thomas Mtobi Mapikela

"You cannot build ... [what you] like.
Everything is dictated by the municipality."
2 December 1940, 222ff

In Bloemfontein you will find that the building contractors in the native Locations are all natives, and the main qualification is that they are able to do the work. None of the houses in the Location are built by white men; they are all built by natives. I am an old man today and cannot do this hard work anymore, but some years ago most of these contracts were carried out by me.... The very same thing which Councilor Thema mentioned here, that these contracts should be handled by natives, exists in Bloemfontein. Now take those houses in Orlando—that kind of work should be done by natives, and I am very much surprised indeed to hear that these contracts are being carried out by Europeans.... In these Locations here I have noticed that you cannot build a house for yourself where you like. Everything is dictated by the municipality; even the size of the room is dictated.... You may have two rooms or perhaps three rooms, no more, but in these days of civilization when a man wants to live decently we want good houses, we want to be allowed to make our own plans. And because the money is borrowed by the municipality from the government, the stand holders are involved and they have to do as they are told.... But after all the money for the houses in all these places ... that money comes from the natives themselves. If we can be given this money direct we shall be able to take up the contracts ourselves.... In Bloemfontein this scheme enables the people to build their own houses and people can build them in the way they like, but according to plan.

Richard Grenville Baloyi

"There [are] no doors ... there is no flooring."
2 November 1940, 224ff

If you will go to places like Orlando or the Western Native Townships and examine these places, there you will find that conditions are by no means satisfactory. When a house is put up no doors are put in—there are no doors between one room and another. They just put up the wall and the roof and they leave things like that. In the Western Native Townships there is a case pending about this. Only the wall were put up ... there was only one door and that was in the front. There were no doors between one room and another. Yet if one puts in the doors and leaves a house like that some time later, one has to leave the doors there, one is not allowed to take them away. There is no flooring in a place like that. The man taking the house has to put in the flooring himself. All that sort of thing is wrong. And I say that people should be allowed to put up houses according the their own wishes and their own plans.... I say that the government must please try and improve this condition so that the natives may be able to lead better lives.

George Champion

"We did not feel ... there was any necessity
for a white gentleman to become the ... ruler of our settlement."
6 May 1943, 153–54

The motion says that the office of a superintendant of a Location shall be held for a fixed period of time and that the election of a superintendant shall be voted for by the residents of the Location concerned. In seconding this motion I have in mind some discussions which took place as far back as 1923 when the Urban Areas Act was explained to the natives in many places. Many natives submitted that the position of a Location superintendant should be held by a native. A Location is a sort of native settlement where a white man is not required. It was explained to us that as a compromise, Europeans of good standing would be appointed.... Well, we agreed under protest. We did not feel disposed to agree that while we were put in our segregated homes away from the towns there was any necessity to condemn anyone to become the practical ruler of our settlement.... Now the question arose as to what qualifications such a man was to have.... Some of these Locations are the size of Utrecht and Vryheid. Yet some of the officers in charge are not whole-time officers but part-time officers. They combine the office of brewers of *kaffir* beer, messengers of the Court, town clerks and so on. And generally these people are recruited from among old police officers. Some of these people know nothing about the natives and they look upon the natives as nothing but nuisances.... They prefer to deal with kraal natives who are quite prepared to submit to everything they tell them. Such a condition was never anticipated when the provisions of the Urban Areas Act were explained to the natives. We were told that because we were living in the slum parts of the towns we were going to be given good places where we could live happily with our families. But you know how the position has deteriorated. We have been explaining it to you all morning, and I don't think you want to hear any more about it…. I say rather than have a man who is a stranger, whose qualifications are unknown, whose sentiments are unknown—the only thing we know about him is that he is a policeman and that he looks upon everyone in the way a policeman does…. The Location superintendents are known to many as the uncrowned kings of the Locations. Now I have said that the present native superintendants are usually old policemen. Are policemen the right type of person for these duties? I am speaking as a member of the native advisory board of the Lamont Location. And I know what I am speaking about, and I say it is unwise to take just any white man, just any white man who has no education, who is not matriculated, and bring him into contact with the natives, give him control over men of education such as Councilor Mosaka, Councilor Matthews and others…. The position of a superintendant is an extremely important one, and his qualifications should be almost equal to those of a native commissioner…. Why should not similar qualifications be demanded of a man entrusted with the charge of large numbers of natives, with the very lives of natives and their families? It is particularly in the small towns that it is essential that we should have the greatest care exercised in these appointments. The powers given to these superintendents are such that they can do the greatest harm to the natives.

Richard Hobbs Godlo

"We roundly condemn any legislation
which is designed to keep a race in perpetual servitude."
24 April 1946, 44–48

We came to the conclusion that the [Urban Areas] Act proposed to set up certain types of accommodation, namely hostels, Locations and native villages. And we found again that the cardinal feature of these types of accommodation was the African was only to be allowed to occupy them under conditions which guarantee him no security of tenure. He must always be regarded as a temporary dweller in the Locations, as a person who has no right to be there and can only be there on sufferance, although he is there to minister to the needs of the European community of the town, and we roundly condemn any legislation which is designed to keep a race in perpetual servitude, a race of servants, a race of people who cannot rise to any level of progress…. We … demand some sort of legislation, legislation that will regard the African as a rightful resident of the towns, just as other members of other racial groups are regarded as rightful inhabitants of the towns which they have helped to build. Here in Cape Town we have seen with our own eyes the shocking conditions which prevail in these urban areas. We find that the African has no right to participate in the local government ... they have no say in their own Locations, except that advisory boards are set up in those Locations—advisory boards that have no functions and no powers whatever, advisory boards that are more often than not completely ignored by the municipalities. If you were to tour the smaller towns of the Karroo and of the Midlands of the Cape, you would be surprised to find the position in respect of some of these advisory boards. We discovered again a well-known fact that the Africans cannot own their own homes in the urban areas. I have already referred to that, and I shall not bore this meeting by repeating myself. The fact of the matter is that the African has no right to come and go as he wants to.... Sometimes—more often than not—we come to the conclusion, rightly or wrongly, that the policy of the government is to force the Africans to go to the farms to work there for next to nothing because the farmers are complaining that they are short of labor. Now I say again that this type of legislation aims at forcing the Africans to offer their services to the farmers. That is all that is behind it.

Sam P. Sesedi

"A Location is a place where you have no rights, no security of tenure."
6 January 1950, 50

The word Location has become a sort of stigma, and one would have thought that ... as far as the natives are concerned, it ... is a word which has a number of bad ideas connected with it. It even goes to the extent of people living in a village looking down on those who live in Locations. In a Location there is no security of tenure—you are not master of your own home. The police can come into your home at any time without knocking. They can kick the door open and go in, and they can do all sorts of things; they can search the place and no one can raise any objections. We have come to detest this word "Location," because it brings upon us this stigma of inferiority.... A Location is a place where you have no rights, no security of tenure, and if the authorities could eliminate this word altogether, it would be a very good thing indeed.

8

Taxes

During the period in which the NRC functioned, 1937–1950, there were two types of taxation levied on Africans. The first and more important was the poll tax. This tax was payable by all African males from the ages of eighteen to sixty-five years, fixed at one pound per year. The second type of tax was made up of various local taxes, paid mainly in the rural areas. They varied from the dog tax to the hut tax. The later was paid only in Natal and was implemented in order to discourage the Zulus from having more than one wife, because it was the custom that each wife had to have a separate hut provided for her.[1]

The local tax was used in the area in which it was collected. Only one-fifth of the poll tax was used directly for the benefit of Africans, notwithstanding the fact that the poll tax was the only source of funding for African facilities of every kind. The provincial authorities were expected to provide health and educational facilities for blacks from this tax. The provinces by 1937 had made it clear to the government that they were not able adequately to provide either health or educational facilities if they had to depend on the meager sums allotted to them from the poll tax.[2] The attacks by the Council against the local taxes were not nearly as vociferous as those made against the poll tax. The Council tabled numerous resolutions calling for the abolition of the poll tax and its replacement by income tax. Councilors protested that blacks were singled out for a tax that no other section of the population was expected to pay. In 1945 only about forty Africans earned enough to pay income tax.[3]

The threat of prosecution for tax evasion forced African men to seek employment that gave them a cash wage. This necessity was regarded by the Council as forced labor, a view shared by Smit, the secretary of native affairs, although he said that there could be no advantage in asking for its removal as long as it provided the only source of funds for such essentials as black education. It was for this reason that the motion put forward in 1939 for the abolition of this tax was defeated.[4] To ensure that the poll tax was paid, the Native Taxation Act gave legal sanction to such measures as police raids (which frequently took place at night) to check on tax receipts. Ndhlovu complained that in a particular part of Natal, while waiting their turn to pay the local native commissioner, Africans were humiliated by having to kneel before him.[5] Tax receipts had to be produced before an African could get employment on the mines. Although the Department of Native Affairs protested that this was not a legal requirement, the councilors were adamant that it was enforced. Much time was spent by the councilors trying to get the authorities to agree not to jail the defaulters and to limit the amount for which they were liable. Not surprisingly, tax evasion was common, even on the part of the councilors themselves. Msomi, for example, said that he had not paid his taxes for three years. Mapikela said that his own son passed himself off as a colored man in order to avoid paying this tax. Thema claimed that the one advantage that Africans conceded in the learning of Afrikaans was that it enabled them to pass as coloreds and thus avoid paying.[6] Certain stringent measures were considered in order to counteract this tax evasion, such as the use of detention camps for tax defaulter and the start of better methods for collecting the tax, such a paying chiefs and headmen bonuses.[7] Taxpaying was also made a part of the electoral process, in that Africans who had no tax receipts could not vote for the NRC. The NRC stated that the principle on which Africans were taxed was wrong. If they did not earn enough money to pay income tax, they should not be taxed at all and the poll tax should be abolished.[8]

Richard Hobbs Godlo

"Africans [did] not pay the tax ... because they were unable to do so."
29 November 1938, 581

When we had to deal with the estimates, the chairman rightly pointed out that in the present year he was embarrassed because of the inadequacy of funds available for native development in this country. The chairman also mentions the fact that owing to political activities for the abolition of the poll tax, there was a shortfall of 60,000 pounds. If, as the motion requests, the general poll tax was done away with and native development in all directions were to depend on monies obtained from the general revenue of the country, I am sure our chairman would not be in the same embarrassment as he is in today. People tell us, "Well, if natives want development they must expect to pay for it," but we hope and I think ...

that we do contribute to the general revenue of this country.... Now we contend that the amount of service rendered to the Africans should not be assessed in terms of the amount of taxation we contribute towards the State, and it is well known ... that those who are least able to pay should receive the benefit of the taxes paid by those who are able to pay. It is a well-known fact, and it goes without saying, that the Africans are the poorest and least able to pay. It has been shown by the recent report of the Board of Trade and Industry that the earnings of the Africans in the towns and in the reserves do not justify the imposition of a general tax of this nature. I just want to point out that this resolution has not been caused by any agitation for the abolition of the tax which has taken place elsewhere. It has nothing whatsoever to do with the difficulty you have experienced in the collection of your taxes, sir. I can assure you that if there was any agitation for the abolition of the tax, there were a number of Africans who could not pay the tax, not because they did not want to but because they were unable to do so.

Richard Hobbs Godlo

"The chief menace ... is the menace of ignorance."
7 May 1943, 203

Our people have been asking this question—"What is the use of our contributing to the State coffers in the form of the poll tax?"—because rightly or wrongly they understood the position to be that when the poll tax was introduced the idea was to improve native education generally, but now they say that the coloreds and Indians are not contributing 1d. [one penny] directly to the revenue of this country, yet they have all the facilities; they have all the buildings; there is no understaffing in their schools. But we Africans are taxed directly, in addition to the many forms of indirect taxation we are subjected to in common with the other sections of the population.... It is common knowledge that even if the proceeds of the whole of the poll tax was handed over for native education it would not meet the requirements of our people, and we therefore appeal to you to give the matter your support. We feel that the chief menace to Western civilization is the menace of ignorance. If we were to educate our people, to obtain facilities for them, to relive understaffing in our schools, there would be very little for the police to do. The wave of crime would be considerably reduced, and we would hear little about these forms of unrest. We are strongly of the opinion that our people need education and more education, and that facilities for such should be made available.

Saul Mabude
"All that, he has to pay out of his meager earnings."
18 August 1945, 137

We asked for certain information that was never supplied to us, and we are now asked to sanction a policy of further taxing the African people whom we represent. To put the matter briefly, we feel that we have been seriously ignored by the government; we feel that the government is merely making this council into a kind of rubber stamp, and naturally we resent that most strongly. We feel that as men chosen by the people to represent them, the very least that the government can do is to respect our decisions. It was only reasonable to ask the government for an extension of time after the government had summoned us so hurriedly to discuss a particular bill with all its implications ... implications that would cause serious difficulties if we were to agree to further taxation being imposed on our African people, on the lines of the poll tax system to which we have so often referred the government, and which we have so often asked the government to revise. Further, we feel that when the Financial Relations Act was passed, the matter of allowing the provincial councils to tax the Africans must have been fully gone into, and when it was decided that the provincial councils were not to be allowed to tax the Africans, that decision was arrived at after very careful consideration by Parliament itself. Now we would naturally have liked to have been told by the government why that decision, that policy, is now to be altered.... It is a very hard thing for us to agree to, when we have to sanction a system which ... savors of the poll tax system. In the Transkei, for instance, there are various other taxes which the African people are required to pay, taxes for local purposes. Possibly people think that the African only has to pay poll tax and perhaps a local tax, that is to say ten shillings, but let me tell the Council this in some cases he has to pay quitrent. In all cases he has to pay stock rent, and there is a special rate for dipping [of stock]. All that, he has to pay out of his meager earnings.

Lancelot Peter Msomi
"The people are full of the spirit of hope."
2 May 1945, 33–34

I met a few members of the community in which I live and they wanted to know ... why I had been called to Pretoria ... and they all had very bright hopes—the people are full of the spirit of hope, that they have something bright in store for them for the future.... And all the time we were called together to discuss the most painful subject of all as far as our people are concerned: taxation. The position is made very difficult for our people. It is now considered that they should be forced to pay more than a £1 tax, which they are paying now. There is another hardship our people are suffering; that is, they are made to pay their tax from the age of eighteen. They are the only people who have to pay that tax at eighteen. All other sections of the community have to pay their taxes when they attain the age of twenty-one. All these things bring more and more burdens on our people.... Any casual reader of what happens today will say, there they are again—they want everything to be done for them; they want to be spoon-fed. They are opposing the very small charge of only two shillings and sixpence extra. But the fact is that if only they knew what that two shillings and six pence means to a native, they would know that it is really a big sum of money. But we will be told that we are not willing to cooperate. We want to cooperate, but we should be enabled to do so. As has already been pointed out, a serious departure has been made by the suggestion that once more the provinces should be allowed to tax our people. The past history of their dealings with our people does not justify that they should have anything to do with us at all

Richard Hobbs Godlo

"The ox is only to be asked whether it prefers to be roasted or cooked."
18 August 1945, 140

A Xhosa man said to me, "Now you tell me that the government has decided to impose this tax. I would liken this to telling an ox that you have finally decided to have it slaughtered and your consultation is like asking the ox whether it would prefer to be roasted or cooked—because the decision to have it slaughtered has already been taken." ... Whatever advice we tender to the authorities, to the various provincial councils, the tax will remain, the amount of the tax will remain and the manner in which the tax will be collected will not be altered because the tax will be collected ... in the same way as the poll tax. The ox is only to be asked whether it prefers to be roasted or cooked. I feel that in the circumstances we are now grasping the shadow when the substance has gone. It is for these reasons, Mr. Chairman, that we feel that any discussion of these draft ordinances will be a waste of time.... We have been ignored, and in fact I do not think that I am disclosing a secret if I say that we feel that the time has come for us to lodge our strongest protest by word of mouth, and also by action if necessary. We come to this council in the hope that we are at least doing a service to our people, but the more we speak the more we endeavor to express what we believe to be the feelings of our people on legislation and policy, the more we are ignored, the more we are treated as a rubber stamp by the government. I would only repeat, Mr. Chairman, what I feel is the feeling of the whole Council, that we strongly resent not being consulted, in fact, being ignored, when measures of this kind are passed in this way—measures which so vitally affect the people who have sent us here to look after their interests.

9

Wages

From the early sessions of the NRC, the wage issue was given great prominence. In 1939, at the specific request of the Council, an official from the Department of Labor addressed them on the issue. He explained that the industrial legislation in South Africa excluded from its provisions agricultural employment and domestic employment in private households. This meant that a large section of the black work force was not working under any kind of minimum wage scale. However, with few exceptions all agreements entered into by white trade unions contained provisions for the wages of black unskilled labor. This system was only applied to industries with their own white trade unions. Most of these wage agreements were for workers in the urban areas, and very few applied outside the principal towns. The efforts of the wage board that made these determinations were unpopular with white employers, and this was reflected in the reluctance of local authorities to implement the Wage Board's minimum recommendations. Municipalities asked to be exempted from this determination. Such an exemption as this was granted to the Pretoria municipal council. When the workers heard this, it caused a riot in Pretoria among the municipal workers who were unable to understand how the government could publish a wage determination and almost immediately thereafter grant exemptions from it.[1] There was also an emphasis by the councilors on improving the wages of teachers.[2] The NRC concerned itself with miners' wages because these were taken as the basis upon which black labor was paid in other instances. For example, the earnings of soldiers in the Second World War were calculated on this basis[3] because it was considered of the utmost importance not to take potential workers away from the mining industry with the offer of better wages elsewhere.[4] In 1936 the ILO had laid down that the ongoing fare of miners must be paid by their employers. This resolution was consistently cited by the councilors in their attempts to have this fare, which amounted to one and a half month's wages of the miners, be paid by the mines. Smit, the secretary of native affairs, pointed out that South Africa did not recognize the ILO and consequently did not regard itself as bound by its decisions.[5] In 1941 Jabavu asked that chief's salaries be raised to two pounds a month. Councilors pointed out that in some cases chiefs received less pay than miners. The government's unwillingness to increase the payment of chiefs led the NRC to conclude that the real authority in the rural areas lay with the white native commissioners and that the low salaries paid to chiefs were an indication of the low priority the government gave their cooperation.[6] The assumption by the government that Africans in rural areas could make do with less money than urban Africans was material to the rural wage structure. This was Smuts' justification, for example, for the low pay of the black soldiers, 90 percent of whom he said came from rural areas. This argument was also used to justify the low wages of laborers in the Transkei.[7] The significance of wages was highlighted in the early years of the Council when the rumor was current that in the event of a Nazi victory, the black worker would be paid ten shillings a day.[8] Nothing was heard about the abolition of passes or the provision of housing or free education. The emphasis was on wages.

William Washington Ndhlovu

"Compelled to resort to thieving ways to make ends meet."
9 December 1937, 179

Most of the matters that this council deals with have some economic aspect.... We think that if the wages of the natives could be improved many of the ills amongst them would disappear, the circulation of money would be increased and the country as a whole would benefit. Owing to the poorness of the wages paid to our people, they are practically compelled to resort to thieving ways to make ends meet. The average wage where I come from is thirty shillings per head per month and out of that the people have to send their children to school, clothe them, feed them and keep their family generally, and when the month is ended they find their wages totally inadequate and there have been instances where our people have resorted to thieving in order to supplement their income.... The Regent (Mishiyeni) has been inundated with appeals from his people to do something about this matter.... I know from my own personal experience that the matter is serious and that is why I rise to support the Regent in this matter.

Elijah Qamata

"We have passed the stage where we are only an asset ... as laborers."
9 December 1937, 179–82

The question [of wages] is of vital importance to the native people as a whole. It is not only a question for urban [people] but also those working on the farms. As it is known, the Reserves are so congested that people today are forced to go out and work.... We find in the urban areas that unless a man is paid six pounds and ten shillings he could not, if he has a family of five, live without debt. We know that there are sections of the European people who think that if they [Africans] were paid more money they would become rich and they would not work and that they could in effect bring about the impoverishment of a large section of the European population. I think that we have passed the stage where we are only an asset to South Africa as laborers. Today we have become consumers, and I think as consumers we should be treated differently to those forefathers who were perhaps ... not consumers. Today we buy the things that Europeans produce and our money, if we are paid, would circulate in the country and does not go out of this country.... We are cash buyers.... You have a city like Johannesburg where you find people who have stores only for natives, and they grow fat. We clothe ourselves, we eat the best we can afford, and if we were paid more we would be able to purchase more and therefore we are going to be ... a real asset in that respect. As a race, we are really an uncultivated home market to which European people should turn their eyes, the farmers as well.... I doubt that even with the improvements that have taken place in the Reserves the people who are going to live there ... would be able to save for a rainy day.... As I say, if we are paid well we would all have motorcars, and the motor car industry would expand, and the Europeans would get more employment.... If we are well paid, the people who deal in textiles and hardware would be able to increase and expand their business, with the result that there would be employment for everybody. We think we have passed the stage in our development in South Africa that a man, because he is black, should be paid just this and no more. I am not appealing for equal wages. What I am appealing for is that he should be paid a wage that would enable him to live comfortably and be in a position to save for rainy days.

Thomas Mtobi Mapikela

"It breaks our people's health—low wages everywhere."
25 November 1940, 182–83

Conditions have changed. I grew up in the Free State. In the olden days when I went out, I got my piece of bread and milk, but these farmers of today they do not care what we eat. They only give us a bag of *mielie* meal. We get ten shillings, fifteen shillings a month and little food. We get a few acres which we cannot live on, and it is time the government should know that the native of today is not the native of old. They want to educate their children; they would rather sacrifice everything and educate their children These farmers should be asked to put up schools where the children can be educated.... You hear the farmers crying, but you just go to the farms and see yourself how the people are treated—no man can live.... Let the farmers have a labor bureau ... this is one of the things that should be considered. It breaks our people's health—low wages everywhere.

Richard Victor Selope Thema

"We are asking for a minimum wage for the farm laborer."
14 August 1944, 124–25

South Africa is a big country, and it should be able to produce more food. We are starving today. Other farmers in other countries do much better work than the farmers in this country. Yet they have no black labor. When I was a little boy I used to work on a farm. The Oubaas used to sit on the stoep [verandah] directing the people, and that is the attitude of a great many people today.... That is not the way to do things.... We are asking for a minimum wage for the farm laborer. We are not concerned whether they are small farmers or big farmers. That has nothing to do with us. The small man who cannot afford it has no business to employ anyone and he should do his own work in his own way. I have no servants because I cannot pay them.... And when we ask that the farmers should be brought under the Wage Determination Act of this country we know very well that we are going to be told that the farmers cannot afford it—the farmers have no money. Well, let me say this, no one has the right to employ anyone else if he has no money. If the farmers have money they must pay. When we gave evidence before the Mining Commission we said that if the mines could not pay they must close down. We are not going to allow our people to work for nothing. When we were told that the mines could not pay more we said, "Very well, close the mines, and let our people go somewhere else—rather let them die of starvation than of tuberculosis and miners' phthisis for nothing." After all there is no difference between ourselves and the white people—the only difference is that we are black. What the white man has we have. The native lives and breathes in the same way as the white man does—we suffer, we have our feelings in the same way as the white people have; we are human beings like the white people, and if we work we are entitled to be remunerated and given better treatment.

George Champion
"The Department of Native Affairs
is there only to establish control over the natives."
10 August 1945, 106–07

We have in Natal the sugar industry as well as the coal industry, and if we in Natal try to organize our labor force to make the employer pay us better wages, they immediately turn round and bring into our province labor recruited elsewhere, labor which has no say at all about their wages. Their wages are fixed far away from Natal, and they come to Natal as recruited labor. Those people in the majority of cases come from the Transkei. The same thing applies to the gold mining industry, where I myself spent several years as a miner. We know that when the gold mines want to get cheap labor they turn to the Transkei. I say this now, that if the gold mining industry, the sugar industry and the coal mining industry were to find out that an industrial scheme was being started somewhere in the Reserves, competition would at once arise. Many of us have come to believe that the Department of Native Affairs is there only to establish control over the natives. I have heard it said very often that that is the object with which the Department of Native Affairs has been established ... people speaking like that are often not very far wrong.

Lancelot Peter Msomi
"They have to ... work...; [they] are not paid. [It] is tantamount to slavery."
21 August 1945, 354–55

Since the war broke out a large number of people who were carrying out business in town ... and some in the country as well, have embarked on acquiring farms, they have either leased or bought farms. The lessees have adopted the painful practice of using free labor in running their businesses, which they have in the urban areas. Some of these people have been carrying on businesses in towns-businesses like those of a general dealer and so on. Some of them run garages, run butcheries and bakeries. They take a large number of boys and girls and bring them into town and get them to work in these businesses, and they do not pay them. They even work in day shifts and night shifts and though they have to work hard, they are not paid. That is done in bakeries for instance. And those who work in butcheries are engaged as delivery boys and as helpers in the abattoirs and they are not paid either. Some of these people—I am now referring to the men who have acquired these farms—take contracts in the wattle plantations. They undertake to strip the bark off the trees and take it to the nearest station, have it loaded into railway trucks—and they use free farm labor for which they pay nothing, although they amass large sums of money out of these contracts. Some of these people contract to make bricks for the erection of buildings in native Locations and such like. A large number of men are employed in making these bricks; again the contractor is paid large sums of money but he does not pay his laborers. The labor which he uses is labor acquired from the farm which he has either bought or leased. As a result, many of these people, these Africans, have been reduced to a state of great poverty. Now, this is a very grave complaint, and this is not the first time that I have brought this matter to the notice of the Council. We have done so before and we had hoped that a commission of inquiry of some kind would be set up, but nothing has been done. This sort of thing is causing great suffering because we find that not only do these people use the labor for themselves, they even sell the labor of these boys. They transfer them to others; they have to go and work for other people ... but the men who do the work are not paid.... We feel that such a state of affairs is tantamount to slavery.

10

Trade Unions

In 1937, at the time of the first session of the NRC, the trade union movement among Africans was of little importance. Communist attempts in this direction had been unsuccessful, and the ICU had disintegrated as a movement. Champion was the only one in 1937 who contested his seat on the ICU platform alone, and he lost that election.[1] The ICU was considered by the Africans to have had two virtues, namely a dynamic leadership and the fact that it was an indigenous movement, "not a radio controlled robot of some countries overseas."[2] Anton Lembede wanted the ICU to act as the workers' wing of the ANC.[3] The importance of the ICU to the trade union movement from 1937 to 1951 lay in the manner of its demise rather than in any threats posed by its possible revival. The government and particularly the Chamber of Mines were convinced that the ICU had failed as a trade union movement because the government had refused to give it any recognition. It was accordingly of the opinion that if new trade unions of the 1940s were treated in a like manner, they too would disintegrate in time and no longer pose a threat either politically or economically. It was this attitude that the NRC had to contend with in its dealings on the question of black trade union recognition, a recognition that councilors insisted must include the African mine workers. The thrust of NRC resolutions on recognition precluded any discussion of other aspects of trade unionism. The Council made it clear that they approved of militancy and coercion on the part of union organizers, if this was found to be necessary. The minister of mines in 1943 held that the granting of recognition would only produce new elements of dissatisfaction and even conflict between black and white. He regarded as illusory the idea that black trade unions would be amenable to control by either the Department of Native Affairs or the Department of Labor or that recognition could be confined to certain sections of the African workers and withheld from black miners. The Mozambique Convention, which the South African government had signed with Portugal, precluded trade union activities among blacks from the Portuguese territories. It was thought as highly probable that the organizers of these trade unions would be white militant communists. Certainly Max Gordon, perhaps the most successful of these organizers in the late 1930s, was a communist—as were others.[4] Smit in 1942, perhaps as a result of NRC resolutions on the matter, placed the blame for industrial strife not on the communists but on the poverty of the workers. Bertha Solomon in Parliament was right when she said that what the government called communist propaganda was really labor problems amongst the Africans.[5] Both the NRC and the ANC saw no reason to abstain from gaining every possible benefit, including economic, from the war situation, which, by implication, included strike action.[6] No recognition of any kind was given to African workers until apartheid began to disintegrate, many years later.

George Champion

"The seeds that we planted in 1918 are now shooting out."
8 May 1943, 203–05

For the last twenty years, I have been connected with these efforts to improve the conditions of the native workers, to improve their conditions of pay, living on the mines, as well as outside the mines.... As I was sitting here listening to this debate since yesterday, my mind went back to the days of 1918 when the first strike of the municipal workers took place in Johannesburg. I can still remember that poor group of native laborers being brought before the magistrate. The magistrate's name was McPhie. "You have got to go and work in jail because you don't want to work for your employers." That was the beginning of the movement, which has spread all over without interruption. And as I am speaking to you now, my mind, my thoughts are in Dundee, where a crowd of my men are to parade before a judge of the Supreme Court for the same reason.... The chief native commissioner of Johannesburg, Mr. Lowe, says that you must make it possible for the workers to combine so that the leaders will not exploit their own people. Well, sir, all these things are caused by the fact that our government is determined to govern the native in a separate way, separate from other people. They want to divide the civilization of this country into two parts—the one ... for the Bantu, the other for the other section of the population. I ask you how long that position will continue without creating a state of affairs such as we are rapidly approaching now? Ever since 1918 ... this thing has been going on. In those days there were very few ... people who stood for the movement ... today we have an army of people. We have an army of people ready to speak for the others.... The seeds that we planted in 1918 are now shooting out, and there is only one remedy for the position which is of your own making and that is the one we submitted in 1918. Remove the barriers in regard to the color of a person. Remove the color bar. It has been urged that the mining industry should be relieved from the operator of this trade union arrangement. Why so? ... What right does the mining industry have to get people as cheaply as they can, and do get, from the country areas, from the Transkei, from Basutoland, from outside the borders of the Union? What right have they to get this concession? The leaders of the world ... in their convention at Geneva said that they had no right to do so. A man in every part of the world should have the right and the opportunity of selling his labor in the best market. But we have in this country, because of circumstances that have never been explained, a set of people, capitalists, mining magnates, who are buying the labor of our people as cheaply as they possibly can. How many people are they going to buy this year, when the Africans are starving because they cannot get *mielies*? And then we are told that the trade unionists are not to have any say. These people from the Transkei get into the train from Mabela, and at Stutterheim, and then they are sent to the mines. I am speaking here as a miner of long standing. I am speaking as a man who has organized the miners in the mines, and I claim that no one has better experience of these matters than I have. I have always claimed that. I have studied these questions as a miner and I have made a special study of the whole matter. I have studied the position of the working miner and of the employer. And I hope that what is taking place today will be a force to open the minds of those who keep the keys to the welfare of this country. You have invited us to go and meet the soldiers who are fighting for King and Country.... I ask you what is our feeling in this country when some of our people right from 1918 are still being told that they can go so far and no further in asking for an improvement in their conditions? We have a strike in Durban, which called for an ... increase in the wages of railway workers. That strike was complete. Yes, if there is a strike we must have pickets, and what is wrong with pickets? When a man is stubborn and does not want to fall in line, he is made to fall into line. When we had that strike there was no bloodshed, there was no disorder and there was no violence. Well, we were promised increases and when we were promised these things, we sat down. And ... what was the outcome of it all? We saw ... the police, and they said to us, "You are going to do as you are told," and the men were forced back at the point of the bayonet.... Let me say this at once, we are not afraid of you, we are not afraid of the police. But when a man in my position, working for the people, tries to show ... that the department is wrong—what happens? He is described as an agitator.... Now these statements did not come from the police but from the Department of Native Affairs. These men in the department were selected because of their knowledge of our customs. Our customs do not enter into labor questions at all.... I belong to the great force of the ICU, which once shook the four corners of this country.... Why do we still have these strikes taking place today? You can send people to their death—you can send them to jail—but no matter what you do the people will continue to organize and they will always go on organizing. Did I not spend three years outside my own province and for no other reason than that I tried to improve the conditions of my people? But, sir, I came back to my people, and my people still want me, and now they have sent me to Pretoria. Why? I shall tell you why. It is because you are trying to kill a spirit which will never die, a spirit of freedom, a spirit of freedom which lives and which will continue to live in the hearts and minds of our people. Our home is in this country. I cannot go to Europe or India.... I can only stay here in this world as long as God allows me to stay here. But I have my people, and I want to serve my people and to do my duty by them. My mind and my thoughts today are in Dundee where the coal workers are being prosecuted for no other reason than that they want an improvement in their conditions. Damage has been done to property as the result to their demands. Well, that sort of thing is bound to happen. You cannot stop that by simply talking to them. It can only be stopped in one way. We know what that way is.

Paul Mosaka

"If 300,000 ... are to be excluded,
what exactly will be the value of recognizing ... 3,000?"
10 December 1942, 193–95

Mosaka was given a mandate by the African trade unions to introduce this motion:

"That the Industrial Conciliation Act be amended to give African Trade Unions the same recognition and rights as European, Indian and Colored Workers Union."

The African trade unions want to be recognized directly under the Industrial Conciliation Act of 1937.... Now the Trade Union Council in Johannesburg, as indeed all the trade unions in the country, had received an assurance from the minister before that some form of recognition would be given. And just recently, the government has expressed itself very emphatically that it is now no longer considering full recognition of

African trade unions. What they are considering ... as a condition for any kind of recognition is that the mining industry shall be excluded from the recommendations regarding the recognition of trade unions. Now, if 300,000 workers in one of the most important and basic industries in the country are to be excluded, what exactly will be the value of recognizing a few trade unions consisting of 100, 200 or even 2,000 or 3,000 people? ... In our opinion the exclusion of the mine workers from the right to organize trade unions in effect will exclude something like 2,000,000 to 3,000,000 who directly and indirectly benefit from the mines to get the full advantage of the organization of trade unions. It will mean that there will be no raising of the standard of living in the Transkei and Basutoland and in the native Reserves; it will mean that the conditions of poverty, of want and ill health which exist there, will continue to exist. Now it is important to realize that the effect of an organized trade union among the African people is not merely a benefit to members of that trade union. When groups of men or women workers organize so that they can bargain with the employers for better conditions of work and better rates of pay, they make available to their families and the communities in which they live more money; they bring into circulation more money, which finally is for the good of the community.

Richard Hobbs Godlo

"What is causing disturbance ...
in the industrial areas ... is want, poverty and starvation."
10 December 1942, 197

I have no desire to repeat what Councilor Mosaka has so ably put before the Council, but ... leading trade unionists of this country are agreed that we shall never have peace in this country unless our people are given the same opportunities, and are given the same legal status in industry, as the other sections of the population. From the government quarters there is always the talk of communists, people who are regarded as the worst enemies not only of the employers but of the workers themselves. I am not a communist myself, but I think that communists are the most honest people one could ever hope to see in this country. If the cause of complaint is eliminated I can assure you that no communist or other organization will disturb the peace of our people in the urban areas.... What is causing disturbance, more especially in the industrial areas of this country, is want, poverty and starvation; and if these are removed, and if the people are given the opportunity of forming trade unions ... everything will go smoothly in this country so far as the workers are concerned.

Z.K. Matthews

"I have not got the pathetic faith which I notice
in some quarters in regard to ... departments of state."
8 May 1943, 208

I am glad that reference has been made to the fact that the Department of Native Affairs, in the disputes that have taken place between workers and employers, has used its influence to protect the leaders of the trade unions. I think that rightly conceived it is the work of the Department of Native Affairs to protect the native people against those who want to exploit them.... I feel that we are indebted to the department for this new view which is being taken of the functions of the department. It has been the impression of the native people for many years that their department is one that exists to control and regulate but not to protect, and this new note is a very good thing indeed.... Personally I have not got the pathetic faith which I notice in some quarters in regard to various departments of state. It seems to me that when we are dealing with the native in the country every department seems to be just as bad as the next one.... But the native people will not accept trade unions that are solely under the Department of Native Affairs. All they want is that this department of state, which has been set up to look after these interests, should include the Africans in all its activities and operations.... The Department of Labor shall treat the African people as they treat all other sections of the population.

11

Social Welfare

Much emphasis was placed by the Council on social welfare resolutions. In 1941, for example, out of 96 motions presented, 35 were resolutions of this kind.[1] In 1941, Mapikela, Qamata and Sililo presented their views to the minister of social welfare, J.H. Hofmeyr. They were to discuss such measures as allowances for war widows, tuberculosis sufferers, injured miners and phthisis sufferers, with their main focus being on the question of providing old age pensions.[2] The crux of their demands was to achieve parity with the other groups in South Africa. They were strengthened in their belief that such measures would be granted by the fact that every year saw the adoption by the government of at least one of their social welfare resolutions, in stark contrast to the fate of the majority of the other resolutions passed by the NRC.[3]

Dr. James Moroka
"No man ... can speak with authority about native drugs."
7 May 1943, 187

It will be a long time before we shall get the native people of this country to believe in European doctors. I have been practicing for quite a long time in South Africa, and I find that even in Thaba 'Nchu there are many who will pass my door and go and consult native doctors. I am of the opinion that before we take the step of saying that the native man must not be allowed to sell herbs, we shall have to educate them first and show them that their herbs and medicines are of no use. At the present moment, there is no man who can speak with authority about native drugs or native herbs. There is no European doctor who can tell me that all native medicines are no good. In the meantime, I think that what should be done is this, that seeing that the European doctors are allowed to sell native medicines, we should not stop others.

John Dube

"White people have not taken the trouble to study their science."
29 November 1938, 592

The people in our part of the country suffer more that these people do because these people wish to be recognized, but under the Natal Code we were recognized years ago—but the government has been cutting down the number of these men a great deal. Between the years 1927–1935, one thousand native medicine men have been scrapped and not allowed to renew their licenses ... and the native people regard this as unjust treatment. They say that the white people have not taken the trouble to study their science. They think that medical science recognized by the Western civilization should make research and find out the good in native medicine men. Prior to the coming of the white people in this country, we had these medicine men and they were able to help the people. They discovered various kinds of herbs and medicines, but it must be admitted that nowadays there are people who abuse this profession of native herbalist—but in all professions there are bad men. Even the white people have found it necessary to have people to look after these doctors, who have taken years and years of training, to see that they do not do anything that is unscrupulous.... There is a great deal of feeling in our part of the country with regard to these people and even the government ... must realize that it is a native custom. I heard one official say that he did not see any good in these fats being smeared on people and things like that, but the native people like it and it is an old custom and has existed from time immemorial and we do not want it taken away from us.... If European medical science is superior, which no one doubts, why not give the natives the liberty to have their own science?

William Washington Ndhlovu

"A very kindly gesture."
29 November 1938, 587ff

Mr. Chairman and councilors, I have been requested by the chief regent to move this motion. This is an old standing complaint from the Zulu people because most of their kings belonging to the Zulu dynasty have been buried in the [same] neighborhood. I remember at a meeting of chiefs in Maritzburg, there was a resolution ... to ask the government to buy these farms where our Zulu kings lay. That resolution was passed by acclamation.... We realize that there is nothing impossible for the government. Although these farms are in a European area, the Zulus would look upon the granting of these farms by the government as a very kindly gesture, especially in view of what Chief Mshiyeni, upon whom we look as our king, has done for the government—and he still intends to do more.

John Dube
"Being burnt and trodden on by cattle is very degrading."
29 November 1938, 588

For the native people to see the graves of their old chiefs being burnt and trodden on by cattle is very degrading indeed. What we are asking for, as the Zulu people, is something that will be like Thaba Basigo in Basutoland, where all the kings are sent to be buried. In this question it may not have been necessary to bring it here but we want the support of this council in our plea that the government may buy the three farms, and the Europeans who own these farms are quite willing to sell their farms, and they border with the exception of one, I think, on native areas.

Charles Sakwe
"If anyone wants to behold poverty..."
11 November 1944, 86–87

That owing to the high prices being charged by traders for *mielies* in native reserves, the government is requested to make available supplies of maize to natives in those areas where there is a food shortage. It has been found very difficult in our province to obtain *mielies* at a low price ... charges have been made by traders up to as much as one pound five shillings per bag. And the Department of Native Affairs has done all it possibly could do to make traders come down to a more reasonable price. That is a fact that we appreciate very much. But it does not alter the fact that if the government were to rail *mielies* to certain centers in the reserves, or to magistrates in the reserves, it would go a long way to alleviate any suffering of our people. Some of our people have gone to the Transvaal to get supplies of *mielies,* and the *mielies* have taken as much as two or three weeks before arriving at rail head, and there has been difficulty in getting the *mielies* transported to its destination on account of congestion.... There are shortages in Nongoma, Mahlabatini and also in Vryheid. Our people have no green *mielies* at all.... If anyone wants to behold poverty, if anyone wants to see with the naked eye the condition in which these people find themselves, he should go to the Transkei, here he will see piccanins [small children], shivering with cold, two or three of them covered under one blanket; there he will see people who have no means, who are unable to earn money, because there are no industries there to give them employment; and those who depend on a few morgan [about five acres in modern terms] to eke out a miserable existence. These people cannot even be called peasant farmers; they have to live from hand to mouth. And that is the state of affairs which exists among the people in many native reserves, and not only in the area in which I am concerned. Now let those people who speak so eloquently about the well-to-do in the reserves go to the reserve areas and see for themselves. They would find that the ... people living in the reserves are overburdened by debts ... that they have incurred with the traders. If the traders were not so sympathetic—if they did not want to help the Africans, the situation would be absolutely desperate.... They have patience with us and they put up with long periods of debt. And I want to say that a statement [in Parliament] that our people are rich is, to put it mildly, inaccurate and foolish.

Richard Hobbs Godlo

"If a law is made ... it has to be observed."
2 December 1940, 232

This matter [allowing Africans to trade in the Locations] is one of the hardy annuals of this council as well as of the congress of advisory boards.... Deputation after deputation has been sent to the authorities to place the case of our people [to the right of trading in the Locations] before the minister of native affairs. As far back as 1934 or 1935, if I remember correctly, Councilor Mapikela and myself went on a deputation to the secretary of native affairs in regard to this important matter.... In the first place we pointed out that to allow the municipalities to have their way in this matter would have a very bad effect upon the minds of our people because the reaction would be that as far as the Europeans are concerned, the law can be ignored; whereas in the case of our African people, they were required to observe the spirit and letter of the law. We must give credit where credit is due, and I think the Transvaal as a whole on this matter derives to be congratulated in that the people in the majority of the towns in the Transvaal are allowed to trade among their own people. But the Orange Free State has consistently maintained that it will not allow Africans to trade throughout the Orange Free State as a whole. We feel, sir, that if a law is made ... it has to be observed, and no matter whether the people are white, no matter what the local authorities are, they have to see to it that the law is observed and carried out.

Richard Victor Selope Thema
"Every house is a canteen today."
2 December 1940, 240–41

Personally, I think we must face the facts. We must face the facts as a race and deal with the evil which is before us. Some people say that because beer was brewed in the past for our ancestors, therefore we must drink it as much as we like. I am afraid that today *kaffir* beer has become commercialized. The fact is—whether we like it or not—not a single woman will not brew beer for her husband unless she can get money from the sale of *kaffir* beer. She is not going to brew it for her husband alone, which does not pay.... And that being so, I say that home brewing has failed. That is a fact we have to face whether we like it or not. And then I say that the municipal brewing of beer has a degrading effect on the African people. All of us know that our ancestors never drank *kaffir* beer in the way it is being drunk today. In the olden days whenever beer was brewed it was brewed for a certain festive occasion, or for ceremonial purposes. For instance, it was brewed when ploughing had to be done or when a house was built or for some special occasion like that. You would find for instance that there was no brewing during the week ... but today beer is brewed in almost every house and every home. Yes, sir, every house is a canteen today.... And I say that as a race we cannot allow such a thing to continue. It is degrading us.

Bertram Buxton Xiniwe
"The more you restrict people in regard
to liquor, the more trouble you [will] cause."
2 December 1940, 245

Councilor Thema spoke about home brewing and the abuses which are indulged in, in the Transvaal. I want to say that as far as Kingwilliamstown is concerned, home brewing there is being done by the municipality; as far as I can see and hear there has never been any abuse or complaint of home brewing. The people there are allowed to brew four gallons of beer from Monday to Saturday, and on Sunday there is no home brewing. The people there have been so law-abiding that there has been no abuse whatsoever of the enterprise, and home brewing is doing very well indeed, and is meeting the purpose. I can only say that the more restrictions you impose upon a person, the more you make that person go in for the illicit liquor traffic. During the Boer War when martial law was in force, no one was allowed to drink—that restriction applied to both black and white. But in spite of that you could see large numbers of people in the streets dead drunk. How they got hold of their drink, no one seemed to know, but they got it all the same. The explanation is that people got bottles of brandy from the hotels, and being afraid of the liquor being found on them they drank it straight off and got drunk. Well, sir, that was the result of these restrictions being imposed—they led to greater drunkenness. That is the position everywhere.... It has always been my contention that the more you restrict people in regard to liquor, the more trouble you are going to cause.

Richard Hobbs Godlo

"I welcome the difference of opinion in this matter."
2 December 1940, 246–48

In view of the sharp division of opinion which prevails on this question [of beer brewing and municipal beer halls], I feel as a measure of justice that you should give me a few minutes to reply to the points raised. I welcome the difference of opinion on this matter. It shows one thing, and that is that in this council there is no such thing as following one another blindly. And that is healthy. It shows that we think for ourselves. Members are speaking in the light of the experiences which they have brought from the various towns and from the various environments that they live in. That is a very welcome sign because it shows that we are all thinking and are all trying to help our people to the best of our ability. First of all I should like to say this, that in my opinion and in my heart of hearts I do not believe that there is such a thing as an ideal system for brewing *kaffir* beer, or for that matter European beer.... Personally I have nothing whatever to do with beer of any kind. I decided long ago that the only ideal thing is to close the door between the nose and the chin, so far as intoxicating liquor is concerned. But we are here to serve our people who perhaps do not think that it would be in their interest to abstain altogether.... Now, may I just refer to some remarks that were made about exaggerated language insofar as drunkenness is concerned. I can assure the chief native commissioners for the Witwatersrand that there is no desire on the part of members of this council to exaggerate matters or to put matters in a worse light then they should be put. All we are doing is to present our case as we find it—we want to put the facts before this Council, and there can be no gainsaying the fact that municipal brewing has not had the result which was expected of it, namely of destroying illicit liquor everywhere. In fact, the illicit liquor trade is increasing.... And I want to point this out: We Africans know the condition prevailing in our Locations better than a European can ever hope to do. After all, these highly placed officials can only see what is on the surface. They are only acquainted with the external appearance of conditions in the Locations. They only know very largely what they are told.... We know what the position is very much better than our native commissioners do. We know the position as it exists in the present Locations. But I can tell you that ever since the municipal canteens were introduced drunkenness has increased, convictions have increased and the amounts of money paid in fines have increased.... That is all I have to say in reply to the very interesting discussions which my motion has evoked.

R.V. Selope Thema
"Even angels would not submit to laws of this kind."
20 August 1945, 358–61

African people like their beer, beer was part of their father's food, and when the Europeans say, "You shall not drink beer except the beer which is made by the municipality," they simply show that they do not understand the position. As far as European liquor is concerned, the government of this country, in order to recognize the loyalty of the Chinese people, suddenly said, "The Chinese can have drink," and when a number of Indian soldiers won the V.C. [Victoria Cross] the government said the Indians could also go and buy in the bottle stores. Now these Indians and Chinese are living among us and the police, when searching for liquor, may find Africans who have been supplied by Chinese; and men and women are arrested and sent to jail. A far as I can see that does not provide the police with a solution to the problem of crime. What it does is this—that the police on the Rand and in Pretoria are failing to detect crime because they go in for one method of detecting crime—and that is the raiding and arresting of people at the weekends.... We have this fact: that most of our big criminals today are taught crime in the jails—the first time they were sent to jail was on account of a contravention of the Pass Laws or of the municipal regulations. But surely the breaking of these regulations or of these Pass Laws is not a crime at all. If one man is allowed to drink I cannot see any reason why another man should be prevented from having a drink just because he is black.... If people had the right to drink they would drink like gentlemen, and we would not have this disturbance which we see today. I am not one of those who hold that view that our African people are angels, or can be turned into angels.... But I say this: that we have human qualities which are being destroyed by the laws which are being inflicted on us. These human qualities are respect for the law, respect for authority—those qualities which are traditional with us are being destroyed. How can people respect laws of the kind which we have in this country? Even angels would not submit to laws of this kind, and I therefore say that these laws are demoralizing in their effects. What are we going to reap as a result of these laws? We shall reap something evil.... A man is put into jail because he has left his tax receipt or his pass at home, or because he is found with a glass of beer in his hand. They are all put in jail.... They are arrested in front of their homes. It does not help a man saying to a policeman, "This is my home, and I have left my pass inside." The police do not wait for the man to produce his pass, they simply pitch him into jail.... The contravention of these regulations does not harm anyone. Just because a man has gone out without a permit—does that make him a criminal? ... The Africans have learnt, as a result of the treatment meted out to them, that they must stand together, and they are going to defend one another.... Well, if this goes on then the position in this country will get worse and worse.

Richard Hobbs Godlo

"All races, even the chosen race drinks,
yet they are not subjected to these raids."
20 August 1945, 362–63

The position obtaining on the Witwatersrand and Pretoria is, I am afraid, extending to all the big industrial centers—people being arrested for statutory offences, for breaking laws that do not apply to members of other races. For example, the Pass Laws do not apply to Europeans, the Indians or the coloreds. The result is that the colored townships and the Indian quarters of the towns are never invaded by the police—there are no mass arrests there. There are no raids during weekends, as there are in the native Locations. Law-abiding people are also affected, because my experience of these raids in every town is that if the policeman enters a house because it is suspect—because it is suspected that there is beer in the house—and if he fails to find liquor in that house the policeman will demand the poll tax receipt, and if that is produced he will demand something else, such as the service contract, and if the man has that then the policeman will yet demand something further.... For these reasons we appeal to the powers to stop this.... Now the position is that people do drink. But our people, Mr. Chairman, are not the only people who drink. All races, even including the chosen race, drink, yet they are not subjected to these raids. With these few words, I support the motion.

Z.K. Matthews

"When they are altering a section of the law ... we should be consulted."
25 May 1945, 45–46

You know, sir, that the government is in no doubt at all about the fact that the African people are opposed to the beer halls.... The profits made from these beer halls were not being used to the best advantage. I should like to direct your attention to ... the report of the commission which says: "The tendency to exploit beer hall profits to meet recurring expenditure on ordinary municipal services, i.e., roads, lighting ... and other items, which ... should more properly be financed by the general account...." To our surprise today, we find that the amendment passed only last year is to be radically altered.... I feel that it is the plain duty on the part of the department when they are altering a section of the law to which we have agreed, that we should be consulted.

Richard Hobbs Godlo

"Perhaps we would welcome segregation based on terms of equal treatment."
2 December 1940, 227ff

Godlo moves that the Council endorses the resolutions passed by the Advisory Boards Congress on 20 December 1939:

That the (Advisory Boards) Congress strongly opposes the attitude adopted by the municipalities throughout the Union towards the native revenue account; that is, that the African population must for themselves provide the whole of the revenue for running the native Locations or villages either from rents or from the sale of beer; and that no improvements or social services can be provided in Locations and villages unless they can be paid for by the African people, who are the poorest section of the population; that this congress holds this financial segregation to be indefensible and only a convenient way of enabling the European people to escape moral and financial responsibility for contributing their share of the costs of decent housing and adequate social services in the Locations and villages. That the Congress declares that in any case the African people are contributing though their labor and other activities and are entitled to a far greater share of the fruits of their labor in such forms as higher wages, better housing and more social services.... The mere fact that the government proposed that all moneys collected from our people should be set aside to be used only for their services did not mean that the municipalities should not do their duty by financing the necessary services of our people. As is pointed out, it is a well-known fact that our people in these Locations are the poorest section of the community. Commerce and industry have chosen to keep the economic conditions of our people at the very lowest ebb.... The municipalities and the government are the worst offenders in this respect because our people cannot afford to carry all the services that are needed in the maintenance of these Locations ... and whenever representations are made to the municipalities, the answer is invariably we are using all the moneys collected from natives and that the expenditure of the Native Revenue Account exceeds the income, and that is about the best we can do. We hope that the employers of labor which include the municipalities will realize they have a moral responsibility for carrying out the services in these Locations. We in common with the rest of our people are opposed to any scheme of financial segregation. Perhaps we would welcome segregation in all its aspects if it was a segregation based on terms of equal treatment. If our people were paid on the same basis as the Europeans. If the policy of the government and of commerce and industry were one of equal pay for equal work there would have been no need for the presentation of such a request to you. Our people are making their contributions. Their cheap labor ... is a contribution towards the services in these Locations.

Victor Poto

"It is within the power of the government
to provide ways and means for the people to live."
8 December 1942, 92

We have some difficulty in finding a way whereby industries could be established in the reserves. It is now quite clear that there are certain ways in which they could be established in the places where people live. We shall keep on saying that it is within the power of the government to provide ways and means for the people to live. And we do not expect the reports issued by the various committees to be shelved, never to see the sun and never to reach the people.

Victor Poto

"Trying to depart from our native customs and traditions."
3 May 1943, 92–93

This matter of old age pensions for Africans has been brought to the Council on many occasions without any success. It has also been before the Transkeian General Council. There, too, it has never been successful. With regard to these poor people, their case is always answered by the authorities in this way—that they are now trying to depart from our native customs and traditions. Namely, that we are now saying that we are not able to support our helpless and old people. The authorities always lose sight of the fact that these old people have given a great deal of service to the government, and in addition, they are also supporting their families. The only way in which the authorities suggest that they may be met is by exempting them from the tax liability. Their exemption from the tax liability does not help them at all in regard to their maintenance and support. The old native traditions or customs do not work at all in these modern times, because times now prevailing make things very difficult, the high cost of living prevents other people from helping these old men—they can no longer lend these old men a beast or do anything for them in that direction. We do sometimes try to help these people by working their lands for them. But experience has shown that people who are helped in this way only suffer as a result because we attend to their lands when the season is almost over.... Let us remember that before the advent of the Europeans in this country the land was governed and administered by native chiefs. In those olden days, the chiefs were in a position to support their people—they were able to look after those of their people who were helpless, aged and infirm. But the conditions have changed and we can no longer rely on the ability of a chief to govern his tribes and to help the infirm. Those days have gone. Today we have to look to the government.... I want to ask the authorities ... to consider this matter from the point of view of the facts which I have advanced.

Richard Hobbs Godlo
"A changing society ... with changing conditions."
4 May 1943, 93

I can add very little to what Chief Poto has said [asking for old age pensions for Africans] except to express the disappointment of the African people generally at the attitude of the Treasury in harping upon a custom impracticable in so far as the farms on the reserves are concerned. There is that well-known hospitality among the African people ... who would never allow a fellow being to suffer. But the position is that we are dealing with a changing society and with changing conditions.... I do not represent a country constituency but I make a point of visiting country Locations, and I compare the conditions existing in urban areas with those prevailing in rural areas, and I have always found that the aged people and the blind people in the country districts are living on a lower scale ... simply because they are finding it difficult to eke out an existence. And one must also remember this that some of these aged people have no sons or daughters to support them, and even those who are supposed to have children to support them find it impossible to do much because they themselves are hardly in a position to make ends meet. So I think the argument that Africans do not require old age pension because of the prevalence of their customs and traditions is worn out.

Bertram Buxton Xiniwe

"I pride myself on my native law and custom."
7 May 1943, 181–82

I must submit that our rural native population has been fully consulted on this matter [native custom of inheritance] as far as the Ciskei is concerned.... The native commissioners—the paramount chief and the chief under him were present. The various tribes were present.... They were all represented and this whole matter was thrashed out.... The views of the people said that if we changed our native law of succession by allowing a widow to take possession of any immovable property or of any cash it would only mean that any man would find it possible to propose to that widow with the view of taking possession of that money. Now let me say that as far as the native law of succession is concerned, there is no abuse and there is no trouble in the appointment of an heir. We represent the majority of the tribal people, and they have said that they do not want any change. Let me say again that I pride myself on my native law and custom.

Charles Sakwe

"We have the right to voice the feelings of the people."
7 May 1943, 179

As far as the Transkeian Territories are concerned I support the recommendations of the committee.... I feel that the rural areas of the Ciskei are also in favor of what is proposed here.... We have been sitting here patiently listening to the grievances that have been advanced by the people who come from the urban areas, but when it comes to a question which affects the people of the rural areas, I think we have the right to voice the feelings of the people from those areas whom we represent.

R.V. Selope Thema

"Women today are asserting their rights."
7 May 1943, 179–81

Councilor Sakwe speaks as if the African people are divided in urban and rural sections. He forgets that the women for whom we speak are the women who come from the rural areas.... He should remember that times have changed. He speaks for the type of man who lived about a hundred years ago, who has what they call a native *kraal,* where the women have to do this, that and the other, and have to obey what their men tell them. I say that whether we like it or not, the women today are asserting their rights, and we are not going to keep them down. They even smoke cigarettes. I don't like it, I hate it; but I cannot prevent it. Your daughter comes to Johannesburg and she smokes cigarettes in spite of your *kraal* traditions.... A far as the Natal Native Code is concerned, we do not want it in the Transvaal.... Whether we like it or not, those ideas of our forefathers in regard to the position of women have long since passed; they have outstayed their usefulness.... And the Natal Native Code cannot even prevent the native women of Natal from advancing.... To consult the chiefs who do not understand the change that has taken place does not help—it does not give the authorities the views of the natives themselves. We, the ordinary natives, may be in the minority, but after all we are the people who count. Let me put it this way. It is the educated man who counts. With the Europeans it is the same.... The ordinary Rooinek and Oom Jan in the street is not the man who counts in the affairs of state. It is the man who is educated who understands what is going on, whose views we must take, and we cannot be driven back to the conditions of the past. We must go ahead and forward with the times.... To say that if the husband dies the husband's brother can take the widow—well surely the time for that sort of thing has passed.... It is all wrong. Let those who want to adhere to these customs do so, but if there is a progressive woman and a progressive man who want to go ahead, let them be allowed to do so and not be kept back by customs which have ceased to have any purpose. Today we do not marry according native custom; we marry according to European rights. I no longer ask my father to look for a wife for me in a certain *kraal*. I look for my own wife.... We want to protect all these women.

George Champion

"We are speaking of civilized women."
7 May 1943, 184

Now let me say that it is the women who are concerned in this matter—the women who lose their husbands—who have worked hard with their husbands, who have acquired a little property and have deposited their money in the bank. When the husband dies, the woman is left in the charge of a guardian. I am not speaking of the women in the *kraals*. I am speaking more particularly about the Christian woman, the civilized women, married according to Christian rites ... we are not discussing the position of the polygamists—we are speaking of civilized women.

John Dube

"We Zulus still cling to our old customs."
7 May 1943, 182

As far as this matter is concerned, let me say that I have dealt with as many as six women who came to complain that they had been taken advantage of and were being cruelly treated by their late husbands' brothers. It is a very difficult matter.... Now, this committee said that the Natal Native Code might be suitably amended if and when the majority of the natives in Natal desire a change. So I do not see why we should oppose the findings of this committee. Of course, I must say that now the majority of the people in Natal are afraid that if they change the present position, their women will start to be the bosses. Our people have been accustomed in their *kraals* to be above the women, to be in charge of everything. A woman after her husband has died may have to appeal to the magistrate for relief or she can make a lot of trouble in the *kraal*.... Now I personally feel that many women in Natal have not been treated properly after their husbands have died.... I know of one case where the brother of the husband who had died wanted the widow to become his wife. She refused. So he went into the *kraal* of the widow, took all the cattle, and said, "If you want any milk from the cattle you can come and live in my *kraal*." But she preferred to live without milk or cattle because she would not become the wife of that man.... We Zulus still cling to our old customs while the generation is moving forward. But it will take time before we before we shall be able to get past these old customs.... This report, as I read it, says that those who wish to remain under these conditions may do so, but the door is left open for those who want to go ahead and become free of their menfolk.

Richard Hobbs Godlo

"We are a changing society."
7 May 1943, 179

The feeling of the meeting [on changing the native law of inheritance]—and I may say that it was not the women who spoke but the men—was that the time had passed for the women to be treated as they had been in the past. In East London I addressed a meeting and explained the proposed legislation, and the people felt that the enlightened element among the women were being penalized, and I do feel that whatever has been done, the position is such that it cannot be said that the majority of the people favor the status quo. Mr. Chairman, let us remember that we are marching with the times and that there are laws which answered quite well in the olden days when applied to our people, but we are a changing society and we must not only look to the tribal African, we must also bear in mind the position of the others who are marching ahead with the times and are progressing.

Saul Mabude

"We are here representing our backward people."
7 May 1943, 184

We have been told that we should look to the educated section of the African people—that is what Councilor Thema told us. I take that to mean that we are not to take any notice of—that we are to ignore the ignorant section. Well, if that is the contention of Councilor Thema, then I must agree to differ from him. We are here representing our backward people—we are here to represent and look after their interests. We are not here to represent the minority. We are here to represent the majority, and the majority of our people are still backward people. The majority of our people are in the Reserves. It is quite clear that there is an apparent anomaly in connection with the property of a deceased man in regard to the immovable property and the money, which has been saved, by a man before his death…. Now, the woman in the ordinary course of events had no power to dispose of his property by herself according to native custom, but it does seem to me that native custom makes adequate provision for her…. It appears to me that there may be some misunderstanding on this point…. There is some injustice done now and again as between an heir and a widow or a woman who has acquired property…. So far as the Transkei is concerned, I might just as well say that it is very, very seldom that difficulties of that type occur. But I do realize that in the urban areas, difficulties of that nature might often arise because women acquire property in their own name and when a woman's husband dies, I can quite see that it may be difficult for the woman to get his money in her name.

Paul Mosaka

"We are concerned."
9 November 1945, 108

We are concerned that we should be rid of the criminal element; we are concerned that there should be proper health conditions in the townships; we are concerned with the small pieces of ground that have been given us in the reserves to plough; we are concerned that these small pieces of land be properly ploughed so that the people can eke out a proper livelihood. We are concerned about our people not becoming an unclean lot of individuals—a useless section of humanity. We want our people to be useful. I have in my mind a particular individual ... he is a perfectly useless fellow. He has joined a criminal gang—the individual happens to be a nephew of mine. He joined a criminal gang while in his teens. He has not had any schooling. He is just a regular jailbird. We cannot get help from any one for these people. They grow up in the streets and in the slums ... they know when to steal where to steal and how to steal ... they have no other work to do. They study the work of the police, they study their opportunities of stealing, and they have become expert in this job—and if the government thinks that by increasing the police force, by building more prisons, by telling the police to shoot if necessary, then I am afraid the government is on the wrong track because that will not solve the problem at all.... It is not often realized how we who live in the Locations are concerned about this problem; let me tell you that we are *more* concerned about the problem because when the white people feel that the situation is getting out of hand ... they have the right to decide for themselves what they shall do. But the native people in the Locations have no right to say anything. What can they do? They can only make representations to the city council, and the next they know is that somebody will come along and arrest everyone under Section 17, and then the trouble starts. The innocent people are arrested and sent to jail. We have no right to control our own affairs in the Locations to see to our own safety; we are in a very much more parlous position that the white section of the population. We are prey to the criminal element to a far greater extent that the white people are.

Piet van der Byl, Minister of Native Affairs

"Many thousands if not millions are expected
to starve to death in the next few months."
April 1946

To put the speeches below into the context of the conditions of that time, I include an extract from the address given by van der Byl at the opening of the sixth NRC session.

We all view with regret the continuation of the drought conditions in many parts of the country, particularly in the Ciskei, where the severest suffering has been experienced.... The shortage of maize in this country is still the main cause of hardship, though every effort is being made to ration our available supplies as fairly as may be and even to augment our supplies from abroad. The Union has managed to get 250,000 bags from Angola, and further supplies are being obtained from the Argentine. To encourage local production a price of 19/- per bag for the following season has been guaranteed.

In the Ciskei, rationing of supplies has been aided by the local committees of natives to ensure equitable distribution of maize at 2 kilos per head of the native population per day. The services put in place by the food controller to distribute essential food from lorries at special minimum prices in the worst affected areas are working well. The 200 cooking centers from which scientifically prepared food is supplied free to pre-school children are all doing their part. The scheme for the ploughing of native land with tractors ... should have a considerable effect in producing a *mielie* meal crop as early as possible. Arrangements have been made ... to supply seed maize at controlled prices. We must bear in mind that there is a very serious food shortage affecting hundreds of millions of people in other parts of the world. Many thousands if not millions are expected to starve to death in the next few months in spite of all efforts to feed them. For this reason the Union cannot make a very strong claim upon supplies.

Paul Mosaka
"Considering the interests of the many as against the interests of the few."
4 May 1943, 48–49

I speak as a trader and as one who represents the trades of the Transvaal. And may I say, I am not only expressing my own views as a trader, but I have consulted a number of advisory boards who do not hail this scheme with any enthusiasm [a government proposal to enable Africans in the townships buy fruit, vegetables and milk at cost].... We feel that the municipalities are always very ready to interfere where they feel they can make money without giving corresponding amenities and that will have the effect of pauperizing the whole of the African community, because it will deprive those few who are struggling to raise the ladder of their means of livelihood.... That is the opinion of the ordinary trader who deals in fruit, vegetables and fuel. Recently we have been told that the municipality of Johannesburg had been given the right to distribute *mielie* meal during these times of great scarcity. And that, I take it, is simply giving them further powers to encroach on the trading field of the retailer. If the government or the municipality have any regard for the people, we have always maintained that home brewing has made it possible for hundreds of families to live decently—but we feel that these means of livelihood have been taken away from the ordinary family, and now we find that the man who can go to these small farms in Orlando and hawk the goods will also be deprived of his means of livelihood—all hawkers of this kind, will be deprived of their means of livelihood. If the municipalities want to help us, let them reduce rents.... There is the humanitarian principle involved—the principle of considering the interests of the many as against the interests of the few. But I think that in this particular case, where the control is not with the people themselves, the position is different; if it were a co-operative society in which Africans had shares, there would be nothing to say against it, but if you hand it over to the municipalities where we are not represented ... you will find that the ordinary man will be opposed to it. In Orlando the advisory board has opposed it. Even in the case of Springs, where the people get their milk a little cheaper, it is only because there is a beer hall there and the milk supply is subsidized by the beer hall; and even there we would rather see that private enterprise were not discouraged.... We feel it should not be allowed.

Lancelot Peter Msomi
"It should not be to the detriment of the public."
4 May 1943, 49

I am sorry that I have to differ from the last speaker in regard to this contemplated scheme by the government, to persuade the municipalities to store quantities of food in Locations so that it should be available to people at cost price. I take it that business people who happen to be in the Locations should run their business there in accordance with the conditions that they find in the Locations. They are not primarily there to make things difficult for the people who are resident in the Locations. Most of these people have made the Locations their permanent homes. They are laborers mostly for the towns and the subject now is one which comes under the heading of "nutrition." We know that many people are in a deplorable condition, their not having sufficient to maintain them. If a step is taken in the light of the recommendation which your committee has made, I think it would be of great material benefit to the people, because they get things cheaper there and are able to buy everything there.... If a businessman chooses to run his business in the Location he should so fix his prices for whatever commodity he sells as to be in accordance with the conditions he finds, but it should not be to the detriment of the public.

James Moroka
"Do the right thing and pay people living wages."
4 May 1943, 49

The whole position is really this: we are approaching this question from the wrong point of view. The reason why the government finds it necessary that these people should be supplied with cheap goods is because of the insufficient pay that these people get. The municipalities and the other organizations which go around supplying food and milk and things of that kind should do the right thing and pay people living wages. It is the insufficiency of wages which is the thing that causes all this trouble. I maintain that if we are going to allow the government or the municipalities to sell these things to the people at these low prices, we are interfering with the native traders. I am looking at it from the point of view that the municipality is out to kill the native trader, and surely that is not right.

Paul Mosaka
"Black markets have developed."
10 August 1945, 92

The position is really very bad. I do not know whether the Department [of Native Affairs] is aware of the extent to which we people in the urban areas are suffering from a shortage of *mielies* and *kaffir* corn. The position has become so bad that with the present system of rationing, black markets have developed, black markets of a serious kind, so that it is necessary for the department, if it is going to be of any assistance, [to] provide some other native foodstuffs. I realize that in the Transkei you have sent rice.... Practically all the *mielies* which we use [in the towns] is used for human consumption. There is a certain amount of illicit liquor brewing and a certain quantity of *mielie* meal is used there.... I should say that over twelve months the number of bags of *mielie* meal which could be made available for human consumption by preventing the municipalities from making *kaffir* beer would be several thousands. So we have a very promising source of relief here.

Bertram Buxton Xiniwe
"It is not right that the men should be fed
while their women and children starve."
10 August 1945, 91–92

I need hardly take up the time of the Council by telling councilors of the conditions which exist in the Ciskei. We have heard from the government officials and cabinet ministers for that matter that there is an acute shortage of *kaffir* corn and *mielies*, and that it will be some time before the distress is alleviated. I am not quite *au fait* with the system relating to the distribution of foodstuff, but what I know is that the little bit of *mielies* and *kaffir* corn, if any, in the country, has to be divided amongst people who want to use this as foodstuff, and that a certain percentage goes to feed animals. I have no quarrel with the feeding of animals from *mielie* products when there is no grass available, but I know that a certain percentage of the *mielies* and *mielie* meal goes to the beer halls.... The point is this—that in the reserves the children are starving, so much so that the government has to step in to introduce a supplementary feeding scheme. The shortage of *mielies* is aggravated by the fact that some of it has to go the beer halls, where the children do not benefit at all. Only men benefit—the men who are in the habit of going to these beer halls. What I propose is that we should ask the government that during this crisis, this time of acute shortage of *mielies* and *mielie* products, the sale of *kaffir* corn and *mielies* be suspended until such time as there is a good supply to go round. Surely it is not right that the men should be fed while their women and children starve. I am not raising hypothetical cases. Only a few weeks ago I attended an auction sale of *mielies* and *mielie* meal. The stuff was being sold by the South African railways, and quite a number of Africans and traders attended that sale because even in town there is a shortage of *mielies*. You cannot buy a bag of *mielies* even if you have the money to pay for it because *mielies* are rationed.... So we all rushed to that sale in the hope of having an opportunity to buy at least a bag of *mielies*. What did we find? We found the superintendant of the Location— who manages the beer hall—at the sale, to compete against us. The result was not a single African got a bag of *mielies* or *mielie* meal at that sale.... Now, sir, that is a very unsatisfactory state of affairs, and I do hope that your department will make the necessary representation to the *mielie* control board ... with a view to this sale of *mielies* to the beer halls being suspended.

Paul Mosaka

"Intolerable burdens placed upon the African people."
17 August 1945, 124

We have had these disputes about Alexandra Township; we have had these disputes about the buses, and the conditions in the suburbs of Pretoria. There was a riot here in Pretoria which resulted in the killing of many people, and that riot clearly demonstrated the conditions under which the African people have to live. We have had these upheavals on the Reef—are not all these things clear evidence of the intolerable conditions, the intolerable burdens placed upon the African people? If all these things are not evidence, incontrovertible evidence, of what is going on, then I want to know what more evidence the government wants. The starvation in the Ciskei in an indication of what is going on. The outbreak of typhus and the spread of smallpox—all these are indications. But these things mean nothing to the government; they simply go on and they continue to legislate as if the Africans are in the most comfortable and most fortunate circumstances. Yet we know what their conditions are, and so should the government. I want to mention another thing to show the lack of sympathy on the part of the government. We have spoken ... in connection to the starvation in the Ciskei, and while I am aware that this whole food position is going to be discussed, I want to say that it is something of which the government must have full knowledge, and when they put up the price of *mielies,* they are adding further burdens on a population which cannot stand any more burdens.... If we had a government which knew the conditions of the African people, which realized the contribution the African people have made to the war, which realized the sacrifices made by our men who have gone to the front; a government which realized, too, the loyalty of the people—or let me put it this way: if you have a government which knows all these facts and yet continues to impose a burden, to impose burden upon burden in regard to essential articles of diet on a poor section of the community, then I say that that government does not appreciate the services which have been rendered—I say that the government is callous to the interests of those people of whom it claims to be the trustee.

Chief Mshiyeni Kwa Dinuzulu

"There is starvation in my country."
27 April 1946, 80–81

There is starvation in my country; we are all hungry, we are dying. There is corruption all over the country. I have seen things in the streets here. I have seen queues of people waiting for bread. We are faced with a very dangerous situation. When food is distributed it should be distributed not through the stores alone. Let some food be sent to the chiefs in the country so that we can distribute it to the people. I want the government to know what is going on, and I therefore want to tell them that throughout my country people are dying of starvation. If you were to visit Nongoma you would be surprised at what you would see there. That is the place where I live, and all over my country the same position prevails. You meet old women, people who have never been to a store before, wending their way to the nearest store, crying because of starvation. Today they have no cattle, their cattle have died, or they are infested with ticks. Our cattle are dying in thousands in Zululand from Ngana. Our native commissioners are continually sending in reports about starvation and famine. Sir, it is true, we are on the point of perishing.... I want the government, and I want you, to go throughout the country to see for yourself what the position is…. We would like to see more food distributed to the people because we hear rumors that there is almost sufficient food in the country. Already there are people who go about making mischief in the country. They come across a man or a woman carrying a small quantity of *mielies* and they take that food away and assault … the people. Whatever the government is thinking of doing let it be done quickly, because people are perishing.

Z.K. Matthews
"One sometimes wonders whether the Europeans have any heart at all."
17 August 1945, 110–11

As to the evil of migratory labor: one sometimes wonders whether the Europeans have any heart at all. When you think of the harm that is done from the social and moral points of view by having these thousands of men and women away from their homes, one wonders what people are thinking about. Those of us who are interested in child welfare in these areas could tell you stories, which, if you are parents, would make you very sad about the effects of these people being away from their homes. It seems to us as if the nation, the European side of our nation, does not care what is going to happen to our children, and to our family life, as a result of people continually leaving their homes and going to and from industrial areas. I feel that anything that can be done to stop people from leaving their homes and going to and from industrial areas … will be worth a great deal to the nation. If we cannot have our people working near the reserves, then we shall have to make it possible for them to live with their families in industrial centers…. If we want to build up a more wholesome race, both black and white, we must do that; and if opportunities for employment can be created for people near their homes so that families can be kept together, that will be worth more than the wages which they might receive by going away from their homes at the expense of their family life.

12

Pass Laws

In 1937 the pass system had not yet been uniformly applied in all the four provinces. In the Transvaal and the Orange Free State, Africans could be required to carry up to nine passes, but this was not the case in the Cape and Natal. In spite of the fact that the implications of the pass system were not fully apparent to the councilors from the latter provinces, the NRC was always unanimous in its condemnation of the system. Members regarded freedom of movement as the basis of a free and democratic society, and passes were regarded by them as a form of slavery.[1] In the constant demand for the abolition of the pass system, there was no difference in attitude between the resentment of the nominated and elected councilors. Chief Victor Poto used the phrase "hunting of the people" when referring to the police pass raids, while Mshiyeni Kwa Dinuzulu pointed out that although the Africans were the original inhabitants of the land, they were the ones whose freedom of movement was being restricted. Mapikela said, "We are supposed to have freedom under a democratic government. Is this our freedom?"[2] The councilors used arguments that they thought would resonate better with the Department of Native Affairs. The latter emphasized native custom when it suited them to do so. Councilors thus argued that the Pass Laws were inconsistent with tribal custom and should be abolished for that reason. They did not argue that they were both an inefficient and an ineffectual method of controlling the African population, which they were. Councilors asked that for at least the duration of the war, the Pass Laws should be abolished or at least suspended on the grounds that this might persuade Africans to join up and fight for their country. Another reason given by them for abolition was that as the war had stopped land purchases for blacks,[3] the congestion in the rural areas was increasing and was forcing Africans into the towns.[4] Initially the NRC had hoped that something might be done about the pass system, but in spite of the protests that had confronted the Department of Native Affairs and the Native Affairs Commission, it all came to nothing in the end.[5] The Pass Laws were more rigorously applied than ever.

R.V. Selope Thema

"It is the law that is at fault, not the police."
21 November 1938, 161–62

Sometimes people condemn the police; they say the police are handling the natives roughly; but I have come to the conclusion that no policeman—even if you get a London policeman, you will find that he will handle the people roughly because our laws themselves are rough, so he cannot be different. There is no way in which these laws can be handled sympathetically. They are harsh, even if you had the deepest sympathy in your heart. It is the law that is at fault, not the police, because if the police were not given the impression that they were doing their duty they would not be harsh. They do not come into contact with the colored people; the result is that there has never been any friction between them and the colored people but that there is always friction between them and the natives because of these laws.

R.H. Godlo

"We advocate the total abolition of these laws."
5 May 1943, 110

We exhausted ourselves this morning on this question, but I want to say again: there can be no compromise on this matter. We advocate the total abolition of these laws. Pass Laws ... we want peace in this country, we want harmony in this country, and we, as leaders of the African community, desire to see all things that are responsible for creating that spirit of hostility between Europeans and Africans removed. When we come to these parts of the country we are generally told that we in the Cape live in a paradise where the Pass Laws are unknown. But ... curfew regulations have the same effect as the Pass Laws. In some towns like East London, they are rigorously enforced.... And for these reasons we find we are unable to draw a line between the curfew regulation and the service contracts—they are all Pass Laws—and they must all be abolished if we want contentment in this country.

W.W. Ndhlovu

"Every time we see a policeman we start dodging him."
21 November 1938, 153

This pass system is very irritating, especially in raids, which are often made in Locations. Innocent people are stopped for hours at times when inquiries are being made. I don't for the life of me see why a pass should be carried by an African in our land of birth, but just to meet the farming community I think one pass should be quite sufficient. A far as our womenfolk are concerned, they should be exempted.... Sometimes it is very difficult for people belonging to other races to quite appreciate how we feel about these pinpricks to which we are subjected; every time we see a policeman we start dodging him because we know we are going to be detained and lose time and we want to be relieved of these indignities.

Chief Victor Poto

"We always consider these things as the hunting of the people."
21 November 1938, 154

When a native comes to us, we always consider these things as the hunting of the people—the raids—merely to produce passes and things like that.... When I came to this council, I went to Umtata to get my railway ticket. The ticket issuer asked me, "Have you got your pass, you have to produce your pass if you are going to the Transvaal." I said to him, "When has that started, I have never carried a pass, I have a document with me indicating that I am a member of the Native Representatives Council." He said, "Notwithstanding that you are a member of the Native Representatives Council, the law insists that you have to carry a pass when you go to those provinces." [Chiefs were not required to carry passes; Poto was just giving an example].... Frankly speaking, sir, I don't think you will find anybody among our native people throughout the whole Union who support the operation of the pass system—not one.... We as natives feel it is a great indignity to us, it is only the black people who are required to carry passes just as though we were cattle going to the dipping tank ... it is a stigma on us.... We do desire that this matter should be righted and simplified, but I do agree with those who say, Let us only carry one document. We should not be made to carry a bag of papers and when you lose one the rest will never save you from being arrested.

Chief Mshiyeni Kwa Dinuzulu

"Pass Laws ... [turn] youths into criminals."
21 November 1938, 151

I support Councilor Baloyi's motion about the Pass Laws, sir. It is quite true that the Pass Laws have the effect of turning the youths into criminals.... If a person is moving about in his own country and he is up to no mischief, he should not be required to carry more than one pass. Now they have to produce special passes; in many instances they are required for people who are quite harmless. Natives who do not belong to this country are not called upon to produce their passes as, for instance, Asiatics and colored people and we who are the aboriginal natives of this country [have to do]. When the white people first came here we had a tussle with them. The government should remember that we are also human beings living the same as other human beings. We are very grateful, sir, to have this opportunity to be able to talk like this in your presence representing the government. I do not say that we are not in need of passes; a person must have some document by which he can be traced if he dies by misadventure.

William Washington Ndlhlovu

"Freedom is impossible..."
7 December 1939, 52

The aim of the state should be to have a satisfied nation, and I submit that this pass system does not contribute to the making of a happy nation.... We want freedom, and freedom is impossible as long as the pass system is in vogue.

James Moroka

"We want to be free to go where we like, free to live like human beings."
5 May 1943, 103

This morning you had a man here who knows more about criminology than any one in South Africa [chief commissioner of the South African Police]. He told us in plain language that passes do not stop people from committing crimes, and he admitted that the Europeans, the colored and the Indians were equally as criminally minded as the native people. So then the question arises why are we singled out, why should be asked to carry passes when others who are equally as bad ... should be allowed to roam about freely? What we want in this land, sir, is freedom, freedom and security. We want to be free to go where we like, free to live like human beings. We want to be free to go to the mines. We want to be free to leave our masters on the farms and to sell our labor to any and everyone who is prepared to pay for our labor. We do not want our hands to be tied to one man; we do not want a condition of affairs under which when a man is not prepared to give us a pass we have only one solution left to us, namely to run away from that man and to expose ourselves to the risk of getting into the hands of the police and being sent to prison. We know what that means. Once we get into prison we are given a pass for a few days and after that we again land in prison. We ... are not criminals either by nature or by inclination, and my contention is that if we cannot be free in this land, in this South Africa of ours, we can be free nowhere else. I put this question to you: Where else can we be free if we cannot be free in our own country? Can you blame the native people in the circumstances for thinking that the Europeans are out to keep them down, are out to exploit them, are out to do everything they can possibly do to keep them as backward as possible, so that they may do with them as they like? ... I say this and I say it openly and plainly, that the people who make laws like these are not fit and proper people to look after the interests of the African people of this land.

Charles Sakwe
"Poll tax—a tax let me say—which is a racial tax."
5 May 1943, 109

We are not here to force matters. We are here to express our views in regard to matters affecting our country and matters affecting our people. We do not know, as a former speaker has pointed out, what exactly are the intentions of the Pass Laws. If I return home and they ask me, "What reply did you get when you asked the authorities what the purpose of the Pass Laws is, what the reason is why Africans have to carry passes?" Then I can only tell them what I was told here this morning. But I am afraid, Mr. Chairman, that that explanation will not be acceptable to our people. We are told that our men have to carry passes for the purpose of identification.... Men, before leaving home, have to apply to their native commissioners and they have to apply for traveling passes.... They have to be registered and then they have to fulfill their contract. And our people have been asked by the government to pay a special tax in the form of a poll tax—a tax, let me say, which is a racial tax. But in view of all these factors ... all the necessary information is supplied and they are known to the authorities for whom they labor. Yet these round-ups take place and these people are arrested.

Z.K. Matthews
"...breeding within them resentment and hatred of the white man."
5 May 1943

Now, I submit that there is probably nothing in this country which has done more to contribute to a feeling of hostility between black and white than the Pass Laws. The Europeans I feel are not aware—not sufficiently aware—of the extent to which hostility towards the Europeans is developing among the natives in this country. I feel that if that feeling of hostility goes on, we shall not be able to live successfully and peacefully in this country as we are trying to do. What is the good of all the schemes we are developing, which we are promoting for the development of the African people, if at the same time we have got some agency here which is breeding within them resentment and hatred of the white man? It has been said here that the police could possibly administer the Pass Laws in a different way. They could administer them in a less vexatious way. I submit that the police cannot administer these laws in any other way than they are doing now, and the relaxation ... which the minister of justice has supported has not done anything to reduce this feeling, this growing feeling of resentment towards the white man arising out of these Pass Laws....

I want to say again that quite apart from whether the Pass Laws stop criminality and quite apart from the question whether they can be administered humanely, on the sole ground that they poison the relations between black and white, something should be done towards ... their total abolition.

Richard Victor Selope Thema

"They always force him into the hands of the police..."
5 May 1943, 96–98

Those who still want to maintain the Pass Laws argue that they are a protection to the African and also a protection to the Europeans—an argument which is rather ambiguous.... But those of us who have studied these laws and their operation have definitely discovered that they are responsible for the criminalization of the African people. They do not protect the African in any way—they always force him into the hands of the police.... If the African walks along a street, he can walk along until he meets a policeman, and the policeman will immediately demand him to produce his pass.... One will invariably find that the first time an African goes to jail is through the Pass Laws. An African leaves his tribe and he gets a travelling pass.... He has to wait a few days before he gets his travelling pass. When he eventually gets it he proceeds to a particular place, say Johannesburg.... He is just a little ignorant farm boy and he thinks that the travelling pass which he has obtained ... is all he needs. He is perhaps a day or two in Johannesburg looking for work, and then he gets into trouble. The police ask for his pass and he produces his travelling pass.... He is sent to jail and spends seven days there. When he comes out of jail, he does not find it immediately and is again arrested and again sent to jail. It is these Pass Laws which are responsible for the African becoming acquainted with jail life. And these young fellows feel that they have committed no crime ... and they are suffering from a sense of injustice. And gradually they develop the feeling that it is better to commit a crime and be sent to jail for a crime rather than be sent there for nothing.

I remember the time when the Pass Laws were rigorously enforced, and I think it was the late Mr. Merriman who pointed out that South Africa was sowing the wind and would reap the whirlwind as a result of what she was doing. Restricting the movement of the African people is responsible for what is happening today. How can you expect people who are treated in this way ... to stop them from committing crimes—from becoming criminals—they learn to become criminals.... By nature we are a law-abiding people, and if here in the towns we have become criminals then the blame must be put on the laws under which we live and labor and one of these laws is the Pass Law. I do not think there is any justification for the continuation of these laws.... In the interest of South Africa as a whole, these laws should be repealed. The African has been forced out of his ordinary tribal life. He has learnt that he cannot live otherwise than by the sweat of his brow. It will be argued that the farmers want these laws because without these laws they cannot get the labor of the Africans.... But I say the time has come when the farmers of this country ... must pay them wages.... And then let me say this: the fact of a man having to carry a pass does not prevent him from leaving a farm.... This law was put on the statute book originally to deal with slaves.

James Moroka

"...a serious disadvantage..."
20 August 1945, 152

That in view of the fact that passes are a serious disadvantage economically, besides being a serious flaw in the character of a state under democratic conditions, the Pass Laws be repealed.

James Moroka

"What was the motive behind the introduction of passes?"
20 August 1945, 163

Another thing that I want to find out is why these passes were ever introduced. What was the motive behind the introduction of passes? The African people lived with the white people for a very long time before any passes were introduced, and it would be very interesting for us to know why the passes were introduced.... What were the reasons which made it necessary for the Africans in their own country—the only country they know—to carry passes when other members of the population, such as the Coloreds and Malays and the Europeans, are not supposed to carry passes? We, the Africans, came here first, yet we have this humiliating indignity imposed upon us. I maintain that the white man likes himself more than he likes anyone else. And I say this, that if the white man thought, if he imagined when the passes were introduced, that it was a good thing for people to carry passes, he would have made sure that he himself carried a pass. He says it is a good thing—it protects people— then why does he not carry a pass himself? The very fact that he does not carry a pass is because he knows that no good comes from it. The Africans are fully aware of it. I say again that the obligation to carry a pass is a stigma. You can say what you like, but we are convinced that this pass-carrying business is nothing but an attempt to control the movements of the African people, to humiliate them—and, sir, to get them down to the mines.

Lancelot Peter Msomi

"The police are out to make trouble."
20 August 1945, 162

It is a fact that some of these people who are placed in responsible positions simply use the Pass Laws as a means of humiliating the native. There are many irritations which result from these Pass Laws and which are often followed by arrests. The police are out to make trouble. Sometimes you drive a car and the police ask for your license. When you show them your license they ask for some other document to prove you are capable of driving that car. Then they ask for your pass—they know they will get you somehow. Now that is the kind of thing which we require those in authority to prevent. After all, if there are laws in the country which encroach on the individual liberty of a person, then these laws are not worthy of a democratic state. We have been fighting for freedom, and now that we are on the verge of the end of hostilities throughout the world we expect to enjoy that freedom we fought for, and to be free from the operation of such oppressive laws as the Pass Laws.

Richard Victor Selope Thema

"...and yet the government has turned a deaf ear."
20 August 1945, 154

This question of our Pass Laws has been raised at every session of the Council. These Pass Laws have been condemned by the judges of this country ... who administer the laws of this country—and yet the government has turned a deaf ear to their remarks. Yes, sir, these Pass Laws are the instruments which lead to the disturbances. I know definitely that there is going to be a serious row in this country in the near future. No race of men can be subjected to laws like this and yet remain loyal and obedient to any authority.

Richard Victor Selope Thema
"If the police have no respect for God
then I have no right to belong to a church that is led by a European."
20 August 1945, 157

Mr. Chairman, I used to belong to a church, and I was in the habit of going to church regularly. One afternoon when I came out of the church the police were at the doors. And there was one shout from the police: "Where are your passes?" Imagine! We had our Bibles with us. The police could see that we were good people, but no, the police wanted our passes. It upset me to such an extent that I said to myself, "If the police have no respect for God then I have no right to belong to a church that is led by a European." I feel strongly about this matter. I am a member of a committee which is organizing the people on the question of the Pass Laws....

Is it necessary, Mr. Chairman, to subject one section of the community to such indignities as these? Why must men, decent men, men who are trying to live like good citizens, be subjected to the indignity of producing passes at the behest of some policeman at the corner of the street? If there is one thing we object to it is these passes, and some of us are prepared to go anywhere the government may want to send us just to show our abhorrence of these laws.

George Champion
"Can you expect these people to do anything except resort to rioting?"
20 August 1945, 158

We know that an anti-pass campaign has been engaged upon which sooner or later may enlist the sympathy of every man in the country. Once this happens, the condition of affairs that will arise may not be like the riots which took place in Johannesburg in 1918, or like the riots in Durban; the position may be far worse. When responsible men like councilor Thema try to interview the prime minister and are refused an interview, and what is worse when they are charged before the law courts, and are convicted, the situation becomes dangerous. You get men who have devoted their lived to get the Pass Laws repealed.... Today they dare not even interview the authorities. What must they do? Can you expect these people to do anything except resort to rioting? I say this, that the position becomes dangerous and threatening when a leader of the African people, a member of this council, is sent to jail for wanting to see the prime minister. This thing may look ridiculous, but in the eyes of our public, and to us, it is a very serious matter.

Lancelot Peter Msomi
"We are being unnecessarily singled out."
5 May 1943, 103

I stand up with a feeling of disappointment. My disappointment started this morning when a question was put to the commissioner of police, when he was asked why the native people were the only people who were obliged to carry passes in this country. I had been looking forward for quite a long time to some explanation, because I sincerely believed that there must be something at the root of this whole matter, something known to those who govern this country, something which particularly earmarks us as the people who should carry passes while the other sections of the population are not required to carry similar documents.... We begin to be suspicious and we begin to feel that we are being unnecessarily singled out. I do remember that there was a time in this country when there were no Pass Laws at all. What have we today? The longer we have stayed without masters the stronger has the machinery become of applying the Pass Laws ... and it would appear to us ... that this machinery in regard to the carrying of passes is applied in a way as an instrument to retard our progress, to stifle our progress and in many ways to take advantage of us.

13

Politics

In April 1946 R.V. Selope Thema handed in a motion stating that if the government refused to adopt a policy in keeping with the spirit of the United Nations Charter, then the only policy which might be acceptable to Africans was one that divided South Africa into two separate states, one for whites and the other for blacks, each with its own parliament and prime minister.[1] Eiselen's apartheid divided South Africa into white areas and black areas, the latter given direct representation in those areas called Bantustans. Eiselen did not necessarily have to attend the NRC sessions; he could read the NRC debates in their published form. In addition, he could decide which debates he wanted to attend by perusing the motions handed in before each session. Not all the proposed motions were debated by the Council. This decision was only made once they had arrived in Pretoria.

John Langalibalele Dube
"They should listen to our cries."
29 November 1940, 158ff

It must not be thought that we do not appreciate this new creation in the affairs of South Africa when we are ventilating the grievances of the natives. That does not mean that we are antagonistic and do not want to cooperate. But we live among these people and are their representatives, and they have given us instructions to cry—that is the general term used by the natives. And when we cry in this Council ... then they should listen to our cries. I do not think people should be so touchy when they hear us cry. We are trying to assist the authorities as much as we can, and we hope they will see our point. It is our duty to give them a naked picture of the feelings of the natives. How can we help the position if we do not go to the root? I think the authorities should take notice of the long-suffering people, who have no outlet, no mouthpieces. Now that they have a mouth-piece, their representatives should not be regarded as an opposition to the government, but we are doing our duty when we express the feelings of these long-suffering people.

Richard Hobbs Godlo

"The time has come for individual franchise to be enjoyed by women."
29 November 1938, 584–85

Sir, I do not think that we are all aware of the fact that under the Representation of Natives Act, down our way, African women are eligible for election on electoral committees in the urban areas. For example, they are eligible for election to the native advisory boards, and as such they constitute a voting unit in the area for electing senators and members of the Natives Representative Council. Therefore ... I feel that the time has come for individual franchise to be enjoyed by women in the Cape Province so that they should also take part in the election of members of the House of Assembly. I am glad that this view is also held by the Transkeian General Council, where people are considered to be conservative. In this case the Transkeian Territories is satisfied that the time has come for the extension of individual franchise to the women in the Cape Province; at their last meeting they passed a resolution on this.

Chief Jeremiah Moshesh

"There are many things to be put right."
2 December 1940, 205

I feel proud, sir, to receive this medal at your hands [from Deneys Reitz, minister of native affairs].... When I cast my mind back on the past with its many hardships and when I look at conditions as they are today, my mind feels lighter, and I am happy. I shall carry this medal with a sense of pride and honor.... I wish to thank you most sincerely for your words when you said that there are many things to be put right, and that it was the government's desire to put these things right, although it was quite impossible to do everything at once.... But you have told us that the government is anxious to right many things that are wrong. We look upon that as a promise. There is an old saying among the native races that when a chief promises one a beast one must start building a *kraal*, because one can rely upon the beast being forthcoming. Our chief has now promised to give us a beast. Well, sir, we shall start building a *kraal* for it. I am grateful of the fact that I have seen our chief in this assembly for the first time; I am proud of the fact that on this first occasion I have met him he has seen fit to present me with this medal. That is the first point I wish to emphasize. The second point is that presentation is the first presentation of its kind. The third point is that it has been presented in the presence of the first Natives Representative Council.

Elijah Qamata
"All the native people … want is …
to know that the White people are not here for themselves alone."
2 December 1940, 207

Sir, I must say that I am a young man compared with the grey-hairs that are here, but I may take it that I express the feelings of the Council when I say that the native people of this country here represented by us— I want to assure you, as minister of the crown that our people are and ourselves shall be loyal to the Union government during this time of the greatest crisis that has befallen the world. We are aware that in a country like South Africa with a mixed population there must naturally be misunderstandings, but that these misunderstandings are natural, and must come about. You have advised us that we should proceed steadily. I want to assure you that that is the policy of this council. We shall bring our grievances to the department, but we cannot for a moment expect that they will or can be put right in a day. Rome was not built in a day, the British Empire was not built in a day, the United Kingdom was not built in a day, and likewise we as a people cannot be built in a day. All the native people of this country want is a sympathetic attitude from the white people of this country, an attitude which will encourage the peoples of this country to know that the white people are not here for themselves alone, but that they are here for everybody that constitutes the Union of South Africa.

R.V. Selope Thema
"We have not offered our lives in vain."
14 December 1942, 269

The men who are now fighting our cause up north do not expect to come back, and we do not expect them to come back, to the same conditions as those which existed before…. They want to be able to say, "We have not offered our lives in vain." In the last war many of our people went to France and other parts of the world. Many of them lost their lives in that fight for a better world, in that war to end war. Yet when they came back, nothing was done for them. Sir, all of us want to know and want to know exactly what our position will be after this great struggle. We appreciate your views expressed by yourself at Kingwilliamstown and other

places when you said openly that the color bar laws should be done away
with. We would welcome a statement from the minister to that effect. We
know that you personally would do these things if you had your way.... If
we leave this matter until after the war the result will be that ... the Atlantic
Charter will be regarded and treated as the merest scrap of paper. We
have had experience of that. In the last war there was a charter consisting
of fourteen points which came from the other side of the Atlantic. We
heard a lot about that charter. Everybody knew about President Wilson's
fourteen points; yet what happened? The 1914–1918 war was brought to
an end on these fourteen points, the [League of Nations] was interrupted
until it was respired [*sic*] in 1939.... I think that the time has come when
we should put these things right, so that we can come out of this war and
out of this turmoil with clean hands, and say to the Africans of the continent, "You can look to us for a lead." And so should we play our part that
one day we shall be able to say ... that we do not want any more Europeans
here; when we shall be able to say that those who are here are quite enough,
and we don't want people here who will bring the troubles, difficulties and
the turmoil of Europe to our soil.

Paul Mosaka

"It is too late ... to say we want to get rid
of the white people and drive them into the sea."
14 December 1942, 265–67

In this country where the white people have already got political freedom, they are not very much worried. But as far as the African people are
concerned they realize that they cannot get freedom from want, they cannot get freedom from fear—in other words social and economic freedom
is not possible without political freedom. The place where we want to
have that freedom of speech is in Parliament through the people whom
we appoint to go there.... We are only free to express ourselves when we
use the legislative machinery ... and unless we have that right we shall
never have that freedom which we are aiming at. This is a puppet parliament ... it merely gives us the shadow of the substance, and the only interpretation which will be satisfactory as far as we are concerned is one which
envisages a place for the African people ... in the parliament of the country.
We are beginning to notice that even President Roosevelt and Mr.
Churchill, who met on the Atlantic waters and drafted this document, are
beginning to have divergent interpretations of that charter.... Mr. Churchill
has recently made a statement that he was not going to preside over the
liquidation of the British Empire. It was not intended that this war would

eliminate the British Empire, but it was expected that it would give free-dom to India and other dominions of the British Empire.... Now, this Atlantic Charter has been accepted by the United Nations and South Africa is one of those nations. We, as the underdogs, want to want to know where we stand. We believe that if the Atlantic Charter has any meaning it means liberty, liberty to the underdog.... It says, "They respect the right of all peoples to choose the form of government under which they will live; and they wish to see sovereign rights and self-government restored to those who have been forcibly deprived of them." I do not think that sovereign rights and self-government will be restored to the African people. It is too late for that, so we want what we can get. It is too late of course to say we want to get rid of the white people and drive them into the sea. That is not in our minds.... The right to choose, to choose the form of government, does not merely mean that we want a democratic government or a Nazi government or a communistic form of government. It does mean this: that I shall have the right to influence that group of opinion to which I belong, and the only way of influencing the course of government is by means of the franchise.... The final weapon any man can use in a properly constituted society is the franchise, and this para-graph is the one which has a message for the African people politically. Personally I say that what we want, what we should be given, is political freedom. We should want every type of freedom, but in order to secure those other types of freedom—freedom from want and freedom from oppression—the first thing we want is political freedom.

In 1942 the NRC formed a recess committee that put forward various proposals to make the NRC a more powerful and significant body. Among their proposals were the extension of African representation in urban local authorities and the granting of executive and legislative powers to the NRC, which included the power to pass laws binding only on Africans and subject to the prior consent of the governor-general.[2] The report was ignored by the government.

R.V. Selope Thema

"I hope [it] will not be a cry in the wilderness."
7 May 1943, 166

We are asking that which everyone ... every human being, is entitled to ask for. If we must be governed, it must be with our consent and with our knowledge and with our approval, and I think that is the principle for which people throughout the world are shedding their blood—the right to be heard, the right to be protected by the government of any country.... I hope our request will not be a cry in the wilderness.

R.V. Selope Thema

"Let me tell the White man that
if he enslaves us he is enslaving himself as well."
9 August 1944, 41

We believe that this country should be a free country, free in the eyes of the world and free to those whose heritage is in the soil of the country. And let me tell the white man that if he enslaves us he is enslaving himself as well.... Are people who are deprived of the benefits of freedom going to give South Africa the benefits which the country needs ... are they going to help South Africa in the way it should be helped? ... Why should 8,000,000 people be at the mercy of 2,000,000 people? ... We want South Africa to take a leading part in the development of the continent, but can South Africa take that leading part? ... We say "no" and we say so because of these laws to which we object. Before South Africa can ... direct the destination of this continent, it will have to rid itself of these pernicious laws; it will have to rid itself of the Nazi spirit of these laws.... That is the only way.

Richard Hobbs Godlo

"The Council is the official channel ...
to the government ... in all matters affecting Africans."
10 August 1944, 68

The Council has the right to recommend to Parliament or to the provincial authorities any legislation which it considers necessary in the interest of the Africans generally. In other words, the Council is the official channel through which the Africans can express their views and also their grievances for transmission to the government. This Council occupies the position of advisor to the government in all matters affecting Africans in this country.... There is nothing that the Council cannot place before the authorities.

The importance of the NRC in politics was not then challenged by the ANC, which remained a very small organization in spite of the considerable efforts of the councilors to increase membership. In 1945 ANC membership in Natal was only 707 members and in the Orange Free State, 1823.[3] The state of the organization can best be illustrated by the activities of the Springs branch when it held a meeting to elect a new committee for 1945. No one except members of the old committee arrived at the meeting. As it was the rule that only ANC members who had paid their dues could vote, it was found that the majority of the committee could not even re-elect themselves, because even they had not paid their dues.[4] In 1945 the NRC asked Smuts to explain his government's postwar policy towards Africans. He refused, although the Department of Native Affairs had by 1945 realized how important this was and made every effort in this direction. By November 1945, however, it was clear that Smuts was not going to address them.[5]

Z.K. Matthews

"[Chiefs did not exercise] unfettered despotism
as a normal form of government."
14 August 1945, 207

The conception of supreme chieftainship and its exploitation for purposes of native administration originated at a time when there was no settled peace between the Europeans and the Zulus in Natal. It was supposed at that time, and it is still so thought in official quarters, that such dictatorial powers were enjoyed by the Zulu kings as a normal right. Whatever may have been the right at the time of the great Zulu kings, it cannot be stated that the position was the same among the other Bantu tribes, on whom this conception has been imposed without qualification. It has not been established to the satisfaction ... of the African people in general that the Zulu kings or any other Bantu kings ever exercised such unfettered despotism as a normal form of government. At all events your committee desires to state categorically that the continual use of this conception in native administration is a violation of the elementary principle of justice. When it is remembered that the governor-general is empowered under Section 24 of the act to amend the code of native law, by proclamation, thus making it possible for him to add indefinitely to his powers as supreme chief, the despotic character of this section becomes ever more apparent. As has been well said, "Nowhere in the world does there exist a system of executive despotism similar to the administration of native Affairs in South Africa, except in totalitarian countries."

R.V. Selope Thema

"A Pitso[6] ... was the element of democracy."
14 August 1945, 209–10

This native administration act gives the impression that the Africans in South Africa know nothing about the elements of democracy, which gives the impression that as a people we have been ruled by tyrants—yet that is not true. In the olden days we had a form of government at the head of which was the chief. The chief had his counselors, he had his Indunas and his brothers; he also had his headman. If he was a paramount chief he also had the chiefs of other tribes within his domain, and he could not arbitrarily order a man from one place to another without having consulted his councilors. Whenever there was a matter on which the whole nation had to be informed, a Pitso was called. This was the element of democracy. It is true that we did not vote for the members of the Pitso, but every man was consulted. It was better than your voting system because everyone went to Parliament. The Zulu people produced a man who was powerful—a man whom we might refer to as a Hitler, a man who had changed the system of government. Well, that man was the man who built up the Zulu nation. His name was Chaka [*sic*]. The very fact that Chaka's own people turned against him and against the system that he practiced shows that his system was a foreign system to his people. And when Dr. Shepstone came along he said: "You people have been accustomed to be ruled in this way, very well, I am now the supreme chief, I have now assumed the powers of Ceteswayo [the previous Zulu king] and you have to look to me, I am the chief." In fact, Dr. Shepstone made himself the uncrowned king of Zululand, and he is the man who is responsible for the system which today prevails. This policy was also introduced by the British after the war. The republic did not know anything about it, but when Dr. Shepstone came here, he introduced this policy and usurped the powers of the chiefs, and he governed the people with a rod of iron.... Now the Americans and the Russians and the English are trying to rebuild a system which Hitler had destroyed.... They did not say to the Germans, "Now you have been ruled by Hitler in this way ... we are also going to rule you in the same way"—they did nothing of the kind.... Why should it be the case in South Africa, why should we in South Africa follow the practice which was followed by other people whom you described as despots in the past? This is supposed to be a civilized country.

R.V. Selope Thema
"Our efforts should be recognized."
17 August 1945, 115–17

We remind you, because we have helped you to build up this beautiful country. We have cooperated in many ways; we have shown that we want to be loyal—had we not cooperated you would not have produced a country such as you have now. When this country was in a critical position we did nothing to hinder your war effort; we did nothing to stop you from contributing to the victory in Europe; in fact, we did everything to help you to make that contribution which has given you that place in the councils of the nations. We feel that as we have helped in that way our efforts should be recognized, and it is the duty of the white people of this country to say: "Well, let us free these people from these oppressive laws." Would that not be a wonderful gesture in the spirit of the San Francisco Charter? It is not right that people should talk about the peace of the world, about freedom, about human rights, and yet refuse to give other people who have stood by them those very human rights which they have fought for. We have no right to say to the world: "You shall go this way or the other way to freedom," when in this country there are millions of men and women who are not free. In the eyes of God we can only have peace; we can only demand rights for ourselves, if we do unto others as we want to be done by. This saying ... was brought to this country by the Europeans, and what we are asking now, is that white South Africa should do unto us as they would like us to do unto them. I feel strongly about this. I see no reason why we should be treated in the way we are treated today. What is the difference between us and the white people? Some Europeans have tried to find the difference, but personally I have found none—the only difference is that of color. Some Europeans have stated that there is a difference in our brain power— a difference in our energies. I fail to see it. We have all the things, all the qualities which you people have. If the white man feels hungry, I have the same feeling; if the white man feels cold, I can also feel cold, and if the white man wants to be free from oppression, I see no reason why any other being should be subject to oppression. We know that other nations have not taken part in this war of liberation; they remained neutral, and they only declared war on Germany when German was down and out. Let me say this—this world cannot be made safe for all people if certain sections of human beings are left out, and I am afraid that the world will never be able to live in peace if the non-Europeans are left out—if they are not given their share in this freedom for which this war has been fought. We have to see to it that every member of the human family is liberated and is not oppressed.

Saul Mabude
"Our boys have ... shed their blood."
17 August 1945, 119

For the past thirty-three years we have labored under these difficult conditions. As a matter of fact, ever since Union there has been continual oppression of the Africans through legislation. But we hope that now that our boys have been to the Front and have shed their blood—now that they have been side by side with their white brothers in war—it will be possible for them to come back as brothers. They were brothers in arms with their white comrades, and I can only say that they should be brothers in peace as well.

Paul Mosaka
"Our participation in the war ... was intended
to safeguard the rights of freedom and political liberty."
17 August 1945, 122

The appreciation of the work of the African soldier has been very well expressed by members of the Council. We maintain that our participation in the war, as indeed the participation of any people in it, was intended to safeguard the rights of freedom and political liberty. Our participation was intended to make sure that the people who fought, fought for something which made life worthwhile for them. We are not fighting for the primary right to exist merely in the same sense that an animal wants to live. We are not fighting for the mere right to have our daily bread. That is something which we expect should be given to every human being. I don't think that is a very high ideal for a government to set itself. These are the primary necessities of life which must be supplied to all human beings, whatever the form of government, whether it be a democratic or a socialist government. When our people went to war, it is true that they did not have these primary rights, but they were ... expecting to be given freedom of movement, freedom from want, freedom to elect their own people in the municipal and provincial councils, and to be more adequately represented in the House of Assembly and the Senate. These are the things for which our people fought.... I am afraid the government has so far not made any gesture of any kind which can be interpreted as a token of appreciation of the services rendered by the African people. In fact, far from doing so, under conditions which have become increasingly more difficult, under conditions which have led to starvation, such as we see in the Transkei today, under conditions which have led to disease, such as we have experienced recently in the spread of typhus and smallpox and which have led to a number of upheavals in the mines and in urban areas, showing the unrest which exists among the African people—under those very conditions the government has shown a complete indifference.

Z.K. Matthews

"The growing tendency to ignore
the accredited representatives of the African people."
25 May 1945, 22

The members of the Council have noticed with grave concern that legislation has from time to time been introduced into Parliament without prior consultation with this Council as required by the act. We would refer particularly as far as the present session of Parliament is concerned to the [Urban Areas] Consolidation Bill, a matter which in terms of Section Twenty-Seven (1) (a) should have been referred to the Council. Furthermore, in regard to measures affecting the population as a whole which the legislature obviously regarded as a matter for consultation with the Representative Council ... this Council has not been consulted; for example, the Work Colonies Bill, the Workmen's Compensation Act Amendment

Bill, the Phthisis Act Amendment Bill, etc. The growing tendency to ignore the accredited representatives of the African people in legislating on matters affecting their interests directly or indirectly is not calculated to inspire confidence on the part of the people, either in the Council in particular, or in the government in general. With regard to the particular matter submitted to this Council for consideration ... this Council desires to take exception to the hurried manner in which the Council has been convened and the insufficient time within which the Council is expected to report upon a measure of such far-reaching importance.

Paul Mosaka
"The Act made it a right [for us] to be consulted."
25 May 1945, 41–44

I want to say again that I feel very sorry that a matter of this importance [beer profits] should be sprung on us in the manner in which it has been done. In the first place, we have not the actual amendment before us in that it was read out, and secondly we understand that it is simply a matter of courtesy that it has been introduced into this Council today. Then I take it that all matters are introduced to us as a matter of courtesy. But I thought that the act made it a right, whatever our views, to be consulted, and if Parliament takes the view that it is merely courtesy, then the consultation is a farce. I personally feel that this is not a matter for this Council to discuss when they have already told us that it is simply a matter of courtesy.... I think we would feel better if the Department of Native Affairs did not pretend to consult us on this matter when once it has made up its mind that it is not a matter for discussion with the Council.

James Moroka
"Why is it that ... the black man ... looks upon [the white man] as an enemy?"
9 November 1945, 101

Why is it that today, when the black man meets the white man, he so often looks upon him as an enemy? Why is it? My own opinion is that if a man treats me well, whether he is a white man, an Indian or a colored, I look upon him as a human being—if he treats me well I look upon him as a friend ... and shall be quite prepared to work along with him. Now what happens in South Africa? We are not blind. We see what happens. We see large sums of money spent on European education, we see large sums of money spent on Indian education and we see large sums of money spent on colored education, but against that we see very little spent on native education.... If you are fair-minded you cannot help thinking that there is something wrong somewhere, that justice is not done. If a man is not prepared to see that, then I say he is not prepared to see the truth. What I am pleading for and what the African people are pleading for is fair play. We do not ask for equality, we do not want to be like the white man, and we don't want to stay in the towns.... We want equal opportunity; that is what we want. We want to be treated on exactly the same lines ... so that the white man in the long run will not be able to say that he is better than we are. Everything must be done purely on merit.

> The political speeches that follow in 1946 were given after the August NRC adjournment when the Council refused to continue unless and until all discriminatory legislation was abolished. In November 1946 the councilors gathered to hear the government's reply. They had expected at the very least that the government would raise the status of the NRC.[7]
>
> The deputy prime minister, Jan Hofmeyr, addressed them at the opening of this sitting in November 1946. His speech was a tabulation of what the African people received from the government; it made no concessions and could thus not even be regarded as a reply to the adjournment motion. Hofmeyr left the hall immediately after making his speech, not listening to the councilors' replies.[8] Already by 1942 Smuts, then South African prime minister, had realized that black leaders could no longer be fobbed off (as he put it) with substantial economic and social improvements. What they wanted were not improvements but rights.[9] In 1943 Smit, the secretary of native affairs and NRC chair for six years, had realized that educated Africans such as those with whom he was in contact in the NRC, had only one ambition and that was political equality. He wrote to his wife that they would be satisfied with nothing less and would not say thank you for anything else.[10] So it ought to have been realized by Smuts, who played the major part in the formulation of this reply to the first adjournment in August 1946, that Hofmeyr's speech would receive no favorable reception from the councilors. During the course of this sitting, councilors made it clear that they could never subscribe to the subordination of the majority by the minority, that they would never be satisfied until they were in a position to make laws and to have Africans represent them in the House of Assembly. They emphasized that as the only legitimate representatives of the Africans, freely elected by them, they had no intention of resigning but would wait for the government to give a satisfactory reply to their demands.

L.P. Msomi

"The native is treated as a person who has no rights ... he has no vote."
25 April 1946, 51–52

And now we are called upon to agree to a policy whereby the native is to be stopped from establishing himself in the towns. We have the greatest respect for the government, which consists of people who have a very great background in the history of democracy, and we have no reason to believe that these people in anything they do are actuated by motives of fear. Yet in every action the government takes, we find that the native is treated as a person who has no rights—and that is simply due to the fact that he has no vote. If the native had a vote the government would realize that if they treated the natives in the way they are doing, the consequences would not be long in making themselves felt. There is only one conclusion we can come to, and that is that because we have no vote the government can do with us as they please. We have no pull on the government; that is the whole trouble.... There is no reason why we should not be given a fair share of the good things of this country. The goldfields of the Free State, the industrial wealth of this country, should be shared by the Europeans and the Africans in fair proportions. The natives cannot ruin the wealth that God has given this country.... We want freedom of movement in this country, which is our country. And we believe we can live happily and prosperously side by side with you. Why are you always against us; why do you always make us carry passes? Give us freedom of movement. We want to live in this country, our country free from want, free from fear; we want to be given facilities to exploit every chance that presents itself for our good, and in these circumstances we are not able to assist in passing a law like this.

> This was the first sitting of the NRC attended by Albert Luthuli, later president-general of the ANC, who was awarded the Nobel Peace Prize in 1960. He won his seat at the by-election after the death of John Dube. Given that his first attendance was after the adjournment resolution, it was unlikely that he could distinguish himself in the NRC.

Chief Albert Luthuli
"Shout a little louder."
26 November 1946, 67–70

Some of us have come to this Council as new members, but we are not new to the matters affecting the welfare of our people—we are merely new to this Council. One must say, speaking as one who has been outside the Council but who has been reading the resolutions of this Council from time to time, that the Council as a council has tried its very best to cooperate with the government. That we, as outsiders, can testify to; although not much has come from the representations that have been made here, we felt that in this Council was a body of men who were sent here to represent our views, and there is no doubt that they tried their best in as moderate a manner as possible to present the needs, the minimum needs, of the African people. I think it is a fact that very little if anything has come from the representations made by the councilors here; very little, if anything, can be pointed out as a tangible result to meet the legitimate demands put forward by the representatives here. Even the motion before you breathes of cooperation. This motion does not imply that this Council intends not to cooperate in the future. It merely indicates the desire to bring strongly to the notice of the authorities the needs of the African people, and this motion has been introduced for the purpose of bringing those needs prominently to the notice of the authorities. We want to cooperate with the authorities, but we want the authorities also to cooperate with us. I feel that a time has come when one realizes that something more has to be one, when one has to shout a little louder to make oneself heard. If I shout at a man and he does not listen to me, I am entitled to shout a little louder to make him hear me, and I think this motion is intended to shout just a little louder. Some of us have just emerged from an election fight.... I am one of those, and that is one of the main reasons why I want to make a contribution to this debate. During this election one of the questions constantly flung at me was this: "You want to be elected to the Council, what will you do?" I must frankly say that the only reply I could give was this: "Well, I can only try to help by shouting a little louder." I was unable to say that I was going to be successful, seeing that abler and better men than I have not been able to persuade the government to do something. If I had said, "I shall do something ... succeed where others have failed," I would have said too much, so what I said was this: "Elect me and I shall try and I shall do my best to let my voice be a little louder than that of the others; I shall try and shout a little louder." Those of us who handle our people as chiefs and as leaders ... can testify to the fact that in recent years, as a result of the neglect of the legitimate desires and wishes of the people, a deep sense of frustration has made itself felt. I recall to mind as further proof of that the words of old Ekeshle, for whom I have a very high regard, a moderate man, even more moderate than the moderates before you. And he said at a meeting, "I am an old man. I have tried my very best to serve the Europeans and I have been a very faithful servant." Now this man works for some government department. I don't want to mention which department. He said, "I have tried my very best to serve the government faithfully and even when my people have wanted to act in a rash manner I have always advised them to be moderate, and I wield a good deal of influence with my chief, but after all these years I feel that I really do not know whether it pays to be moderate because I have got nothing out of it."

Chief Mshiyeni Kwa Dinizulu

"In this country we are looked upon as animals."
26 November 1946, 66–67

Many councilors have already spoken on this matter, and we are all in agreement with what they have said. We do not want you to think that we want to break down this Council of ours. This Council was created for the purpose of giving the African the opportunity of advising the government, and therefore I think you should listen carefully to what is being said here today.... When we come back from Pretoria they ask us what we have been speaking about, and it is quite true that we have always come back with empty hands—we have brought back nothing. Therefore we are asking you to give us replies, to give us some results which we can place before our people when we go back. Today we have not much power. There has been bloodshed, and fighting has taken place on the mines on the Rand.... We went to war to help the government and we did not listen to people who told us not to help the government. But it is a very sad situation when people ask for food and they are shot. In this country we are looked upon as animals. We were given this land by God, we were defeated, and so we became a conquered nation. We admit that. Still, what I saw in Johannesburg is very painful. People are arrested and assaulted. People are shot and they are killed in the streets.... This is very painful, and I hope the government will listen very carefully to what I have to say here. Today there is a feeling that every time an African tries to ask for food he is assaulted or shot at. Sir, it is a terrible thing for our people to be shot at.... That is what we feel. We want to run away, but we don't know where we must run.... I once spoke here and said that there was an animal that had two colors. One of its colors is white and the other is black. But that animal has only one tongue, and with that tongue it licks both colors. Therefore I think that what we say in our Council should be listened to. Our people at home know that their chiefs and paramount chiefs have come here to speak for them and to plead their cause.... I want you to know that we do not want to leave the work of the Council, but we want a reply, and we want it quickly.

George Champion
"We are not interested in that policy of robbing Peter to pay Paul."
24 November 1946, 50ff

The battle royal is still proceeding ... because there was never agreement between the natives and the white government of South Africa. First, the people of the Cape complained that an attack was made on their entrenched rights without any justification, and we from the other provinces were asked to come and rejoice because we were to be given the right to vote for certain people to represent us in Parliament. We submit that we are not interested in that policy of robbing Peter to pay Paul. We would rather wait than take part in taking away the entrenched rights of other people in order to give ourselves rights that are questionable.... We were told that the land was crowded and that the government was going to buy large portions of land as an extension of our existing native reserves. I notice that the minister did not use the word "reserves." He used the words "crown lands." I don't know whether the minister knows the difference between crown lands and native reserves. We did not own the crown lands. They belong to the Department of Lands and we have no say over them. Hundreds of people throughout Zululand ... have been shifted by the Department of Lands, and worse: still they are using the Department of Native Affairs to carry out this Christian business.... I want to say that the Native Representation Act has to be scrapped. It is an act which is not in our interests. Despite the fact that we get $10 per month and a first class ticket to Pretoria, and tea and transport, when I weigh all these things—they have no meaning to me if the intention is to shut up our people without giving them an opportunity to make direct representation to the highest sovereign [body] in the state. That is the attitude which I adopt, and that is the attitude which I would like all civilized people of the country to take up.

Z.K. Matthews

"The government's breach of faith towards the African people."
25 November 1946, 35–41

You will remember that last August this council adjourned in protest against what is called the government's breach of faith towards the African people. In order to understand the meaning of that adjournment I think it is necessary for us to go back a little and to remind ourselves of the purpose for which this council was created.

This council was created in order to give ... the African people ... the principle of consultation in government. By creating this council the government admitted not only to the African people but [to] the world in general that it recognized the fact that government without consultation was not government but despotism, however benevolent that despotism might be. But the South African government, by creating this council, also put forward their contention that in the South African context the principle of consultation can best be given effect to by the creation of separate governmental institutions for the different racial groups represented in this country.... The African people at that time warned the South African nation that this council was likely to prove an attempt to shunt the claims of African interests on the attention of the state into a blind alley, there to remain out of sight, while the claims of European interests receive undisturbed and undivided attention.... Nevertheless, although the African people did not agree with the decision arrived at in 1936, they decided to try out the machinery of consultation. Now I should like to ask the question: what do we understand by consultation? We understand by consultation that on every question of importance affecting the African people, this council would be consulted before a final decision was made.... Secondly, when the views of the council have been obtained, serious consideration would be given to them; and thirdly, that when for any reason it was not possible to accept or act upon the advice of the council, full reasons would be given as to why its advice was not acceptable. Now, what the Council did in August 1946 was to say that they did not feel that consultation as understood in that sense was being given effect to. Our view is that it would appear that what this council is expected to do is to help the government to entrench a policy of white domination and discrimination, and to persuade the African people to be satisfied with such a policy and with such crumbs as may happen to fall from the white man's table.... I want to say that the statement of policy which was made by the acting prime minister does not seem to show any intention on the part of the government to recognize the changed conditions under which we are living today.... It seemed to us that all we are told to do is to pour new wine of modern native life into the old bottles of the policy which was dictated by the conditions prevailing immediately after the South African War.

Z.K. Matthews

"To a voteless and defenseless people, that is their only weapon."
25 November 1946, 38–41

In his opening remarks the acting prime minister [Jan Hofmeyr] said that the government noted with regret and surprise the violent and exaggerated statements made in support of the resolution.... Having regard to the increasingly repressive character of union native policy and its effect on the people we represent, and having further regard to the political impotence of this council, we repudiate the suggestion of extremism and recklessness on our part. On the contrary, these charges could more fittingly be applied to the methods of the government in suppressing the African mineworkers' strike by the unprovoked use of brute force, resulting in the death of several Africans. Even if it is admitted that objections might be taken to the terms of the resolution, the intolerable conditions to which the African people we represent are subjected in this country ... demand condemnation in the strongest possible terms. To a voteless and defenseless people, that is their only weapon. At all events ... the action of the Council has not only met with universal approval among the African people, but has in small measure restored among them that confidence in their representatives which had been undermined by the continued disregard by the government of the advice of the Council.... We must confess a sense of disappointment with the statement made by the acting prime minister. To us it seemed merely an apologia for the status quo.... The statement makes no attempt to deal with some of the burning questions of the day such as the Pass Laws, the color bar in industry, the political rights of non-Europeans in the Union, etc., and in effect it raises no hopes for the future as far as the African people are concerned. The resolution of the Council was intended as a challenge to the government to indicate to what extent if any, it was prepared ... to adjust its native policy.... From that point of view the government does not seem to have appreciated the full import of the resolution. In his statement the acting prime minister virtually denied that the native policy of the Union is in need of revision and proceeds to justify the policy of segregation and discrimination on the grounds of its supposedly protective character. As an example of this solicitude for the welfare of the African people, the minister cited the creation of the Native Trust, whose function it is to acquire and administer land for the occupation of natives who, it is alleged, would not be able to hold their own in a free competition for the acquisition of land. In our view the converse represents a more accurate interpretation of the situation. The reserve system, far from protecting native land rights, is in fact designed to preserve such rights in the rest of the country exclusively for Europeans.... But the burden of our resolution is not affected by minor concessions granted or denied in this or that aspect of African life. We are more concerned with questions of principle and policy. The benefits to which the minister has made detailed reference to do not affect the fundamentals of the policy of white domination in a country, the population of which is 80 percent non-white. The permanent subordination of the bulk of the population to a minority, however well intentioned, is a policy to which we cannot subscribe. The denial of the right of direct representation in governing bodies such as municipal councils, provincial councils and Parliament, and the establishment for Africans of differential institutions with purely advisory functions, is part of the system for the preservation of white supremacy in South Africa. In our view the time has come for South Africa to abandon this policy, under which it will never be possible to harmonize the legitimate interests of the different racial groups represented in this country. It is our intention to continue to work for the ultimate achievement of this result by all means at our disposal.

George Champion

"You have the native in the hollow of your hand."
25 November 1946, 42ff

I would like to draw the attention particularly ... to the minister's speech [saying that] many of the ... existing laws ... were in fact enacted to protect native interests. In 1911 there was the Mines and Regulations and Recruiting Act of 1911. It created the pass system, the recruiting system, and it creates every means to get the natives to the industries, to the mines, to the sugar plantations, etc.... In 1912 we had the Defense Act, which excludes native men from becoming military citizens of this country. In 1914 when the mines were in full operation ... it became necessary to pay compensation to workers ... for injuries. Again we find that pass-bearing natives were excluded ... I notice from the act that he cannot even claim ... for dying underground. In ... 1923 another act was passed, which I believe is amended every year by Parliament. Even today this council is expected to consult on an amendment. I am referring to the Urban Areas Act, which segregates the natives in towns, and which makes provision for compounds, hostels, Locations where Africans have to live. I notice that the minister in his speech made a mountain of that, whilst in actual fact we are not interested in the figures that government put before us. We are not interested in that. Here we are in a country of our own, through no fault of our own, by right of conquest, we find ourselves face to face with the European races. They are trying to draw us up to the towns to work there for their own convenience.... Though nobody's fault, against our request, we find in the towns that we have to live outside what is known as the European towns. We are forced out to certain camps and Locations, and these Locations are under the control of certain Europeans, of whose qualifications you have often heard in speeches in this council. Not only this, but we have a multiplication of passes, which beats all human intelligence. As I remarked, one is not interested in the amounts which the minister has drawn to our attention. We are looking forward to the time when these hostels and barracks and Locations will be abolished in favor of more secure tenure, and when we will be allowed to buy our land where we like and are in a position to buy. I notice that the minister also referred to the Wage Board ... and want to point out to the council that in 1924 unemployment legislation was passed, the Industrial Conciliation Act, under which agreement between the workers and employers, they can go to the government, and the government rubber stamps the recommendations of the Wage Board crated under that act. That act excludes pass-bearing natives. We cannot benefit from that act. In 1925 we come to the Native Taxation and Development Act. Under that act natives are required to pay taxes. I want to submit that there again we have discrimination against natives. It has always been an accepted principle that there can be no taxation without representation, direct representation. Here in South Africa we are taxed without representation in the House of Assembly—that is direct representation.... Then we come to what has often been called the charter of the Department of Native Affairs, Act 38 of 1927. There the native races of South Africa are handed over holus bolus to the Department of Native Affairs. Administrative powers are granted which are very drastic.... You have the power to pass legislation this morning, to repeal such legislation this afternoon and to reenact it tomorrow morning ... these powers you have under the act. You have the native in the hollow of your hand. I submit that no law of this nature has ever been in existences to control conquered nations. I do not know whether it is now in existence in conquered Nazi Germany. No native can brew *kaffir* beer, which is his own food, even if he owns a farm, without the permission of a police officer or the native commissioner.... Although I am exempted I cannot go to a bottle store or a bar and get a bottle of brandy. A European is allowed to go anywhere and get what he wants. And so is an Indian. This is a discriminatory law. How far is the government going with this sort of thing?

Z.K. Matthews

"We know there is method in this madness."
25 April 1946, 55–56

We know why the government is not interested in overhauling the whole system; there is method in their madness. No reasonable man can understand why the government should legislate in such a way as to force people out of the reserves and force them into the towns and then pass legislation to force them out of the towns. It seems most unreasonable. But we know there is method in this madness.... We know that the whole intention of forcing people out of the towns has as its foundation a desire to make people go to the European farms, and to the gold mines, and because there is this deep-rooted self interest on the part of the government, we should not think that talk of consistency will have any effect on the government. If we wanted to be logical and consistent, the right thing for us as members of this council would be to resign ... because as a matter of fact we have opposed the Native Representation Act. And the right thing to say to the government: We have consistently opposed these things, and we have been trying to get the government to effect certain adjustments, but they have not done so, and if we were consistent say, "We shall have nothing to do with this Native Representatives Council."

The first adjournment of the NRC took place at the August 1946 session. It was here that their "freedom resolution" was formulated, mainly by Matthews, and presented by Moroka. Neither the concomitant failed miners' strike nor the riots at the Lovedale secondary school had anything to do with the resolution. Unfortunately they are still cited as the cause of the NRC adjournment.[11] It was emphasized on a number of occasions that both these events were merely cited as additional evidence, if such were needed, that the protest resolution of the NRC was justified.[12] The events at Lovedale in particular were of minimal importance, being one of many similar events signaling African dissatisfaction with mission education.[13]

Z.K. Matthews
"If a system does not produce fruits ... it must be hewn down."
26 November 1946, 62–66

I think this is the first time in the history of this council, or indeed of any other body which has been created for the African people, through which they might exercise their views on matters affecting their welfare—it is the first time that a motion of this nature has ever been brought before such bodies.... But I would say that if I were in the responsible position occupied by the government and a motion of this nature were brought forward, I would sit up and take notice of the motion. The people who are gathered here before you are not irresponsible people. We are grownup men engaged in various occupations of a very responsible nature throughout the country, and we would not lightly come to a decision to place such a motion before the government.... Now, when you have provided for machinery for consultation and co-operation, it does seem as if you are in honor bound to make these systems work, and the only way in which these systems can be made to work is that they must produce fruits, and if a system does not produce fruits and if the tree does not produce fruits, it must be hewn down. Now I would like particularly to deal with that side of this question which may be said to be the credit side. I am sure that if the government were called upon to reply to this motion they would undoubtedly put before us certain things which they regard as being on the credit side, certain definite benefits which they would say have accrued to the native people, as a result of the machinery which was set up in 1936.

Now, what is the credit side? What has happened to the African people since this council was established? I think it would probably be said that a number of new benefits have come into being.... Old age pensions have been introduced, blind pensions ... invalidity [sic] pensions have been introduced. To start with, to say to any person that you have to be old, you have to be blind, and you have to be an invalid before I do something for you is not very encouraging. But the system under which these pensions are operated is such that in many cases people do not even get these benefits. You know that these pensions are hedged about with all kinds of conditions and methods by which the very meager pensions are reduced. I don't know if you have ever been, as some of us have been, at meetings where native commissioners have considered applications for these pensions. A paltry ten shillings a month—and how much trouble is taken to see whether these old women or old men really should get this ten shillings. Elaborate precautions are taken to see that the individual does not get three pennies more than he deserves. The precautions taken to see whether he has a beast or whether he has a cow and by how much the pension must be reduced if he has this or that.... I want to say quite definitely, as a person who has travelled extensively through the rural areas, that the people do not appreciate the way that this pension system is conducted. Then you know that one of the important things which the government has done is to appoint a number of important commissions to investigate native affairs.... But I do not think that anyone can maintain that the recommendations of these commissions have been given effect to by the government.... The most recent example is the Miners Phthisis Commission. Here we have a commission which made a recommendation supported by a recommendation passed by this council ... that silicosis benefits to Africans should be put on a pension basis instead of on the lump sum basis which we have had for so many years and which is unsatisfactory. That was the recommendation of the majority of the commission. It was turned down. Then we have the most recent example. This beer profits system which was investigated by the Native Affairs Commission ... and they recommended against the use of beer profits for ordinary municipal business services, and the necessary legislation was introduced; it was discussed in this council and a recommendation was made in regard to putting that legislation into effect. And wherever I have been, and have been questioned ... it has been put to me, "What have you people in the Council ever achieved," and I have pointed to that one thing. Now, there was one thing which we succeeded in getting.... But before legislation was passed, the government appointed another committee, whose report we are to consider this session, reversing the policy ... which was set down by this council. Now I can go on to refer to the question of education.... We have pointed out again and again in this council that the funds spent by the government on African education are totally inadequate to deal with the situation, and the government has so far refused to accept the principle of compulsory education for all African children in this country.... Even the two million or so which is spent on education is totally inadequate—totally inadequate to provide buildings, proper salaries for teachers, etc.... The African people are a very patient people; I do not think that can be denied by anyone, and the people sitting in front of us here, who are the administrators of Native Affairs, will bear me out that the African people are a patient people. Not only that; the demands they make on the government are not many and are not high. They are very easily satisfied.... I think perhaps it is this characteristic that has led the African people to the position that they find themselves in today. The white people in this country, I feel, think that the situation will continue forever, but I want to say that it will not continue forever. The most dangerous man to deal with in any situation is the patient man when he loses his patience, and I am afraid, Mr. Chairman, that we are getting to the point where the African people are losing their patience. We, as their leaders, have done our best to encourage them in that patience. Our very presence here is an indication of our attempts to encourage our people to go on trusting the government, being patient and keeping up their hopes that the time will come when things will change for the better; but what is happening now is this. When we go round the country, as we are duty bound to do as their representatives ... at meetings people get up and say, "These are the very ones who are cooperating with the government in oppressing us, as we are being oppressed today." They say to people like Sakwe: "Now you have gone up to the Bunga[14]; what have they done for us, what have they done about the demands we have made—down with the Bunga, down with the Advisory Boards, down with this council." To you, Mr. Chairman, this may just be an item in your administrative work; to us it is a very serious thing that we should today be looked upon by our own people, as people who are selling them to the government. I want to say that speaking for myself—and I am sure I am speaking for all the councilors in this council—we have genuinely tried our best; we have made sacrifices—personal sacrifices—in the interest of the cause of our people; and unless we find that the government is prepared to take urgent steps to reform certain things in the life of the people, we will not be able to continue with this work. We cannot continue with this work. I think the urgent things to which the government must give serious attention are the following: The question of the Pass Laws ... the recognition of the trade unions ... the question of proper health services for our people.... It is a pity that our minister [of native affairs] is so busy with his affairs ...

that he cannot spare the time apparently to come here and hear for himself how the people feel. I think that it s a tragedy that we have had two councils—this is the second council—yet I do not think that any members of this council are even known personally to the people who have to decide these things.... They just assume that we are agitators, and I, for one, repudiate that expression as applying to myself. I am not an agitator. But even if we were agitators, I think the people who are responsible for dealing with the questions brought up at this council should know and hear us. They should not feel it is below their dignity to come to a council like this and to hear the leaders of the African people. You may not think so, but I assure you we yield considerable influence among our people, and if we were to direct that influence on the wrong side I think it would be a serious thing for this country. We do not want to do so. We want to put our influence on the right side. Now, as a result of this motion we are going to adjourn this council, and as I said before, we feel that we cannot carry on unless we have a definite assurance from the heads of the government, from the prime minister downwards, that certain definite steps are going to be taken to improve the situation. Otherwise let the government carry on ... and not make us a party to what it is doing.

> The second NRC adjournment thus began in November 1946. The Council was not called together in 1947 but six of its members met the prime minster, General Smuts, in Cape Town in May 1947. Smuts was in favor of strengthening the NRC because he held that that Council represented black opinion and that it would be unwise to ignore it. The Council would be restructured in such a way that it would manage black affairs, a situation which would accord well with the policy of his government, which was to keep the two sections of South Africa separate in their own residential areas. He then dangled before the Council his plans to present a bill that would give recognition to African trade unions, excluding the largest labor force in the country, namely the miners.... He pointed out, no doubt as an incentive for the NRC to return to its duties, that this bill could not be passed by Parliament until the NRC sat and considered it. As nothing was said about abolishing discriminatory legislation, it was unlikely that any negotiations with the NRC would succeed. The general trend of his proposals was to give greater power and responsibility to blacks in their own areas. As Mosaka commented, the adjournment had been a matter of policy and to ask the councilors now to help in the administration of a policy which they did not support was to ask them to police their own people. It was an attempt to let blacks administer their own domination.[15] There seems to have been an attempt by the government to put the proposals as a means to a more grandiose end. A major South African newspaper interpreted this to mean that the Council would, to a limited extent, become a black parliament, which (its editorial noted) could hardly fail to impress the UN.[16] The parliamentary opposition, which was proposing to enter the 1948 general elections with their policy of apartheid, made capital of the Smuts proposals. Smuts, they maintained, wanted to form a black parliament which would consolidate the eight million Africans under anti-white leadership.[17] The councilors were from the start on guard against being fobbed off by Smuts with something that was essentially the same

as previous policy. They also realized that if they put up no opposition now, then Smuts would go to the UN and say that his proposals were being received with genuine approval.[18] Besides providing for an extended Natives Representative Council, they also provided new opportunities for Africans to gain skills and knowledge to practice in the reserves, a feature similar to that proposed by apartheid and the only feature favorably received by some Africans, although not the NRC.[19] These proposals would have given white domination another lease on life rather than ushering in political change leading to equality, which was what the Africans wanted.[20] They were rejected because they showed no radical progressive change in "native policy."[21] It can be argued that political expediency, influenced by the proximity of the 1948 general elections, was responsible for Prime Minister Smuts' document on "native policy." The election manifesto of the National Party under Dr. Malan and apartheid emphasized racial separation and white supremacy and was being presented to South Africa, when not only had India been given independence but Africans were also being included by the colonial powers in the discussions on the granting of self-government. The election manifestos of both parties on the color question were by 1948 considerably out of kilter with a continent in the throes of decolonization. Africans did not consider there to be a significant difference between the policies of the two white political parties. Apartheid was considered to have the same meaning as segregation. It was merely a new name for an old policy. Z.K. Matthews maintained that what could be expected in the future was a more overt and perhaps cruder application of a policy that past governments had been at pains to disguise with various euphemistic expressions.[22] It was thus not immediately obvious to everyone, including the councilors, that the National Party victory might be more disadvantageous to blacks than a United Party victory under Smuts. Msimang and Champion both believed that the National Party at least offered some advancement to Africans in their own areas.[23] Africans were in favor of the continued adjournment of the Council until such time as all discriminatory legislation had been removed. The significance of this demand was that it did not center on the abolition of some aspects of discriminatory legislation, such as the demand for the recognition of black trade unions or the abolition of passes, but asked for the complete abolition of all such legislation. For this reason it can be regarded as a historic and momentous occasion.

The abolition of the NRC had been a part of the National Party's election manifesto, and it was to have been expected that once they won the election, they would indeed have abolished the Council; but nothing was done. It seems that the National Party, having become the government, was now not ready to abolish the Council. Indeed, from the time of the appointment of Eiselen as secretary of state, extraordinary efforts were made to keep the NRC rather than abolish it. These efforts were made not only made by Eiselen but also by the newly appointed minister of native affairs, H.F. Verwoerd. The seventh session of the NRC took place in January 1949. It was stated right from the start that the government would not accede to the demand for the abolition of discriminatory legislation. It was then left it to the councilors themselves to decide whether or not they wanted to continue with the meeting.[24]

H. Selby Msimang

"What is ... behind the abolition of the Natives Representative Council?"
5 January 1949, 30

I have been studying the records of this council for the last ten years.... Somehow or other the government seemed to have a fear that this road of cooperation would lead to a state of equality or perhaps threaten the domination of the white race over the black, and therefore this council became a source of danger to the country, just because the Council endeavored to put before the government the proven facts of the case. Now what is there exactly behind the abolition of the Natives Representatives Council? Personally, with my knowledge of conditions in Natal, I am inclined to believe that the government has found itself in a position which it can no longer face up to, and that the Council has been so useful to the people generally as to be a danger to the government itself.... Now, sir, I feel that the government is deliberately instilling a spirit—is diligently inflaming a spirit of hatred among the races. I feel, as I stand here, that it is difficult to differentiate as between my friends and my enemies among the whites, because after all the government is constituted on the will of the whole of the white population of this country. If the government of this country is not prepared to do justice to me, to provide me with a place under the sun, or give me the natural privileges I require, then it means that the whole of the white population has declared a policy of hatred against my race, and I am afraid that I must [give] my own word of warning to the white race of this country and that I must tell the people of this country that within a very short time, there will arise in this country a very serious and dangerous state of affairs. I speak that word of warning.... But when we feel that we have lost everything—that even hope has been lost—then the position becomes one where the African has to find a way out for himself. And that is what the government says to us, in fact— we must find a way out for ourselves ... well, if that is the appeal which we have to make, that we have to find our own way out, then that appeal would go far among the African people of this country.

James Moroka

"What have we done in this Council, what have we achieved?"
5 January 1949, 52

I am very happy to have the opportunity of saying something this afternoon. To me this day is a day which we, the sons of this land, will never forget.... Now sir, let me put this question, what have we done in this council, what have we achieved? We have brought before you on very many occasions resolutions of the people whom we represent, and I think I am entitled to say that we have been most moderate in the manner in which we put forward the resolutions and the demands of the people. I happen to come from the reserves. I was born in the reserves and I have lived in the reserves all my life.... And what has happened in the reserves since the passing of the 1936 act? Let me put this question bluntly. Have the people improved? Have they got more land? Have they been protected? Can you answer that in the affirmative? In your address to us you say that the people are protected. I take it by that you mean that the Europeans will not be allowed to buy land in the reserves and the Africans will not be allowed to buy land outside the reserves. But what does that mean? What it means is this: that the white people of this land want to preserve for themselves 80 percent of this land. They want to keep for themselves and their children and their great-grandchildren 80 percent of this land and only allow the non-Europeans of this country, the Africans of this country, a matter of 15 percent. But, sir, even that 15 percent does not belong to them. It is still in the hands of the white people of this country. You will not find any reserves where a native can go in and buy land in spite of all we have been told. You will not find anywhere where a native, since 1936, has been allowed to buy even a matter of fifty by fifty yards just to put up his house. The Europeans of this country are very clever people—they are responsible people. Do you honestly believe that they would accept a thing like that on behalf of their people ... and is it possible—do you think it likely that the people assembled here would be satisfied to accept a condition of affairs such as I have outlined? And yet, if they do not accept it they are told they are communists, and that they are agitators, and that in fact, they are not the true leaders of their people. That is what we are told here. We have been told that we are here not to advise our people in the right way but that we must tell them that everything is all right; that they must be content to stay in the reserves ... that it is all right for them not to be represented by their own people in the highest council of the land, it is all right for them to be obliged to carry passes, that it is quite all right for them not to own even the land on which their houses stand. That is what we are expected to tell our people—we are expected to tell them that that is the right thing. How can we? Now is it possible that the white people hate us because of our color? Surely that is not the position.... The position is that the white people of this land ... do not want to see an African advance in civilization. They want the Africans to be there to work for them and they want to be able to exploit them. They want them so that they can go to the mines and work for four shillings and six pence a day so that the profits of the mines can go right up and the owners of the mines can sit back and smoke cigars. And they want the Africans to be there so that they can be called upon to work for the Europeans, and always be in a subservient position. That is their idea.

Paul Mosaka

"The Minister has ... [no] intention to honor the spirit of the law."
5 January 1949, 15ff

I wish now to address myself to the main point at issue: the abolition of the Natives Representative Council. We have been told that this present session of the Natives Representative Council has been convened as a mere legal formality, that the minister has neither the desire to meet the councilors nor the intention to honor the spirit of the law. I should like to suggest that this confession on the part of the minister is long overdue. The trouble is that since its inception, the Natives Representative Council has met as a mere legal formality and the attitude of the government has consistently been one of indifference and apathy. Now at last we have exposed the fraud which this council really is; the minister of native affairs has at last confessed the complete futility of this council and has expressed his intention of abolishing it. The African people have never concurred with the view that it is possible to have a parliament within another parliament—no more than we can have a civilization of the African, primitive and untarnished within the framework of Western civilization.... Let it be repeated that this experiment has failed not only because of the difficulties inherent in a policy of dual political control but also because the government which alone could put life into this institution to make the Council work—it was just a toy telephone, and today the African baby for whom this toy was intended has passed the stage of playing at parliament-making. In this, Dr. Jansen [minister of native affairs in 1949] concurs. We welcome therefore the intention to abolish this council, but let us be clear that this admission of the experiment of parallel differential institutions such as the Native Representatives Council is, in fact, the failure of the policy of segregation, or apartheid.... The present government can be under no illusion that it does not enjoy the confidence of the African people. For the first time, the Nationalist Party has in the recent election [in 1948], held under the Native Representation Act of 1936, pitted its candidates against candidates of other schools of political thought. And in every case the Nationalist candidates not only lost the election, but also lost their deposits—a fact that the prime minster [Dr. Malan] in his "mature judgment" referred to as "most encouraging." Because of the African electorates' unmistakable declaration of no confidence in the Nationalist Party, we are strengthened in our demand that all proposals must be the subject of consultation and negotiation between the government and ourselves as the mouthpiece of the African people.... Finally, I wish to issue a word of warning to the European people of this land in whom the immediate destiny of this country rests. We have today a government which believes in white domination. This policy, as preached, interpreted and applied by its supporters, means the total abolition of all political and civil rights— it means that there shall be no mouthpiece of the African people freely elected by the people either within or without Parliament; it is the prelude to the complete muzzling of African opinion, the forerunner to a state of fascism without freedom of expression, freedom of movement, freedom of assembly and organization, so that the oppressor shall rule like a tyrant over the 8,000,000 Africans of this land whose state of slavery shall be complete. I issue this warning as a member of a subject race, at present in large numbers but powerless in might to face the oppressor. The lessons of history cannot be untruths. The Dutch, the French, the German, the British, the principal elements of the European stock in this country, know full well the results of such a policy. In their own mother countries they have resisted oppression in all its forms, and they claim today, as their inalienable heritage, the principles of democracy, which they cherish as the pillars of a true and lasting civilization. Think you not that ... if ... you trample down ... the principles of freedom of speech, conscience and government in their application to the non-European peoples of this country, what future can there be for the European in South Africa or in the whole of Africa? You have the choice to make us brothers or beasts and take the consequences. In the end the powers of good must prevail over evil, and the empty bubble of race pride shall vanish like mist before the rising sun.

James Moroka

"Only if we stand together can South Africa go ahead."
5 January 1949, 52

Whether you destroy this body or not, whether you keep it going or not, there is only one goal. We can play about and fool one another, but there is only one goal for all of us.... In the long run, the Europeans will see what the position is, that we are all living together in this country and we must all work together.... I hope that the white people of this country will act intelligently and use wisdom in their dealings with the African people.... We are human beings, just as well as other people. My grandfather mixed well with the Voortrekkers.[25] He mixed so well with them that he fought side by side with the sons of the Voortrekkers.... You cannot find a single instance where we, the Africans, have differentiated against anyone ... we do not differentiate against a man's color. That is the attitude which we have always adopted and which we will continue to adopt until you people come right back to us and until you realize that only if we stand together can South Africa go ahead.

Sam Mabude
"The avowed intention of the present government
[is] to intensify its measures of oppression."
5 January 1949, 21–23

To many of us the so-called apartheid policy of the present government and the outmoded segregation policy which reached its zenith in 1936, and which has been weighed and found wanting, have never been clarified.... We can only infer that the difference lies in the avowed intention of the present government to intensify its measures of oppression as disclosed in election speeches. If Western civilization can sink so low in regard to its policy of governing powerless, vote-less and voiceless races, then I am afraid it is not worth preservation by mankind. I suggest, sir, that to make a general election issue of racial prejudices—even prejudices against the non-Europeans as was done during the last general election— was to place South African politics at its lowest place. To the African people, complete equality of political rights will provide the only guarantee of justice in relations between the races of this country. Complete democracy—the removal of all color bars and equality of rights and opportunities for all races—should be the basis of our harmonious relations and complete elimination of the racial strife in this country. I realize that white South Africa abhors political equality between the races and regards it as a kind of taboo or something beyond comprehension—but this is the only goal towards racial harmony. The rights of man are inherent in his human nature, irrespective of race or color, and mankind has resisted and always will resist any tampering with his human rights. The African is no exception to this general law of self-preservation.

George Champion
"We, the people of South Africa, have come to realize
that Afrikaner people are cowards."
5 January 1949, 41

Now, sir, the point has been raised as to why the minister of native affairs has failed to come here.... You invited him here to come and address this council and he deliberately refused to come.... This is the first time that we, the people of South Africa, have come to realize that Afrikaner people are cowards.... When the nationalist government took over the reins of office, the first thing they did was the get the prime minister— and I think he is an Afrikaner—to refuse to go to UNO, where he would have had to face the statesmen of the world. I refer to Dr. Malan. The second thing they did when the Indian congress—which for many years for many years had enjoyed the confidence of the South African government ... and which at one time enjoyed the presences of the present prime minister—they got Dr. Donges to refuse to attend this congress. That was the act of a coward.... I am not surprised, not in the least, that our present minister of native affairs has refused to come here, although it is his duty to come here to address us.... No bill to abolish this assembly can be passed through Parliament without first being referred to us, and we first of all have to express our opinion on it. Apparently that is not to be done and the law is to be broken. There are threats contained in this document, in this opening address of yours, and those threats will live for many years after you are dead.... Strange as it may sound, we read the reports of the debates in the House of Assembly as well as in the Senate. Don't we know that the Nationalist Party won the last election because they told the country they were going to ... abolish this council—that they were going to take away the representatives of the natives in the House of Assembly, don't we know it? Don't you think that a self-respecting man like the Minister of Native Affairs.... The plain fact is that he is afraid to come here. Yet our resolution in the reply to your address asks him to come here. We want him to come and make an explanation.

George Champion
"You will have to face the same people..."
5 January 1949, 41

No matter whether you decide to abolish this council and to establish new councils in this country, you will have to face the same people as you have before you this afternoon. We pay our poll tax and we enjoy the confidence of the people who sent us here; we enjoy the confidence of our chiefs and of the ordinary natives, whether in the reserves or the locations or in the towns or on privately owned land. We are here as their representatives, and I claim we enjoy their confidence.

G.S. Dana
"The future of white civilization is based on the consent
and goodwill of the non–Europeans of this country."
5 January 1949, 58

Those people who study the problem of race relations will readily admit that in a country like South Africa, which has a mixed population, of different colors, all classes should be represented in the supreme legislature of the country.... There is hardly any law passed by Parliament which does not directly or indirectly affect the native people of this country. Take customs matters, educational matters, industrial and social legislation—the native people are affected by all legislation passed in respect of these matters. The native people are either included in the effects ... or they are specifically excluded. The South Africa Act is not only an act of Parliament, it is a treaty entered into by the four states which constitute the Union of South Africa.... I want to make an appeal to the white people of this country to honor the moral obligations implicit in the Act of Union. Once a section of the community has been given franchise rights, and exercised those rights, those rights should not be taken away unless there is adequate justification for it. We shall never have a sound native policy unless it is based on consent. The future of white civilization is based on the consent and the goodwill of the non–Europeans of this country.

George Champion

"I prophesy that one day these laws will be wiped out."
5 January 1949, 41

I want to assure you that one day these laws, these discriminatory laws, will be abolished; today the fifth of January 1949 I assure you, I prophesy that one day these laws will be wiped out. If not by agreement, then by right of conquest. It may appear a dream, it may appear an insult, but if we have been created by God in his own image and placed in Africa and surrounded by the oceans to live here, for what it is worth, we have committed no sin and if we are to have occupations which mean that we are to be exploited and are to be kept on our feet from early morning till late at night well, then I must tell you that we are not prepared to submit to that. We are not slaves ... we are the rightful owners of the land and, sir, I say emphatically that we are the true Afrikaners.... If it has been found possible to get the Europeans to retreat from India after 200 or 300 years, just so will it be possible for the Europeans to be made to retreat from this country—I don't know after how many years, but ... the day will come when you will be called upon to retreat from this land.... Let me say again, before this body is abolished, that there has been laid down by law that no legislation affecting the interests of the natives shall be passed without having been placed before the Native Representatives Council for its consideration and report.... What the government is doing today is to lay up a store of trouble, trouble which is likely to develop in years to come; it may be soon or it may be in fifty years time, or longer.

R.V. Selope Thema

"We have now come to the parting of the ways."
5 January 1949, 24

Mr. Chairman, I feel that we have now come to the parting of the ways, and if we have come to that stage, then members of the white race in South Africa will excuse us if we speak plainly to them. Over three hundred years ago people in Europe, stirred by their greed for wealth, came down the Atlantic in search of gold and other things; they went to places where they had heard that there was such wealth. That story is well known and there is no need to repeat it.... At the end of the last war, we saw and we heard of the retreat of Europe, of the people from Europe, from Asia. That retreat must be of significance to the people of Africa and of South Africa. What does it mean to them? What does it mean to the world? We have seen that those people who went to Asia to grab the wealth of the Asiatics are retreating, are going back to Europe, and the descendants of those who came to South Africa ... may not be realizing today what this retreat means. But the day will come when they will realize it.... What does the freedom of Asia mean to this continent of ours? It means that the eastern coast of Africa is open to Asia.... You, Mr. Chairman, said yesterday that you wish that the native people would cooperate with the white people. Yes, we know that that is your wish and we wish that the object could be achieved, but how can we cooperate with people who trample on us? We can only cooperate with those people who help us and who are prepared to give us those rights which they enjoy themselves.

Paul Mosaka

"We as a Council cannot be easily duped by the cheap policy of apartheid."
5 January 1949, 15ff

Asking for the minister of native affairs to address them on the policy of apartheid:

The observation of the simple courtesies even to members of the lowest class in the land would detract nothing from the respect and prestige of the minister of the Crown. It is in fact possible that such a display of courtesy would at least be used to indicate the doctrine of the inherent superiority of the white race. He should moreover have the courage of his convictions and not hide behind the secretary of native affairs. If there is a forum for the discussion of native problems, this is the forum. [If] the honorary minister does not even consult the Native Affairs Commission even on so vital an issue as the fate of the Natives Representative Council, with whom does the minister discuss native affairs? At least let the minister be honest and conscientious. The present government has made so much noise about apartheid and native policy that the native people and indeed the whole country expected that on the first opportunity the responsible minister would expound to the Council the meaning of the much-vaunted policy of apartheid. We are not afraid to be told that an adverse policy is to be adopted against us—we have always credited the National Party with courage and honesty. It now appears that both virtues are wanting and that the government ... either considers it below its dignity to expound its policy to a council which represents approximately eight million people, or in its political bankruptcy it has no serious policy to offer. Indeed I am satisfied that the responsible minister knows that we as a council cannot be easily duped by the cheap policy of apartheid which he and his colleagues have hawked so freely on the platteland [rural areas]. That much credit to our intelligence we must grant him. I feel certain that many ardent followers of the nationalist cause will agree with me in condemning the minister for losing this grand opportunity to tell this so-called agitator council just what the government has in store for them—and for all who will question their supreme authority. I submit that the minister is not acting in the spirit of the high portfolio he holds by lightly dismissing this council and by refusing to address it. I can conceive of nothing more calculated to sow seeds of deep hatred and mistrust that this attitude of the minister towards an institution to which a population of eight million has, by an act of Parliament, been made to look with great respect and hope.

In December 1949 James Moroka, the councilor who had passed what was then termed the "freedom resolution," namely the demand for the abolition of discriminatory legislation, became the next African National Congress president-general. He himself said that the resolution had not been formulated by him but that he knew and approved of it, and when he was asked to present it at the August 1946 NRC meeting he did so. The councilors were not immune to arrest (both Paul Mosaka and R.V. Selope Thema had recently been arrested), and nearly all of them had so-called "agitator" numbers. Dr. J. Moroka was a medical man with an independent practice and least likely to suffer any repercussions from such a presentation.[26]

Eiselen was appointed secretary of native affairs in 1950. As has been noted, Eiselen had attended many sessions of the Council in previous years when he was head of black education in the Transvaal. He had been well received by the councilors, seemingly having a great understanding of their problems and aspirations in connection with education, and when he chose to participate in debates with some other matters as well.[27] His subsequent efforts to retain the NRC indicate that the ideas behind the apartheid policy were not set in stone. In fact it seems that both Eiselen and Verwoerd wanted to give blacks a greater share in their own administration, i.e., self-government in black areas, but under a reconstituted NRC.[28] Immediately after his appointment he contacted Matthews and asked the NRC to hold an informal meeting to consider ways of overcoming the impasse. Matthews was under the impression that he would attend the meeting.[29] There was no publicity, and no report of the meeting was made available. The councilors at this meeting asked that the minister of native affairs meet them and explain the new government's policy towards the Africans, namely to explain the policy of apartheid. Eiselen, however, knew that Jansen, then minister of native affairs, was not favorably inclined towards the NRC, and such a meeting had no hopes of ending the deadlock.[30] He then called another informal meeting in August 1950. Although it is true that the government had given no formal indication that they were considering using the NRC as a channel for the implementation of apartheid, the renewed attempts by the government to heal the breach certainly indicate that Eiselen was considering something like this.[31] Eiselen explained his actions by stating that he had been dismayed in 1949 when he read that the newly elected council (the third NRC elections had taken place in 1948) had passed the same resolution as the old one. When he became secretary of native affairs he thought that he could remedy matters, and as a result of a discussion with Matthews decided to attend this informal meeting with the councilors. He believed he could talk more openly at an informal meeting. However, he assured councilors that the government would call a formal meeting later in the year. Eiselen maintained that the councilors did not have the moral right to decide that because they did not like the policy followed by the government, they were no longer willing to serve their people. It was not the government that had suspended the Council; it was the councilors themselves that had taken from the people the only representation they had. He ended by asking them to withdraw their adjournment resolutions, indicating at the same time that great benefits would accrue to Africans under apartheid. The councilors refused to withdraw the adjournment resolutions, at least until they had met the minister of native affairs and the policy had been explained to them.[32] Eiselen subsequently wrote to Albert Luthuli expressing his appreciation of the cooperative spirit in which the councilors had approached the problem.[33] The last session of the NRC opened on 5 December 1950. The meeting was regarded as of great significance because if the NRC cooperated with the government, the NRC would not be abolished. This in turn was dependent on the minister of native affairs making a statement that would satisfy the councilors and enable them to withdraw their previous standpoint. The major newspapers of that time held that the success or failure of the whole of the apartheid policy might depend on this meeting.[34] On it would depend the question of whether the future for blacks would be citizenship by reform or by revolution.[35] It was generally understood that they had been called together to hear an exposition on apartheid, the first (and as it later turned out, only) time that this was addressed to the people to whom the policy was applied.[36] At this, the last session of the Council, the opening address was given on 5 December by the newly appointed minister of native affairs, Hendrik Verwoerd.

H.F. Verwoerd, Minister of Native Affairs

"They will not be prepared to sacrifice White supremacy in South Africa." Speech
translated from the original, given in Afrikaans
5 December 1950, 13ff

You have often heard that the policy of apartheid means oppression. Is that really true? The easiest thing on earth is to poison people's minds by the misuse of words. It is not the word itself that counts. It is the idea behind it—it is what one wants to do that counts.... The word is only a vehicle carrying a meaning, the word apartheid, which could just as well have been expressed as separateness—has been poisoned.... Let us examine calmly what it means and what will be done in actual practice by the government who believes in that policy, and what will be done by me, who as minister of native affairs has promoted this policy. I cannot deal with all the details, as you will realize, but I hope I shall be able to deal sufficiently clearly with the fundamentals and with certain steps that have to be taken so that you will not be able to say that I am vague and that you don't know what is going to happen. I don't wish to be vague. There is nothing I wish to hide. I have no ulterior motives. The policy I believe in is open for everybody to see. And I say again that although I know that the Bantu won't easily believe that the European has no ulterior motives, the only real and valuable motive we have is this. We believe that if that policy is not carried out, both the European and the Bantu will suffer in the future. This may be the selfishness of the white man, if you wish to call it so. At the same time it would serve the selfishness or self-interest of the black man because I believe each will serve his own nation best by following this policy.

Let us face openly what the problem is. That problem is simply this. What will lead to a better South Africa in the future, a development of the Bantu and the European on the basis of an intermixed, intermingled, integrated society—use whatever words you like, words don't count with me, ideas do.... Is that better for South Africa and for both population groups, or is separateness, to the greatest practical extent—the policy to support? ... Let us ask ourselves for a moment what is going to be the consequences of an intermixed and intermingled society? You have experienced it in your own lives when in the society which we have founded on the "let things develop" basis, you have often and often found yourselves involved in clashes and competition with the white man. You have often experienced unpleasantness in your everyday life. The intermixing and intermingling of our society has, however, not proceeded very far as yet. If these clashes have come about in the course of this relatively small degree of intermixing, how do you think these clashes will be if this intermixed society continues and develops further? The more the intermixing, the more the interrelationships, the greater the clashes must be—so one must expect. Seen from your standpoint, the European has the advantage. He is in a stronger position. You will be the sufferer more than he, although he will also suffer. We cannot have two population groups living together with one suffering and the other going scot-free. It never happens; both suffer. But in any clashes which arise in an intermingled society, you yourselves know better than I can tell how great the advantage of the European can be. You cannot desire these clashes. You can only desire the possibility of these things being eliminated.

Let me illustrate my point in the political sphere of which you have often thought and spoken. Supposing we let this intermixed society, this integrated society, develop in the future to a greater and greater extent. What sort of society will it be? Will they want communal representation as the integration grows? Will they be satisfied with that? I am sure they will not.... I am sure that as time goes by their pressure for a full franchise, for full participation in the country's parliament will grow.... They will no longer be satisfied to be represented by white people. They will want to be represented by their own people in such a parliament.... But let me look at that from a white man's point of view.... The supporters of the present government say very clearly—not because of any bad feeling, but because they face facts as facts should be faced—that they are against that, that they will not be prepared to sacrifice white supremacy in South Africa. They say so very clearly and very definitely. When they do say that, they also say something else which is always left out when people talk about this policy. This is what they say: "Just as we want supremacy in our areas, so we are prepared to grant the same supremacy to the Bantu in his areas. We don't want for ourselves what we are not prepared to cede to others...." Now, don't forget that. When this one group says very clearly that white supremacy in its ideal, it says that is its ideal in its own portion of the country, and it is prepared to give exactly the same to the native people in their own portion of the country.... That portion of the European population, English and Afrikaans, which is ready to give representation to the Bantu in the government of the country, wants to give nothing more than communal representation, and that on a quite limited basis. They do not yet realize that by so doing, the balance of power could be given to the non–Europeans.... I say with great confidence that when the time comes, when the implication of communal representation is felt, you will find that this portion of the population will combine with the other portion of the white population to resist.... The efforts and desires and aims of all Europeans and of all the Bantu people will thereupon be mutually opposed. Such a clash of interests could only bring unhappiness and misery to both. If we do not want this future strife, which seems to me inevitable, when you have your intermixed society, what is the alternative? There is only one alternative, and that is: Instead of having an intermixed society you should have a society in South Africa in which there is separation, giving the fullest opportunities of development to the one, just as to the other.... How can we attain that? If one could put the clock back and arrange an ideal society in South Africa in which these troubles do not appear, then one would say that having separate states—a state for the Bantu and a state for the Europeans—would be the easiest.... But you cannot turn the facts of history back ... the facts are otherwise. We have to take into consideration the position as we find it. We may make use of that theoretically ideal situation as a measure by which we can judge how we have to deal with the problems which we have to meet in everyday life.... The reserve, the white man can say, should fully become its own by the gradual withdrawal of the white man, as he is no longer needed by the black man. However, only just more than one third of the native population of the Union of South Africa still lives there. Slightly more than one third of the native population lives in our rural areas, either in Locations, adjoining villages or on farms, and something like less than one third of the native population live in European areas. These are facts which no policy can get away from—and which no policy tries to get away from, in spite of the fact that it has sometimes been said that the policy of apartheid does not recognize this fact. That is perfectly untrue. The policy of apartheid has always recognized this fact, and wishes to deal with it in the way I am going to show. What I was saying to you now is not something new. It is just what we have always said.... Let us therefore try to picture to ourselves what can be done. At the present moment everybody knows that it is perfectly impossible for those native areas to carry economically and to make prosperous the people who live there—not to speak of the generations to come. The native areas push off continually those for whom no livelihood is to be found in those areas. And why? The answer given in the past was "there is not enough land for all." But there is not enough land for all white men in the European portions of South Africa.... Present day civilized society is not built on the basis of land for all, and it must be quite clear to everybody that in future our policy must be based on a clear issue; that land for all ... cannot be the policy which is going to save the Bantu population from poverty and frustration.... Instead of most of these people living on economically impossible pieces of land on which they cannot make a livelihood, those who remain on the land must be given the type of cattle and the extent of land which will provide them with the opportunity to live as they should live and to cultivate their land in the way good farmers should cultivate their land. For those for whom there is not sufficient land, that means in the first instance the development of certain industries, in the native areas. The native of his own accord, the Bantu, cannot on the whole yet provide for that. It will be my duty, as minister of native affairs, to see to it that the Union of South Africa provides such instruments as will, under the duty of wardship, which we have resting upon us, ensure that industrial development for natives will come into being.... We shall have to recognize that ultimately those industries in what [are] native areas must be theirs and theirs alone because there will ultimately have accumulated the necessary funds and they will have gained the necessary experience. That is very clear and that is apartheid— seeing that every man has every chance in his own area to develop and stand on his own feet. One of the main problems to be faced there is that there are a number of what have been called black spots. You find a native-owned area or native-taken area within what is white man's land. Apartheid does certainly try to exchange those areas for other areas adjacent to actual native areas so that they can all be grouped together. And when I say this, I say the opposite too. That is that there are white spots in native areas, and there one must say exactly the same thing as I have said in regard to black spots in European areas.... The white spots will have to be taken away from native areas just as the black spots will be taken away from the European areas. What we want for the one we want for the other—and that is apartheid.

... When you take all this into consideration you will understand why the policy of apartheid also aims at providing suitable education for the native people. It is so often said that we are against education for the Bantu people. Let me tell you here that that is not true. We are against that form of education which ... makes a person into a frustrated man without any possibilities of earning a decent living.... We are not against an education which makes a man a worker in the service of his own nation, and we believe that what the Bantu needs more than anything else is vocational training.... There is one clear proviso and that is that when he is educated he may not use that education to slip out of the company of his fellow Bantu and try to go among the white man to use his knowledge there.... I have tried to give you as clear a view as I can in a short address of what the policy of apartheid means. If anyone after what I have said says that that is oppression, then he just shows that he does not know what oppression means.

> Verwoerd clearly made a great effort to overcome the deadlock, but his sympathetic explanation of apartheid and his invitation to talk over their problems with him was overshadowed by his injunction against political discussions. This was due to the new interpretation given by his government to the NRC as being an administrative and legislative but not political body. When the four bills to be discussed were distributed to the NRC it was explained that discussion on them would be limited to details only. The NRC would thus be expected to discuss bills and policies which would give effect

to apartheid without being able to discuss apartheid itself. Although Verwoerd had left the hall before the councilors could reply to his opening address, he had made it clear to them that they could debate his address later on. At the same time, however, he had made it clear that they could not discuss politics. How then could the NRC have discussed apartheid?[37] The councilors argued that the intention of the Natives Representatives Act of 1936, which had led to the formation of the Council, was that new legislation had to be given to the NRC before being placed on the table of the House of Assembly. The NRC was thus the third chamber of the political structure of South Africa and as such the intention had been that the NRC would discuss politics.[38]

Verwoerd then sent a reply to the NRC:

H.F. Verwoerd
"Discussion of ... general principles of high politics [will] lead nowhere."
5 December 1950, 36–37

Do not let words or interpretations of words to lead to unnecessary misunderstandings.... Deal with ideas and facts. Now I understand that the word "politics" has given you reason to feel worried.... From the context of my address it should be quite clear that I only do not wish the Council to spend its time in useless—to it and to the Bantu people—discussion of party political differences which should be fought out elsewhere, or of general principles of high politics which might have led, or would lead, nowhere or lead to disruption, as they did before. Therefore I insisted that the agenda should be systematically dealt with based on the provisions of the law.... It would be foolish to make your work impossible by denying the right of full and unfettered discussion of such a bill or any item on the budget. The chairman must necessarily see to it that discussion is to the point.... The right thing to do would be to test what is intended by proceeding with the agenda systematically and finding out in actual practice if unjustifiable curtailment of debate takes place. I am sure that if, just as in Parliament, you submit to the discipline of the Order Paper, you will find that your apparent difficulties vanish.

W.W.M. Eiselen
"The Council will proceed with its work
in the order determined by the chairman."
6 December 1950, 38

As it is apparent from the statement of the minister, this council will not be precluded from discussing, whenever it is appropriate, any political issues that may be involved, when our legislation, our contemplated legislation, is under discussion in the Council. Neither will Council be debarred from placing on the order paper further points which they wish to discuss; but in the meantime the Council will proceed with its work in the order determined by the chairman.

George Champion

"We ... ask to be released from this false position in which we find ourselves."
5 December 1950, 32ff

We have been living under the understanding that this was the third chamber of the political structure of this country. The very fact that you like to place before us the bills which have to go to the House of Assembly has always led us and the country to believe that this was a political institution. We were told in 1949 by your predecessor that we have attended too much to politics. We replied to him. And we were told it again this morning in a different language [by Verwoerd in Afrikaans] that we are councilors this morning but leaders of the people this afternoon. Therefore it is our bounden duty to ask whether we like it or not, in the interests of this country, to ask to be released from this false position in which we find ourselves. We do not say that it is through your doing that this position exists, but as I have said it is attributable to the machinery that was placed in the statute book. Our opinions are well known. In 1949 when were told that this council was going to be abolished for certain reasons, we said we were not interested in these reasons.... We have our reasons too, which we put forward very carefully, and one is thankful that the new government has been good enough and has been kind enough to send a minister of the Crown to explain to us the policy of the government in power. This government could do no better to the natives of this country as a whole, because the whole country has been wondering what is the policy.... You have pointed out that whatever we say as political leaders ... is a waste of time, or is tantamount to a waste of the time of the Council. Some of us don't want to waste time ... the longer we are here, the greater the waste of time and the greater the cost to the country.

Paul Mosaka

"This body [has] the right to consider questions of policy."
5 December 1950, 33

This council has been in existence now for a considerable period of time, and as the minister said this morning, this is the eleventh session of this body, the Natives Representative Council.... The statement made by the minister and endorsed by you [Eiselen as chairman] this afternoon amounts to a change of the status of this body. As Councilor Matthews has clearly indicated that its status is vested in the law, it is a matter of interpreting the law, and we are not going to accept that interpretation as laid down by the minister or by you, or by anyone in view of the law which has been so clearly stated in the act. We are therefore going to challenge this interpretation of the minister's. Our discussions in the past have not been curtailed, and we have been allowed to propose motions and deal with questions of policy, and our discussions have not been closed down. But today we are faced with the position that in view of the minister having interpreted the law in the way he has done, we are told there are matters for the government and there are matters for the Council—and these are matters for the councilors and these are matters for the leaders of the people. Now we submit that it is within the purview of this council to consider the legislation which you are going to put before us. General Smuts did not question when we met him in Cape Town that this body had the right to consider questions of policy, but today we are told that we could not consider such questions.

R.V. Selope Thema

"We are not going to agree in an indirect way to that policy."
6 December 1950, 42

We all say that the first item on the agenda is the minister's speech because everything we are going to consider is dependent on that speech. We are not going to agree in an indirect way to that policy. If it comes to us in all its nakedness then we know what we are doing, but to be told that we must deal with laws for our people, and to be trapped by the fact that these laws will be passed on that policy laid down in the minister's speech—that is something we can never agree to.

S.P. Sesedi

"It is that spirit which I do not like, that spirit of prejudging us."
7 December 1950, 60

Supposing there were certain advantages to our people in apartheid, supposing there were good things about it—do you think I would refuse it if I realized it and I were made to see that there were benefits in it? Do you think I would say no? But we are prejudged.... It is that spirit which I do not like, that spirit of prejudging us. And I therefore appeal to you, Mr. Chairman, if you will give us the opportunity that the work of this council will be done, and we shall have an opportunity of doing what we have come here to do. As a result of our resolutions, the minister has come to us, and we are thankful to him for having come here, and I am sure that if you will allow us to proceed and discuss the minister's address all obstacles will disappear. That is all we want. This is a special plea. This is all I have to say.

The importance of this meeting for Eiselen and Verwoerd can be seen from these efforts made by Eiselen to make the meeting work and prevent it from ending in the same way as the previous ones. When during the course of this session the councilors refused to form select committees to consider the draft legislation as they had done in previous years, feeling as they did that if they joined a select committee it would automatically mean that they agreed to the policy embodied in that pending legislation, Eiselen then gave it to the full Council to consider. He made it clear that as long as there was a quorum of nine councilors, he would go on with the meeting. On resuming after lunch on the second day, Matthews, Moroka, Mosaka, Mabude and Champion were absent. Eiselen tried to persuade them to return by promising that Verwoerd would meet them if they agreed to conduct their ordinary work. Only Mosaka was willing to return at this stage. The only councilor who was willing to proceed with the business of the Council was Msimang and he could find no one to support him. The Council then adjourned for the fourth and last time.[39]

Paul Mosaka

7 December 1950, 67

Last words

Motion given but not considered before the NRC adjourned:

This Council rejects the ban on political discussion clearly enunciated by the Minister of Native Affairs in his supplementary statement to the Council. Council reaffirms its determination to exercise its unrestricted rights to discuss all matter political and otherwise affecting the interests of the African people.

Chapter Notes

Preface

1. F.J. du T. Spies, et al., eds., *Die Hert-zogspreke*, vol. 5, no. 7, p. 42. Speech made by Hertzog at a Native Conference, 8 December 1925.

Chapter 1

1. M. Roth, *The Natives Representative Council (NRC), 1937–1951*, PhD dissertation, University of the Witwatersrand, 1988.

2. *Political Representation of Africans in the Union of South Africa* (Johannesburg, SAIRR, 1942), 26, ZK Matthews.

3. Roth, *Natives Representative Council*, 574.

4. *Imvo Zabandsundu*, 25 December 1937.

5. B. Willan, *Sol Plaatje: A Biography, Solomon Tchekisho Plaatje 1976–1932* (Johannesburg: Raven, 1984), 242–45.

6. J.C. Smuts Papers (hereafter "Smuts Papers"), 115(4), R.S. Msimang to W.P. Schreiner, High Commissioner for South Africa in London, 10 January 1919; ibid., 115(10), memorandum from Col. L.C.M.S. Amery to the Union government, 17 March 1919; ibid., 115(4), memorandum to General Botha, circa 12 March 1919.

7. Report of the Native Affairs Commission, U.G 17–127; Report of the Native Affairs Commission, U.G. 3–34.

8. M. Roth, *The Formation of the Natives Representative Council*, M.A, University of South Africa, 1979, 23–24, 40–41.

9. *Ibid.*

10. *Government Gazette*, section 19, 30 November 1923; *Umlindi We Nyanga*, 16 January 1937.

11. J.B.M. Hertzog Papers (hereafter "Hertzog Papers"), A32, Box 80, proof copy of Native Representation Bill, February 1935, with alterations in Hertzog's handwriting (Government Archives, Pretoria); ibid., Box 67, I.P. de Villiers, commissioner of police, to J.B.M. Hertzog, memorandum 1929, 4.

12. *Cape Times*, 1 June 1923, Hertzog, leader of the opposition, in the House of Assembly. The House of Assembly did not publish Hansard until 1924. All the proceedings of the House of Assembly until 1924 were reported in the *Cape Times.*

13. Smuts Papers, 263 (110), "Note of conversation with General Hertzog over the Native Bills on 12 March 1928"; ibid., 263(108), "Note of conversation with General Hertzog, 15 February 1928," 4; G. Heaton Nicholls Papers (hereafter, "Nicholls Papers"), MS NIC 2–08-0, Select Committee on the Native Bills, 20.

14. Hertzog Papers, A32, Box 35, "Memorandum on Government Native and Coloured Bills," by General J.C. Smuts, 1929.

15. M. Roth, *Formation of the Natives Representative Council*, 17.

16. Ibid., 16; Smuts Papers, 209(126), Smuts to M. Gillett, 21 August 1929.

17. Roth, *Formation*, 40–53.

18. *Political Representation of Africans in the Union of South Africa*, South African Institute for Race Relations (Johannesburg: SAIRR, 1942); Margaret Ballinger, *From Union to Apartheid: A Trek to Isolation* (Cape Town: Juta, 1969); C.M. Tatz, *Shadow and Substance: A Study in Land and Franchise Policies Affecting Africans 1910–1960* (Pietermaritzburg: Natal University Press, 1962).

19. Ballinger, *From Union to Apartheid*, 28; P. Walshe, *The Rise of African Nationalism in South Africa: The African National Congress 1912–1952* (Berkeley and Los Angeles: University of California Press, 1971), 118.

20. T. Karis and G. Carter, eds., *From Protest to Challenge: A Documentary History of Politics in South Africa*, vol. 4, *Political Profiles* (Stanford: Hoover, 1977), 26, 31, 141, 155; the majority of the errors in volume 4 are due to faulty editing, as a perusal of the original documents in the Karis and Carter Microfilm collection will show.
21. A. Paton, *Hofmeyr* (London: Oxford University Press, 1964), 440.
22. Tatz, *Shadow and Substance*, 96ff.
23. J. Lewin, "The Electoral System in Practice," 2, 13; *Political Representation of Africans in the Union*, 13; compare with the *Government Gazette*, 5 February 1937, 243, 251.
24. Tatz, *Shadow and Substance*, 93ff.
25. M. Lipton, *Capitalism and Apartheid: South Africa, 1910–1986* (Claremont: David Philip, 1985), 273.
26. P. Bonner, ed., *Working Papers in Southern African Studies*, vol. 1 (Johannesburg: Raven, 1977), 291; P.B. Rich, *White Power and the Liberal Conscience: Racial Segregation and South African Liberalism* (Johannesburg: Raven, 1984), 71, 86; Lipton, *Capitalism and Apartheid*, 22, 275; K. Ingham, *Jan Christian Smuts: The Conscience of a South African* (Johannesburg: Jonathan Ball, 1986), 236.
27. For example, Walshe, *Rise of African Nationalism*, 215, 232, 265ff.
28. Dan O'Meara, *The 1946 African Mine Workers' Strike in the Political Economy of South Africa* (Johannesburg: University of the Witwatersrand, 1975), 219; Paton, *Hofmeyr*, 432–33; W.K. Hancock, *Smuts*, vol. 2, *The Fields of Force 1919–1950*, 484, 485.
29. T.R.H. Davenport, *South Africa: A Modern History* (Johannesburg: Macmillan, 1977), 243.
30. James Moroka, interviewed by M. Roth, 4 November 1981.
31. Walshe, *Rise of African Nationalism*, 400–401.
32. A.B. Xuma Papers (hereafter "Xuma Papers"), ABX 361127c, A.B. Xuma to Max Yergan, 27 November 1936; Smuts Papers, 117(12), *Report and Proceedings of the Joint Select Committee...*, 26 November 1931.
33. Davenport, *South Africa*, 232.
34. *Political Representation of Africans*, 31, R.V Selope Thema.
35. W.M. Hailey, *An African Survey: A Study of Problems Arising in Africa South of the Sahara* (London: Oxford University Press, 1938), 160, 162, 163, 170, 172.
36. Ibid., 185, 212, 215.
37. Native Affairs Department, TDL NTS 1781 89/276, S.A.P., report of a meeting held in Ixopo by Mshiyeni Dinuzulu, John Dube and W.W. Ndhlovu, 6 August 1938.

38. Nicholls Papers, KCM 3287, "Some Urgent Problems," by G. Heaton Nicholls.
39. R. H. Godlo, "The NRC," in *Political Representation of Africans in the Union*, ed. South African Institute of Race Relations, 34.
40. F.J. du T. Spies, et al., eds., *Die Hertzogspreke*, vol. 5, no. 7, 42, speech made by Hertzog at a native conference, 8 December 1925.
41. J. Moroka, interviewed by M. Roth, 4 November 1981.
42. Ibid., 31; Thema also attributed this idea to Smuts; *Joint Sitting of Both Houses of Parliament*, 1 April, 1936, col. 866; see, for example, *Umlindi We Nyanga*, 16 December 1940; *Imvo Zabandsundu*, 11 July 1942; *Umteteli Wa Bantu*, 16 December 1939; *Bantu World*, 29 November 1941.
43. *Government Gazette Extraordinary*, no. 2347, 23 April 1936, Act 12 of 1936, Section 29.
44. *House of Assembly Debates*, 4 May 1936, col. 2897, G. Heaton Nicholls.
45. T. Dunbar Moodie, *The Rise of Afrikanerdom: Power, Apartheid and the Afrikaner Civil Religion* (London: University of California Press, 1974), 165.
46. *Government Gazette Extraordinary*, no. 2347, 23 April 1936.
47. Report of the Select Committee on the Subject of the Union Native Council Bill, Coloured Persons Rights Bill, Representation of Natives in Parliament Bill and Natives Land Amendment Bill, SC10–27, 173; *Representation of Africans in the Union of South Africa*, 31, Selope Thema.
48. *Joint Sitting of Both Houses of Parliament*, col. 868, 1936, Dr. D.F. Malan.
49. *NRC Debates*, 26 November 1946, 67–70, Albert Luthuli.

Chapter 2

1. J. Lewin, "The Electoral System in Practice," 2, 13; *Political Representation of Africans*, 13; Compare with the *Government Gazette*, 5 February 1937, 243, 251.
2. Tatz, *Shadow and Substance*, 96ff.
3. Hertzog Papers, A32, Box 81, notes written by J.B.M. Hertzog on the Select Committee meetings; ibid., Box 80, Memorandum No. 20/279, D.L. Smit to J.B.M. Hertzog, 2 July 1935; ibid., Box 67, I.P. de Villiers, commissioner of police, to J.B.M. Hertzog, 2 July 1935.
4. Ibid., Box 81, "Native Parliamentary Bills, Parliamentary Representation."
5. Roth, *Natives Representative Council*, 45.

6. Smuts Papers, 127(7), "Opmerkings oor die wysige wat deur die Naturelle Verteen woordiende Wetsontwerp beoog is"; *Ilanga Lase Natal*, 19 November 1938; *Government Gazette*, 5 February 1937, 250–51.

7. Debates of the Natives Representative Council (hereafter *"NRC Debates"*), 24 November 1938, 401–03.

8. *Government Gazette*, 5 April 1937, 250–51.

9. Hertzog Papers, A32, Box 81, note written by J.B.M. Hertzog on the Select Committee meetings; D.L.Smit Papers (hereafter "Smit Papers"), 63/36, P.G.W. Grobler to E.G. Jansen, 6 October 1938.

10. See Chapter 4, "Members of the Natives Representative Council."

11. *Government Gazette*, 23 April 1936, Act 12 of 1936.

12. See Chapter 4, "Members of the Natives Representative Council."

13. *Umlindi We Nyanga*, 15 July 1937; *Government Gazette*, 5 February 1937, 242–55; Tatz, *Shadow and Substance*, 93; South African Institute of Race Relations, *Political Representation*, 4; ibid., AB Xuma, "Is the Method of Election Satisfactory?" 24; ibid., D.D.T. Jabavu, "Some Criticism of the Act and Its Results," 23; ibid., E. Brookes, "Natives Representatives and the Senate," 14; ibid., D. Molteno, "Political Representation," 12.

14. South African Institute of Race Relations, *Political Representation*, 23, 26.

15. *Guardian,* 21 October 1948; Prime Minister's Papers, URU 1910, minutes, 19 October 1940

16. Xuma Papers, ABX 480131, A.B. Xuma to the editor of an unnamed newspaper, 11 January 1948; ibid., ABX 410927a, A.B. Xuma to T. Mapikela, 27 September 1941.

17. *Umteteli Wa Bantu*, 3 April 1937.

18. *Umteteli Wa Bantu*, 3 April 1937 and 17 April 1937; Lionel Forman Papers (hereafter "Forman Papers"), Bc A1.189, A.W.G. Champion to H. Selby Msimang, 17 August 1942.

19. See NRC election results discussed later in this chapter.

20. *House of Assembly Debates*, 31 January 1952, cols. 445–46, W.H. Stuart; Smit Papers, 31/46, "Notes on Discussions by the Native Affairs Commission at Its Meeting on 27 September 1946 ... in regard to the Natives Representative Council"; Roth, *Formation*, 63, 65.

21. Native Affairs Department, TDL NTS 1781, 89/276, SAP Report to the Secretary of Native Affairs, 1 September 1939; Smit Papers, 40/36, Smit to H. Olmesdahl, 1 August 1936.

22. Ibid.

23. *Umsebenzi*, 8 May 1937.

24. Karis and Carter Microfilm Collection (hereafter "Karis and Carter Microfilm"), 2XC9:94, A.W.G. Champion interviewed by T. Karis, 1964 (Special Collections and Archives, University of South Africa).

25. See Chapter 4, "Members of the Representative Council."

26. This figure shows the reluctance of the urban municipalities to give recognition to Africans as urban dwellers. There were many thousands of Africans in Durban at that time.

27. *Government Gazette*, 16 July 1937, 127–28, 140.

28. Roth, *Formation*, 101ff.

29. Xuma Papers, ABX 420203a, A.B. Xuma to D.L. Smit, 3 February 1942.

30. *Bantu World*, 29 August 1942; *Ilanga Lase Natal*, 12 September 1942.

31. Forman Papers, Bc 581 A1.188, A.W.G. Champion to H. Selby Msimang, 17 August 1942.

32. Native Affairs Department, TDL NTS 8820, 89/362/248, notes of an interview with Samuel Mankuroane on 16 November 1942; ibid., TDL NTS 8820, 89/362/248, memorandum, 16 November 1942; *Bantu World*, 14 December 1942; *Imvo Zabandsundu*, 14 November 1942; SAIRR Papers, Lynn Saffrey Correspondence, W.G. Ballinger to A. Lynn Saffrey, 1 December 1942 (Department of Historical Papers, University of the Witwatersrand).

33. See chapter 4, "Members of the Natives Representative Council."

34. Smuts Papers, 237(196), J.C. Smuts to M.C. Gillette, 6 February 1942.

35. See chapter 3.

36. *Inkundla Ya Bantu*, 12 November 1947, 31 December 1947, 21 August 1947, 24 December 1947.

37. *Government Gazette*, 20 February 1948, 606.

38. *Bantu World*, 24 January 1948.

39. *Government Gazette*, 20 February 1948, 606, 9 April 1948, 114, 16 April 1948, 189.

40. *Guardian*, 15 January 1948; *Inkundla Ya Bantu*, 14 January 1948, 28 January 1948; *Bantu World*, 31 January 1948, 7 February 1948.

41. Karis and Carter Microfilm, 2:AK 5/4:96/4, speech written by Matthews for the first caucus meeting after the election.

Chapter 3

1. Roth, *Formation*, 19.

2. *Umlindi We Nyanga*, 15 January 1938.

3. Smit Papers, 22/37, notes for Smuts' speech at the opening of the Native Representative Council.

4. *Government Gazette*, Representation of Natives Act, Section 28.

5. *Senate Debates*, 23 April, 1941, col. 1622, J.D. Rheinallt Jones; *House of Assembly Debates*, 21 May 1945, col. 2013, P.A. Myburgh; ibid., 13 April 1950, col. 4266, 4751–52, P. van der Byl.

6. Ibid, *House of Assembly Debates*, 21 May 1945, col. 2013, P.A. Myburgh; ibid., 13 April 1950, col. 4266, 4751–52, P. van der Byl.

7. *Joint Sitting of Both Houses of Parliament*, April 1936, col. 897, F.S. Malan.

8. *House of Assembly Debates*, 24 March 1944, cols. 3828–32, Arthur Barlow.

9. *Government Gazette*, no. 2347, 23 April 1936, Act 12 of 1936, Section 29.

10. Smit Papers, 29/46, Edgar Brookes' address to the Native Affairs Commission, 2 September 1946.

11. *NRC Debates*, 13 December 1937, 389, R.V. Selope Thema.

12. Fred Rodseth, interview with M. Roth, 18 March 1978.

13. *NRC Debates*, 28 November 1938, 520, D.L. Smit.

14. *Bantu World*, 28 June 1941.

15. *Umlindi We Nyanga*, 16 November 1940; *Bantu World*, 28 June 1941.

16. This can be verified from the ANC letterheads, where councilors always had "MRC" after their names.

17. *Senate Debates*, 23 April 1941, col. 1659, Deneys Reitz.

18. *Territorial Magazine, Iphepha Ndaba Lezifunda*, February 1940.

19. *Political Representation of Africans*, 24, A.B. Xuma.

20. Department of Native Affairs, TBP NTS 1790 89/276 (3), R.V. Selope Thema's motion for the NRC, undated.

21. Smuts Papers, 164(45), W.J.G. Mears to Smuts' private secretary, 28 March 1946.

22. Ibid., 1794, "The Natives Representative Council. Suggested Formula for Executive Council," undated.

23. *Bantu World*, 29 January 1949.

24. *NRC Debates*, 15 August 1946, 74, James Moroka.

25. Smit Papers, 23/47, "Notes of an Interview Between the Right Honourable Prime Minister and Members of the Natives Representative Council … on 8 May 1947."

26. J.H. Hofmeyr Papers (hereafter "Hofmeyr Papers"), A1 DB, "The Protest of the Natives Representative Council, Outline of the Causes…."

27. *Government Gazette*, 1 November 1946, 394, Proclamation 214 of 1946.

28. *NRC Debates*, 20 November 1946, 1ff.

29. F. Rodseth, interviewed by M. Roth, 1978; *Inkundla Ya Bantu*, Second Fortnight, 1946; Karis and Carter Microfilm, 2:XM66:94, Z.K. Matthews, interviewed by G. Carter in 1965.

30. Hofmeyr Papers, DB A1, telegram, J.C. Smuts to J.H. Hofmeyr, 29 September 1946; ibid., A1 Ca, J.C. Smuts to J.H. Hofmeyr, 17 October 1946.

31. *NRC Debates*, 25 November 1946, 59, A.W.G. Champion, and 65, Z.K. Matthews.

32. Ibid., 72.

33. *NRC Debates*, 22 November 1946, 33, J. Moroka.

34. *Inkundla Ya Bantu*, Second Fortnight, November 1946.

35. Hofmeyr Papers, A1 DB, Natives Representative Council, note of an interview with Prof. Z.K. Matthews, 22 October 1946.

36. *Bantu World*, 18 October 1947; ibid., 22 November 1947; Roth, *Natives Representative Council*, 480–81.

37. Native Affairs Department, TBP NTS 1790, 89/276/(3), Secretary of Labour to Secretary of Native Affairs, 2 July 1947.

38. *Inkundla Ya Bantu*, 10 September 1947. Councilors who attended the Royal visit celebrations did so as members of the ANC, who had been invited.

39. E. Brookes, "Race Relations in 1947," *Race Relations Journal*, vol. 15, nos. 1 and 2 (1948): 2.

40. Department of Native Affairs, TDL NTS 1790, 89/276(2), F. Rodseth, Acting Secretary of Native Affairs, 27 October 1947.

41. Ibid.; *Senate Debates*, 8 April 1947, col. 697, W.M.H. Campbell.

42. *Inkundla Ya Bantu*, 21 August 1947.

43. United Nations, *Official Records of the Second Session of the General Assembly Fourth Trusteeship Committee, Summary Records of Meetings, 25 September 1947*, 5, Rajah Sir Mahoney Singh.

44. Smuts Papers, 237(195), J.C. Smuts to M.C. Gillett, 1 February 1947; *Inkundla Ya Bantu*, 10 July 1947; Brookes, "Race Relations in 1947," 2.

45. Smuts Papers, 237(195), J.C. Smuts to M.C. Gillett, 1 February 1947.

46. Smuts Papers, Ibid., 168(19); Memorandum by the Native Affairs Department Setting Out the Framework for a Progressive Policy Designed to Grant the Natives a Greater Voice in the Administration of Their Own Affairs, 28 March 1947.

47. *Bantu World*, 2 August 1947.

48. *Senate Debates*, 16 April 1947, cols. 1063, 1090, and 1095, P. van der Byl, minister of native affairs.

49. Karis and Carter Microfilm, 2:AK5/12:89/6, "The Smuts Proposals, 1947," statement by Prof. Z.K. Matthews; ibid., 2:AK5/12:31, "Notes of an Interview Between the Right Honorary Prime Minister and Members of the Representative Council on the 8th May 1947."

50. *Transvaler*, 6 January 1947, 14 May 1947.

51. Karis and Carter Microfilm, 2:XC9:41/211, H. Selby Msimang to A.W.G. Champion, 11 November 1948.

52. Ibid., 2:XM66:96/11; Z.K. Matthews interviewed in Basutoland in 1963 by J.H; ibid., 2:AK5/9:89, statement by African members of the Natives Representative Council; *Bantu World*, 7 August 1948, 5 June 1948, and 13 November 1948.

53. *NRC Debates*, 2ff, 4 January 1949.

54. *NRC Debates*, 5 January 1949, 49, A.W.G. Champion.

55. *Government Gazette*, 14 October 1949, 75; ibid., 9 December 1949, 568.

56. *Inkundla Ya Bantu*, 5 March 1949, 30 July 1949, 6 August 1949, 15 October 1949, 29 October 1949.

57. *Inkundla Ya Bantu*, 10 December 1949; Walshe, *Rise of African Nationalism*, 291ff.

58. Walshe, *Rise of African Nationalism*, 291ff.; J. Moroka, interviewed by M. Roth, November 1949.

59. *House of Assembly Debates*, 13 June 1950, cols. 4985, 4994–95, E.G. Jansen.

60. *Ilanga Lase Natal*, December 1950; see Chapter 4, "Members of the Natives Representative Council."

61. See below, chapters 7 and 8.

62. Karis and Carter Microfilm, 2:XC:41/271, circular letter to the councilors from H. Selby Msimang, NRC caucus secretary, 3 February 1950.

63. *House of Assembly Debates*, 20 April 1950, col. 4718, D.L. Smit; *Senate Debates*, 13 June 1950, col. 4990, E.J. Jansen; *Inkundla Ya Bantu*, 15 April 1950; Karis and Carter Microfilm, 2:XC9:41/276, A.W.G. Champion to Z.K. Matthews, 21 April 1950.

64. *Rand Daily Mail*, 4 December 1950; *Bantu World*, 19 August 1950.

65. Native Affairs Department, TDL NTS 1782 89/276(2) W.W.M. Eiselen to A. Luthuli, 16 September 1950.

66. *The Star*, 4 December 1950; *Rand Daily Mail*, 5 December 1950.

67. *Forum*, 8 December 1950.

68. *The Star*, 7 December 1950.

69. *Cape Times*, 7 December 1950; see chapters 7 and 8.

70. See councilors 1950 speeches in chapter 8.

Chapter 4

1. Roth, *Natives Representative Council.*

2. Xuma Papers, ABX 360123, H. Selby Msimang to A.B. Xuma, 23 January 1936; *Bantu World*, 24 October 1942; Walshe, *Rise of African Nationalism*, 256.

3. Roth, *Natives Representative Council*, 113; *Inkundla Ya Bantu*, 21 August 1948, letter to the editor.

4. E. Roux, *Time Longer Than Rope: The Black Man's Struggle for Freedom in Africa* (Madison: Wisconsin University Press, 1974), 306.

5. Department of Native Affairs, TBP NTS 89/276, Police Files, chief deputy for the commissioner of the SAP, to Smit, 24 April, 1948; ibid., E.H.M. Hardiman to Senator P.A. Myburgh, 2 March 1938; ibid., Smit to J.H. Tandy, 10 May 1938; ibid., R. Baloyi to J.D. Rheinallt Jones, 30 May 1938.

6. Department of Native Affairs, TBP NTS 89/276, Police Files; E.H.M. Hardiman to Senator P.A. Myburgh, 2 March 1938; ibid., Smit to J.H. Tandy, 10 May 1938; ibid., R. Baloyi to J.D. Rheinallt Jones, 30 May 1938; ibid., chief deputy for the commissioner of the SAP, to Smit, 24 April 1948.

7. Roth, *Formation*, 111.

8. Karis and Carter, eds., *From Protest to Challenge*, vol. 4, 18.

9. P. la Hausse, "The Dispersal of the Regiments: Radical African Opposition in Durban, 1930," ASI Seminar paper, University of the Witwatersrand, 1986.

10. Karis and Carter Microfilm, 2:XC 9:9/288, Xuma to Champion, 24 February 1949; Karis and Carter, eds., *From Protest to Challenge*, vol. 4, 18.

11. *Inkundla La Bantu*, 24 March 1948.

12. Roth, *Formation*, 131–33, and 133 note 98.

13. Department of Native Affairs, TDL NTS 1781, 89/276, SAP report of a meeting held at Ixopo, 6 August 1938; ibid., 9 August 1938; ibid., SAP report sent to the secretary of native affairs, 1 September 1939.

14. Karis and Carter, eds., *From Protest to Challenge*, vol. 4, 31; *Umlindi We Nyanga*, 15 September 1935.

15. *Umlindi We Nyanga*, 15 March 1937; *Imvo Zabandsundu*, 9 October 1937.

16. Walshe, *Rise of African Nationalism*, 120.

17. *Umlindi We Nyanga*, 15 March 1937; *Imvo Zabandsundu*, 16 October 1937; Roth, *Natives Representative Council*, 111–12.

18. See, for example, *Ciskeian General Council Proceedings*, 19 December 1937, 69, A.M. Jabavu; *Imvo Zabandsundu*, 16 October 1937; *Umlindi We Nyanga*, 15 December

1937; and Karis and Carter, eds., *From Protest to Challenge,* vol. 4, 39.

19. Roth, *Natives Representative Council,* 200–01, 204.

20. A.J. Luthuli Papers (Microfilm), undated telegram informing Luthuli that his candidature as a member of the NRC had been approved by the governor-general (Special Collections and Archives, University of South Africa).

21. Roth, *Natives Representative Council,* 118.

22. Molteno Papers, Bc579 C 6.61, D. Molteno to S. Mabude, 16 May 1945.

23. Roth, *Natives Representative Council,* 128.

24. Donald Molteno Papers (hereafter "Molteno Papers"), Bc579 C6.61, D. Molteno to S. Mabude, 16 May 1947; *Inkundla Ya Bantu,* 27 August 1946.

25. Karis and Carter, eds., *From Protest to Challenge,* vol. 4, 74; *Umlindi we Nyanga,* 15 March 1937, and 16 August 1937; *Imvo Zabandsundu,* 16 October 1937.

26. Karis and Carter, eds., *From Protest to Challenge,* vol. 4, 79–81.

27. Ibid.; Xuma Papers, ABX 420922d, J. Calata to A.B Xuma, 22 September 1942.

28. See, for example, Karis and Carter Microfilm, 2:AK5/1:96/1; Roth, *Natives Representative Council,* 100.

29. Ibid., 105.

30. J.S. Moroka, interviewed by M. Roth, 4 November 1981.

31. See later in this chapter.

32. *Bantu World,* 12 September 1946.

33. J.S. Moroka, interviewed by M. Roth, 4 November 1981; Roth, *Natives Representative Council,* 107.

34. Xuma Papers, ABX 421116b, P. Mosaka to A.B. Xuma, 16 November 1942.

35. Roth, *Natives Representative Council,* 104–05; Karis and Carter, eds., *From Protest to Challenge,* vol. 4, 98.

36. *NRC Debates,* 11 August 1944, 75, J. Alport, chief native commissioner, Transvaal.

37. *NRC Debates,* 25 May 1945, 18.

38. See for example, *NRC Debates,* 9 November 1945, 106; see also Roth, *Natives Representative Council,* 551.

39. *Inkundla Ya Bantu,* 28 January 1948; Roth, *Natives Representative Council,* 123.

40. Roth, *Natives Representative Council,* 123.

41. *Inkundla Ya Bantu,* 14 January 1948, and 28 January 1948; Karis and Carter Microfilm, 2:XC9:41/164, H. Selby Msimang to A.W.G. Champion, 26 January 1948; Roth, *Natives Representative Council,* 121–22.

42. Walshe, *Rise of African Nationalism,* 205; *Government Gazette,* 23 April 1937, 257.

43. Smuts papers, 122(9), Annexure E, "Conference with Natives Held by the Native Affairs Commission...," 7–11.

44. Roth, *Natives Representative Council,* 115–16.

45. See Part 2, Introduction

46. Roth, *Natives Representative Council,* 129; *Transkei General Council Debates,* 22 April 1947, 56; ibid., 19 April 1947, 60; ibid., 26 March 1948, 60.

47. *Inkundla Ya Bantu,* 24 March 1948.

48. *Umlindi We Nyanga,* 16 August 1937.

49. *Bantu World,* 2 April 1949.

50. Roth, *Natives Representative Council,* 126–27.

51. *Umlindi We Nyanga,* 16 August 1937.

52. *Imvo Zabandsundu,* 6 November 1937.

53. Xuma Papers, ABX 410507, A (?) Galileke to Xuma, 7 May 1941; Karis and Carter, eds., *From Protest to Challenge,* vol. 4, 135.

54. Roth, *Natives Representative Council,* 125.

55. *Government Gazette,* 23 April 1937, 256.

56. *NRC Debates,* 30 November 1939, 80, B.B. Xiniwe; Karis and Carter, eds., *From Protest to Challenge,* vol. 4, 164.

57. Roth, *Natives Representative Council,* 117.

58. *Ilanga Lase Natal,* 17 December 1938; Sililo's election manifesto translated from the Zulu by R. Mfeke, University of the Witwatersrand; *Government Gazette,* 20 January 1939, 125.

59. *Government Gazette,* 20 January 1939, 125; Karis and Carter, eds., *From Protest to Challenge,* vol. 4, 125.

60. Ibid.

61. Karis and Carter, eds., *From Protest to Challenge,* vol. 4, 139. This source displays a number of inaccuracies in the dates of the NRC elections. They infer here that the 1948 election occurred in 1949. On other pages they refer to an NRC election which supposedly occurred in 1945 (26). Mapikela is erroneously thought to have held his seat until 1945 (74) and Sililo to have been elected in 1937 instead of the correct date of 1939 (141).

62. Native Affairs Department,TBP NTS 8821, 89/2362/248, Inspector of SA Police, no. 8 De Aar District, to Magistrate, Hopetown, 27 February 1948.

63. Walshe, *Rise of African Nationalism,* 56–60.

64. Ibid., 216.

65. SAIRR Papers, B (51), Autobiographical notes by Selope Thema.

66. Report of the Select Committee, SC10–27, 173.

67. SAIRR Papers, B (51) Autobiographical notes by Selope Thema.

68. *NRC Debates*, 24 November 1941, 15, D.L. Smit; Roth, *Natives Representative Council*, 137–38.

69. South Africa Native Affairs Department, TDL NTS, 8820, 89/362/248, D.L. Smit to M. Ballinger, 28 September 1942.

70. Roth, *Natives Representative Council*, 133–34.

71. Native Affairs Department, TBP NTS 8821, 89/362/248, report of an Interview with Sam Mankuroane, 16 November 1942; ibid., memorandum, 22 August 1948.

72. SAIRR Papers, B2.8.4(1), E. Brookes to D. Buchanan, 10 February 1943.

73. Native Affairs Department, TDL NTS 89/362/248, memorandum, 12 April 1946.

74. *NRC Debates*, 15 August 1946, 72ff ; Department of Native Affairs, TDL NTS 8821, memorandum, 22 August 1948.

75. Department of Native Affairs, TDL NTS 8820, 89/362/248, Additional Native Commissioner Duiwelskloof, to Assistant Native Commissioner, 23 November 1942; ibid., undated memorandum, secretary of native affairs to H. Rogers; *Bantu World*, 18 September 1948.

76. Roth, *Natives Representative Council*, 134.

77. *Forum*, 12 August 1939, 3.

78. *NRC Debates*, 22 November 1940, 400, D.L. Smit.

79. Karis and Carter Microfilm, 2:XD15:44, A.B. Xuma to Chief Mshiyeni, 13 October 1941.

80. See Part Two, Chapter 5.

81. Department of Native Affairs, TBP NTS 8821, 89/362/248, memorandum, 16 March 1948; E.G. Jansen Papers (hereafter "Jansen Papers"), undated memo, "Ndhlovu and Ngwenya"; Jansen Papers, memorandum, 16 March 1948.

82. Roth, *Formation*, 117–18.

83. Roth, *Natives Representative Council*, 136.

84. Department of Native Affairs, TBP NTS 8821, 89/362/248, M.L.C. Liefeldt to W.J.G. Mears, 30 March 1948.

85. *NRC Debates*, 25 May 1945, 14.

86. TDL NTS 8820, 89/362/248, minute no. 912, 12 August 1946; URU 1910, 156, minutes, 7 November 1940.

87. Report of the Native Affairs Department, *U.G. 7–19*, 3; Report of the Select Committee on the Subject of the Union Council Bill, Coloured Persons Rights Bill, Representation of Natives in Parliament Bill and Natives Land Amendment Bill, SC19–27, 166; *Umlindi We Nyanga*, 15 December 1937.

88. *Cape Times*, 3 December 1940; Roth, *Natives Representative Council*, 125; see section on Education.

89. These sessions numbered at least 14, but some sessions, for example their session addressed by the chief commissioner of police, was not published.

90. The Broederbond was an influential Afrikaner secret society, something between an old boys' club and a political think tank.

91. The South African war in Angola in the 1970s.

92. C. Kros, *The Seeds of Separate Development: Origins of Bantu Education* (Pretoria: Unisa, 2010), 124.

93. Ibid., xv–viii.

94. Ibid., 22–24.

95. Ibid., 23ff.

96. J. Seroto, "A Revisionist View of the Contribution of Dr. Eiselen to South African Education: New Perspectives," *Yesterday and Today*, no. 9 (October 2013): 1.

97. Ibid.

98. Kros, *Seeds of Separate Development*, 27.

99. Saul Dubow, *Illicit Union: Scientific Racism in Modern South Africa* (Cambridge: Cambridge University Press, 1995), 278–79.

100. For example, *NRC Debates*, 8 December 1942, 111, and 7 May 1943, 169.

101. *Bantu World*, 22 October 1949; *NRC Debates*, 8 December 1942, 111, and 7 May 1943, 169; *Ilanga Lase Natal*, December 1950.

102. *House of Assembly Debates*, 25 January 1950, cols. 98–100, P. van der Byl; Davenport, *South Africa*, 267, 346; Lipton, *Capitalism and Apartheid*, 26; Dunbar Moodie, *The Rise of Afrikanerdom*, 276.

103. Kros, *Seeds of Separate Development*, 68.

104. *Inkundla Ya Bantu*, 18 December 1948, and 21 August 1948; *Senate Debates*, 24 March 1949, col. 680, E.G. Jansen, minister of native affairs.

105. *Inkundla Ya Bantu*, 18 December 1948.

106. See Verwoerd's speech, in section 13, Politics, part 2, chapter 1.

107. The word "native" and "African" were not used after 1948 because the Afrikaner government regarded themselves as both "Africans" and "natives" of South Africa. In addition, the word "native" had by this time gained an unfavorable connotation.

108. J. Seroto, "A Revisionist View of the Contribution of Dr. Eiselen to South African Education: New Perspectives," *Yesterday and Today*, no. 9 (October 2013), 10.

109. Roth, *Natives Representative Council*, 111.

110. Ibid., 291.

111. Ibid., 292.

112. Ibid., 282.

113. See Part Two.

114. *NRC Debates*, 6 December 1939, 439, 447, and 12 December 1942, 257, 266ff.

115. *NRC Debates*, 7 May 1943, 187, J. Moroka; ibid., 29 November 1938, 592, J. Dube; ibid., 7 May 1943, 182, J. Dube.

116. Kros, *Seeds of Separate Development*, 42, 43.

117. *NRC Debates*, 7 May 1943, 184, W.W.G. Champion.

118. *NRC Debates*, 7 May, 1943, 181–82, B.B. Xiniwe.

119. *NRC Debates*, 21 November, 1938, 19, D.L. Smit, and 7 December 1942, 11, 77; *Transkei General Council Debates*, 27 April, 1944, 3.

120. *NRC Debates*, 7 May 1943, 169, W.W.M. Eiselen; W.W.M. Eiselen, "The Meaning of Apartheid," *Race Relations Journal* 4, no. 3 (1948): 82–83.

121. *NRC Debates*, 25 November 1940, 63–65, Mapikela.

122. *NRC Debates*, 9 December 1937, 167.

123. *NRC Debates*, 10 August 1945, 106–07, W.W.G. Champion.

124. *NRC Debates*, 6 May 1943, 153–54, W.W.G. Champion; *NRC Debates*, 23 November 1938, 246ff, E. Qamata.

125. *Bantu World*, 11 August 1945; *NRC Debates*, 7 November 1945, 7, P. Mosaka.

126. *NRC Debates*, 2 December 1940, 232, R.H. Godlo.

127. Ibid., 232ff.

128. Ibid.

129. One of the new areas for Africans near Johannesburg, later called Soweto.

130. *NRC Debates*, 2 December 1940, 222ff, T.N. Mapikela.

131. *NRC Debates*, 5 May 1943, 116, J. Dube.

132. Traditional homestead in a rural area.

133. *NRC Debates*, 10 August 1945, 85, P. Mosaka.

134. *NRC Debates*, 23 November 1938, 237, and 24 November 1944, 234–35.

135. *NRC Debates*, 7 May 1943, 184, S. Mabude.

136. *NRC Debates*, 20 August 1945, 358–61, R.V. Selope Thema.

137. Kros, *Seeds of Separate Development*, 106.

138. F. Rodseth, interviewed by M. Roth, 1978.

139. NRC, 5 December 1939, 361, 24 December 1938, 337, and 27 November 1941, 144, 154–58.

140. Ibid., 1 December 1941, 307.

141. F. Rodseth, interviewed by M. Roth, 10 July 1978.

142. *NRC Debates*, 5 December 1939, 339, R. Godlo; ibid., 1 December 1941, 308, A.J. Sililo; ibid., 27 November 1941, 151, J. Dube.

143. Roth, *Natives Representative Council*.

144. Kros, *Seeds of Separate Development*.

145. Smuts Papers, vol. 263(110), note of conversation with General Hertzog, 12 March 1928; ibid., vol. 263(108), 15 February 1928.

146. This uprising led to at least 176 deaths and the injury of many thousands.

147. Smit Papers, 11/43, D.L. Smit to Mrs. Smit, 9 May 1943; ibid., 16 May 1943; ibid., 28 November 1944.

148. *Report of the Interdepartmental Committee on the Social, Health and Economic Conditions of the Urban Natives, 1942* (hereafter "Smit Report"), 1ff.

149. Smit Papers, 25/41, R.F.A. Hoernle to D.L. Smit, 31 October 1941.

150. *NRC Debates*, 16 August 1945, 228–229, 248.

151. F. Rodseth, interviewed by M. Roth, 18 July 1978.

152. Ibid.

Chapter 5

1. Roth, *Natives Representative Council*, 272.

2. Dominion Office Papers, DO 35/1172/y701, Sir Evelyn Baring to Viscount Addison, Dominion Office, 29 August 1945.

3. Roth, *Natives Representative Council*, 273.

4. *Race Relations Journal* 8, no. 1 (first quarter 1941): 13.

5. *House of Assembly Debates*, 28 May 1945, col. 2289, J.H. Hofmeyr.

6. Roth, *Natives Representative Council*, 310–11.

Chapter 6

1. *Union Statistics for Fifty Years, 1910–1960*, Government Printer, 10.

2. Z.K. Matthews, *Freedom for My People* (Cape Town: Collins, 1981), 150.

3. UG 35–49, 30–37; ibid., 54–39.

4. Department of Native Affairs, Agricultural Section for the period 1 October 1942 to 30 September 1943, 25.

Chapter 7

1. *House of Assembly Debates*, 9 May 1944, col. 8908, D. Molteno; T.R.H. Davenport and K.S. Hunt, *South Africa and the Right to the Land* (Claremont, Philips, 1974), 62.
2. D. Posel, "Providing for the Legitimate Labor Requirements of the Employers: Secondary Industry, Commerce and the State in South Africa during the 1950s and 1960's," ASI Seminar Paper, University of the Witwatersrand, 1984, 1–3.
3. Roth, *Natives Representative Council*, 397.
4. Ibid.

Chapter 8

1. Smit Papers, 5.1/37, notes by D.L. Smit; *NRC Debates*, 8 December 1938, 650.
2. Smit Papers, 5.1/37, notes by D.L. Smit; *Senate Debates*, 27 March 1940, cols. 509–10, G. Heaton Nicholls.
3. Roth, *Natives Representative Council*, 379.
4. Ibid., 380.
5. Ibid.
6. Ibid.
7. Ibid., 382.
8. Ibid., 383–84.

Chapter 9

1. *NRC Debates*, 1943 Annexure H, Judicial Commission of Inquiry, Pretoria Municipal Riots of 26 December 1943.
2. See chapter on Education; Roth, *Natives Representative Council*, 367.
3. M. Roth, "If You Give Us Rights We Will Fight: Black Involvement in the Second World War," *South African Historical Journal* 15 (November 1983): 96–97.
4. *House of Assembly Debates*, 9 May 1944, col. 6908, D. Molteno.
5. Roth, *Natives Representative Council*, 368.
6. Ibid., 370.
7. *House of Assembly Debates*, 27 August 1943, col. 6372, J.C. Smuts; *NRC Debates*, 6 December 1939, 416, R. Fyfe King, chief native commissioner of the Transkei.
8. Roth, "If You Give Us Rights," 90.

Chapter 10

1. *Umlindi We Nyanga*, 15 March 1937.
2. Anton Lembede, "The ICU and the ANC," *Bantu World*, 26 October 1946.

3. Ibid.
4. *NRC Debates*, 10 May 1943, 203–06, A.W.G. Champion; Smuts Papers, 155(18), "Memorandum by the Minister of Mines on Native Trade Unions."
5. Roth, *Natives Representative Council*, 426.
6. Roth, "If You Give Us Rights," 88–90; Xuma Papers, ABX 171240, ANC Agenda, 17 December 1940.

Chapter 11

1. *NRC Debates*, 24 November–4 December 1941, index.
2. *NRC Debates*, 26 November 1941, 143.
3. The government saw such measures as a way to better African conditions without having to increase wages.

Chapter 12

1. Roth, *Natives Representative Council*, 410–11.
2. *NRC Debates*, 27 November 1941, 199, T. Mapikela.
3. This was an important promise promulgated into law by the 1936 Trust and Land Act.
4. *NRC Debates*, "Verbatim Report of the Committee Proceedings (War Issue)," 5 December 1940, 20, R. Baloyi.
5. The Native Affairs Commission had a statutory obligation to attend NRC sessions. The commission consisted of members of Parliament dealing with the general administration of African affairs.

Chapter 13

1. Roth, *Natives Representative Council*, 450.
2. *NRC Debates*, December 1943, Annexure "E", Recess Committee on Representation of Natives, 2–5.
3. SAIRR Papers, ANC AD 1189, book 5, part 1B, Bloemfontein Conference of the ANC, 14 December 1945.
4. *Ilanga Lase Natal*, 12 May 1945.
5. *NRC Debates*, 16 August 1945, 243, 247–48, and 9 November 1945, 138, F. Rodseth.
6. The Pitso was a traditional gathering of Africans in Lesotho, here equated to an African parliament.
7. Champion Papers, correspondence, H. Selby Msimang to A.W.G. Champion, 21 November 1946.

8. Roth, *Natives Representative Council*, 469–71.

9. Smuts Papers, 237(196), J.C. Smuts to M.C. Gillett, 6 February 1942.

10. Smit Papers, 14/43, D.L. Smit to Mrs. Smit, 16 May 1943; ibid., 9 May 1943.

11. Kros, *Seeds of Separate Development*, 72.

12. Karis and Carter Microfilm, 2:XM66/96/11, Matthews interviewed by J.H., 1963; ibid., 2:XM 66/84/1, *Reasons Why the Natives Representative Council Adjourned*.

13. Roth, *Natives Representative Council*, 292–97.

14. Bunga was the African name for the Transkei General Council.

15. Roth, *Natives Representative Council*, 488ff.

16. *Rand Daily Mail*, 10 May 1947.

17. *Transvaler*, 7 January 1947, and 14 May 1947.

18. SAIRR Papers, AD 1189, ANC notebooks, book 11, part 1, 5 June 1947.

19. *Ilanga Lase Natal*, 21 June 1947.

20. *Inkundla La Bantu*, 12 November 1947.

21. *Bantu World*, 25 October 1947.

22. *Inkundla Ya Bantu*, 30 June 1948, and 7 August 1948; Karis and Carter Microfilm, 2:AK5/4:41/27, "To African Members of the Natives Representatives Council...," 9 June 1948.

23. Ibid., 2:XC9:41/182, A.W.G. Champion to H. Selby Msimang, 13 July 1948.

24. *NRC Debates*, 4 January 1949, 2ff.

25. The Voortrekkers were the Afrikaners who first trekked to the interior of South Africa in 1836.

26. James Moroka, interviewed by M. Roth, November 1981.

27. *Bantu World*, 22 October 1949; *NRC Debates*, 8 December 1942, 111, and 7 May 1943, 169; *Ilanga Lase Natal*, December 1950.

28. Roth, *Natives Representative Council*, 488–89.

29. Karis and Carter Microfilm, 2:XC9:41/271, circular letter to councilors from H. Selby Msimang, 3 February 1950.

30. *Ilanga Lase Natal*, 14 January 1950.

31. *Rand Daily Mail*, 4 December 1950; *Bantu World*, 19 August 1950.

32. *Bantu World*, 19 August 1950; *Umteteli Wa Bantu*, 9 September 1950.

33. Department of Native Affairs, TDL NTS 1782, 89/276 (2), W.W.M. Eiselen to A. Luthuli, 16 September 1950.

34. *The Star*, 4 December 1950; *Rand Daily Mail*, 5 December 1950.

35. *Forum*, 8 December 1950.

36. *The Star*, 7 December 1950.

37. *The Star*, 7 December, 1950, and 8 December 1950; *Rand Daily Mail*, 6 December 1950; *NRC Debates*, 5 December 2ff.

38. *Cape Times*, 6 December 1950 and 7 December 1950; *NRC Debates*, 5 December 1950, 23, 31–33, 6 December 1950, 36–39, and 7 December 1950, 61.

39. *Cape Times*, 7 December 1950; *Die Burger*, 7 December 1950; *NRC Debates*, 6 December 1950, 45, and 7 December 1950, 59.

Bibliography

Primary Sources

Collected Papers

Forman. Lionel Forman Papers. Jagger Library, University of Cape Town.
Hertzog. J.B.M. Hertzog Papers. Government Archives, Pretoria.
Hofmeyr. J.H. Hofmeyr Papers. Department of Historical Papers, University of the Witwatersrand.
Jansen. E.G. Jansen Papers. Institute for Contemporary History, University of the Orange Free State, Bloemfontein.
Jones. David Rheinallt Jones Papers. Department of Historical Papers, University of the Witwatersrand.
Karis and Carter. Karis and Carter Microfilm Collection. Special Collections and Archives, University of South Africa.
Luthuli. A.J. Luthuli Papers (Microfilm). Special Collections and Archives, University of South Africa.
Molteno. Donald Molteno Papers. Jagger Library, University of Cape Town.
Nicholls. G. Heaton Nicholls Papers. Killie Campbell Library, Durban.
Saffrey. A. Lynn Saffrey Correspondence. Department of Historical Papers, University of the Witwatersrand.
SAIRR. South African Institute of Race Relations Papers. Department of Historical Papers, University of the Witwatersrand.
Smit. D.L. Smit Papers. Albany Museum, Grahamstown.
Smuts. J.C. Smuts Papers (public and private). Government Archives, Pretoria.
Xuma. A.B. Xuma Papers. Department of Historical Papers, University of the Witwatersrand.

South African Government Published Primary Sources

Ciskeian General Council Proceedings.
House of Assembly Debates.
Joint Sittings of Both Houses of Parliament Debates.
Senate Debates.
Transkeian Territories General Council Proceedings.
Verbatim Report on the Proceedings of the Natives Representative Council: 6–13 December 1937; 21–29 November 1938; 30 November–8 December 1939; 25 November–6 December 1940; 24 November–6 December 1941; 7–15 December 1942; 3–14 May 1943; 1–9 December 1943; 8–22 August 1944; 22–27 November 1944; 25 May 1945; 8–21 August 1945; 7–14 November 1945; 24–27 April 1946; 14–15 August 1946; 20–26 November 1946; 4–5 January 1949; 5–7 December 1950.

South African Government Official Papers

Native Affairs Department Files, NTS Series. Government Archives, Pretoria.
Native Affairs Departmental Memorandum, 12 April 1946, TDL NTS.
Prime Ministers' Papers, URU Series. Government Archives, Pretoria.
Report and Proceedings of the Joint Committee on the Representation of Native and Coloured Persons in Parliament and Provisional Councils and Acquisition of Land, JC 1–1935.
Report and Proceedings of the Joint Committees on Natives and Coloured Persons During the Period 1930–1934, JC 1–35 (Supplement).
Report of the Interdepartmental Committee on the Social, Health and Economic Conditions of the Urban Natives, 1942 (The Smit Report).
Report of the Native Affairs Commission, U.G. 17–27.
Report of the Native Affairs Commission, U.G. 3–34.
Report of the Native Affairs Commission Appointed to Enquire into the Working of the Provisions of the Natives (Urban Areas) Act Relating to the Use and Supply of Kaffir Beer.
Report of the Native Affairs Department, U.G. 17–19.
Report of the Select Committee on the Subject of the Union Native Council Bill, Coloured Persons Rights Bill, Representation of Natives in Parliament Bill and Natives Land Amendment Bill. SC19–27.

United Nations Official Publication

United Nations. *Official Records of the Second Session of the General Assembly Fourth Trusteeship Committee, Summary Records of Meetings, 25 September 1947.* William Cullen Library, University of the Witwatersrand.

Newspapers and Periodicals

Bantu World
Cape Times
Forum
Government Gazette, Union of South Africa
Guardian
Ilanga Lase Natal
Imvo Zabandsundu
Inkundla Ya Bantu
Race Relations Journal
Rand Daily Mail
The Star
Territorial Magazine (Iphepha Ndaba Lezifunda); from 1940 *Inkundla Ya Bantu*
Transvaler
Umlindi We Nyanga
Umsebenzi
Umteteli Wa Bantu

Interviews

J.S. Moroka, interviewed by M. Roth, 4 November 1981.
F. Rodseth, interviewed by M. Roth, 18 July 1978.

Secondary Sources

Ballinger, M. *From Union to Apartheid: A Trek to Isolation.* Cape Town: Juta, 1969.
Bonner, P., ed. *Working Papers in Southern African Studies.* Johannesburg: Raven; vol. 1, 1977; vol. 2, 1981.

Davenport, T.R.H. *South Africa: A Modern History.* Johannesburg: Macmillan, 1977.

Dunbar Moodie, T. *The Rise of Afrikanerdom: Power, Apartheid and the Afrikaner Civil Religion.* London: University of California Press, 1974.

Hailey, Sir William Malcolm. *An African Survey: A Study of Problems Arising in Africa South of the Sahara.* London: Oxford University Press, 1938.

Hancock, W.K. *Smuts.* Vol. 2, *The Fields of Force, 1919–1950.* Cambridge: Cambridge University Press, 1968.

Ingham, K. *Jan Christian Smuts: The Conscience of a South African.* Johannesburg: Jonathan Ball, 1986.

Karis, T., and G. Carter, eds. *From Protest to Challenge: A Documentary History of Politics in South Africa.* Vol. 4, *Political Profiles.* Stanford: Hoover, 1977.

Kros, Cynthia. The Seeds of Separate Development: Origins of Bantu Education. Pretoria: Unisa, 2010.

Lipton, M. *Capitalism and Apartheid: South Africa, 1910–1986.* Claremont: David Philip, 1985.

Paton, A. *Hofmeyr.* London: Oxford University Press, 1964.

Political Representation of Africans in the Union. Johannesburg: SAIRR, 1942.

Rich, P.B. *White Power and the Liberal Conscience: Racial Segregation and South African Liberalism.* Johannesburg: Raven, 1984.

Roth, M. *The Formation of the Natives Representative Council.* MA thesis, University of South Africa, 1979.

_____. *The Natives Representative Council (NRC), 1937–1951.* PhD dissertation, University of the Witwatersrand, 1988.

Roux, E. *Time Longer Than Rope: The Black Man's Struggle for Freedom in Africa.* Madison: Wisconsin University Press, 1974.

Seroto, J. "A Revisionist View of the Contribution of Dr. Eiselen to South African Education: New Perspectives." *Yesterday and Today*, no. 9 (October 2013): 1.

Spies, F.J. du T., et al., eds. *Die Hertzogspreke*, vol. 5, no. 7. Pretoria: Nasionale Pers, 1962.

Tatz, C.M. *Shadow and Substance in South Africa: A Study in Land and Franchise Policies Affecting Africans 1910–1960.* Pietermaritzburg: Natal University Press, 1962.

Walshe, P. *The Rise of African Nationalism in South Africa: The African National Congress 1912–1952.* Berkeley and Los Angeles: University of California Press, 1971.

Willan, B. *Sol Plaatje: A Biography.* Johannesburg: Raven, 1984.

Index

www.ingramcontent.com/pod-product-compliance
Lightning Source LLC
Chambersburg PA
CBHW031131270326
41929CB00011B/1586